By Django Reinhardt

Transcription by Dennis Baggi, 199
from the Dec. 14, 1937 recording

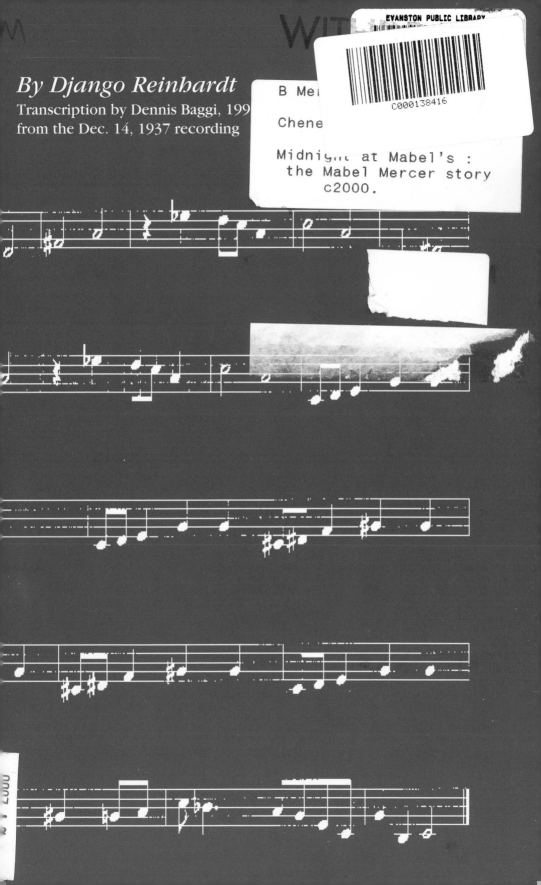

MIDNIGHT at MABEL'S

Dedicated to everyone
afflicted with stage fright.

Also by Margaret Cheney

Tesla: Master of Lightning (with Robert Uth)

Tesla: Man out of Time

Why—The Serial Killer in America

Meanwhile Farm

MIDNIGHT at MABEL'S

The Mabel Mercer Story

Centennial Biography of the Great Song Stylist

by Margaret Cheney

Foreword by
Rex Reed

NEW VOYAGE Publishing
Washington, DC

NEW VOYAGE

NEW VOYAGE Publishing
Washington, DC
www.newvoyagepublishing.com

Library of Congress Control Number: 00-132562
ISBN 0-615-11345-1

Text edited by Robert Uth
Jacket, book design, and page layout
by Radomir and Mary Perica

Printed in the United States of America
04 03 02 01 00   5 4 3 2 1

Centennial Edition

To order additional copies of this book,
a videotape about Mabel Mercer,
or a CD of her work,
visit the Mabel Mercer web site at:
www.mabelmercer.com

Contents

Foreword

As I wandered through an olive grove on a holiday in Tuscany, I came across a ninth century monastery as the monks were beginning to chant their Gregorian vespers. The experience was an escape from the cumulative horrors of the year, and that is exactly how I felt every time I heard Mabel Mercer sing.

She could transport you away from cruelty, ugliness, noise and inhumanity to a place that seemed just and traditional and sane and secure. Whether she was essaying a sad, mournful treatise on betrayal and loss by Alec Wilder, or sassily crooning something naughty by Cole Porter, she illuminated the essence of the heart in all of its pain, wisdom, and frailty. There really was no one quite like her, and every time I heard her I felt privileged to be alive at that moment. I knew and adored Mabel, but never inquired about her past, family, loves gained or lost, or even what she dined on the night before.

We did cross together once on the QE2, and although there were storms at sea so turbulent that her grand piano had to be lashed to the side of the stage for her concert, she never missed a meal and was always the first person on deck in the morning. Lots of amusing gossip occurred at tea on the Quarter Deck and much sharing of musical memories.

And there were, of course, the songs that were particular favorites of mine which nobody else knew but Mabel—songs like "Meat and Potatoes," by Cy Coleman and Dorothy Fields, which was cut from the score of *Seesaw* before anybody ever heard of it—which she would drag out of the piano bench just for me to hear.

And goodness knows I have spent countless nights in every saloon she ever sang in since I arrived in New York in the winter of 1960. But I really don't think I knew very much about the private person, only the public passion that was Mabel Mercer.

Rex Reed

Introduction
What the Stars Said

Among her numerous adopted animals, Mabel Mercer had two stray cats, a mother and a kitten, both of whom she called Minnie—but in different musical tones. A deep chuckling growl brought Minnie kitten, and a lilting soprano called mother Minnie. There was never a moment's confusion on the part of either Mabel or the cats.

Mabel Mercer knew intuitively that all creatures perceive directly through their senses, communicating without syntax. She realized that tonal expressions are understood and are indeed very similar from species to species; that cats are by nature oblique creatures who prefer not to betray their thought processes to human nature. Mabel herself had something of a feline nature—sly, wise, indirect, intuitive, a little lazy, graceful, set in her ways, "not opinionated, but firm," and complicated.

Although I never knew her, one day as I was casting about for a new biographical subject, I happened to listen to a tape collection of popular singers; quite suddenly a voice reached out and electrified me. The accent—the hint of rolling rrrrs, so odd in a popular singer—was it concert training, or perhaps a Scottish burr? What kind of ethnicity was betrayed by the unusual clipping of consonants; was this a studied mannerism? And what sort of person could communicate such an incredible feeling of openness and vulnerability to love, singing out a childlike trust, an adolescent's pain, in the wryly humorous nuances of worldly experience? That voice held longing, insinuation, irony, sophistication, wisdom, naughtiness, and chagrin, but never vulgarity.

The elusive accent turned out to have originated in the swirling gene pool of the English Midlands, with a lyrical overlay of Welsh and African-American, and along the way an exposure to French and German. It was a voice that picked up languages easily; and was definitely so upper-class, so worldly, and so personal that no one could possibly have confused it with another.

Until Mabel Mercer came to America in 1938, popular song was far from a polished art form. Mabel imbued it with a unique melding of her own early experience and survival training, which ranged from European classical and operatic singing to night club revues, minstrel shows, and African-American jazz. Music critics struggled to find adequate descriptive adjectives, and continue to do so.

Mabel taught generations of aspiring stars in every field of entertainment the simple truth that lyrics counted, that they were meant to tell a story, that they deserved to be sung with clarity and phrasing, exquisite diction, naturalness, and above all, honest feeling. During WW II the tiny, tumultuous night clubs of Manhattan provided the atmosphere in which her talents and those of America's greatest popular singers flourished. Crooners, swingers, jazz musicians, song writers, symphony conductors, even opera divas revered the little mulatto from the music halls of the English Midlands. Her style had evolved in the famous Bricktop's Club of "Lost Generation" Paris, where she sang with such talented musicians as Django Reinhardt, the Romany genius of the jazz guitar, and jazz violinists Stephane Grappelli and Eddie South.

Bobby Short, one of her many disciples, said: "I miss the presence of her. She is irreplaceable. She developed enormous style such as I had never heard. It was a wonderfully warming, entertaining, informing presence. I learned a great deal from her. I often saw Sinatra and Billie and Lena and even Piaf in her audience. Barbara Cook and Felicia Saunders. Other, more popular singers listened to Mabel at Tony's and sang the songs and reached the top of the charts."

Cabaret veteran Margaret Whiting, one of her more famous followers, says, "The first time I heard Mabel Mercer sing I knew that my world of music and singing had changed. I think Mabel had the most respect of anyone in entertainment. She was very special and beloved."

Actress Marian Seldes described her singing as "the creative process of discovery shared with us…." Vocalist Johnny Mathis said, "You feel she is telling you, a close and much loved friend, a very personal story…. And she does it all with a regal bearing uncommon in today's casual society."

"Going to the little clubs to hear Mabel," said cabaret singer Pat Carroll, "you felt somehow that you were making a pilgrimage to a special place for some extraordinary reason…."

Comedian Kaye Ballard recalls her first meeting with Mercer, "At first I could not see what all the fuss was about. By the end of the set, I was enthralled. What was magnificent about Mabel was that every second was a treasure. When she sang 'The End Of A Love Affair,' if you had not already gotten there, you were completely destroyed. She was wonderful, gracious, kind… asked for so little in life and gave so much. It hurts my heart when someone doesn't get the recognition they deserve, people who have entertained all their lives." How had this relatively unknown *chanteuse* inspired such passions? I became determined to learn about Mabel Mercer, bearing in mind that discretion was her lifelong guide. She was more stylist than recording star, in time more an actress than a vocalist, but always a beloved and inspiring model for generations of entertainers. The finest jazz groups invited her to sing with them, yet she was not a traditional jazz singer. She was a brilliant occasional concert singer who preferred small New York nightclubs and thus was little known to American jukebox audiences of the mid-twentieth century. Only in later life did she become internationally famous.

All of her friends and disciples were somehow shaped by knowing her. They still miss her, although she died in 1984, and love to talk about her. This made my self-imposed assignment easier than it might otherwise have been. The journey became an enlightenment.

American popular songs have been with us since the advent of recording technology and even before, but the genre is still somewhat elusive. A few years ago Whitney Balliett wrote, "A certifiable body of classic American songs now exists, and we need an elegant and accurate phrase to describe them." They are "not ephemeral" but are "the work of melodists directly descended from Tchaikovsky and Puccini and Rachmaninoff...."

This view of a uniquely American quality was first made clear by composer Alec Wilder and his coauthor James T. Maher in the fifties, and more recently by James R. Morris and others, and is now generally accepted. From 1910 into the fifties, as Morris writes, "a group of composers and lyricists produced songs that were so well crafted in their melodic episodes, so sensitive and responsive in their word set-

11

tings that they stand as distinctive achievements in our culture." These were the great popular classics of Kern, Berlin, Gershwin, Porter, Rodgers, Hart, Hammerstein, Arlen, Carmichael, Fields, Wilder, Sondheim, and numerous others. Morris too believes that there is something different about these songs, "something better than their origins." (Something far better, he might have added, than most of their successors.) Popular songs of this era "sustained and nourished fine melodic writing to a greater degree than did any other musical style."

It is obvious, by now, that we are not likely to get an acceptable descriptive word or phrase that does justice to this genre of American music: classics or standards, pop or show tunes or cabaret. Mabel Mercer loved them all; she learned and sang the lyrics to thousands of songs. Perhaps we could not go far amiss by calling them "Mabel Songs."

For the past several years, the Mabel Mercer Foundation has been dedicated to staging hugely popular music festivals on both coasts of the United States as well as overseas. These weeklong "Cabaret Conventions" in New York, San Francisco, London, and other major cities serve to revive the civilizing fallibilities of the past and create much-needed venues for the young entertainers and the new ballads of today.

As we welcome the 21st century, it seems especially fitting to celebrate the 100th birthday of Mabel Mercer.

Acknowledgments

I am grateful to the many friends and acquaintances of Mabel Mercer, both entertainers and fans, whose reminiscences have made this book a delight to write, especially to Loonis McGlohon, Donald Smith, and William Livingstone; and to my personal friends who have encouraged me in the process.

First of all I thank my talented and hardworking editor, Robert Uth. I am grateful to my loyal friends Barbara Nelson and Jim Kantor for their tactful and generous editorial critiques. I cherish the memory of the late, unforgettable Thelma Carpenter, a lifelong acolyte of Mabel's, a talented big band singer and star of Broadway and Hollywood in her own right. Thelma's friendship and humor, and her reminiscences of Mabel and Billie Holiday are precious. As long as she lived on Central Park West opposite Duke Ellington Drive, a portrait of Lady Day framed in electric lights hung in her kitchen, with a likeness of Mabel nearby.

I also thank Terry Y. Allen, Betty Aberlin, Jean B. Adams, Steve Allen, Read Arnow, Denis L. Baggi, Kaye Ballard, Whitney Balliett, Judy Bell, Fred Bornet, Barbara Bordnick, Charles Bourgeois, Pat Carroll, Margaret E. Cheney, Tom Copi, Stanley Cranston, William Engvick, Eileen Farrell, Muriel Finch, Stan Freeman, Darrell Henline of *Cabaret Scenes*, Bart Howard, Christine Johnson-Smith, Jack Kabulian, the late Madeline Kahn, Orrin Keepnews, Susan Kuralt, Peter

13

Leavy, Pearl Lemert, David Litofsky, Dorothy Loudon, James T. Maher, The Manchester City Librarian, Andrea Marcovicci, Don McCormick and the New York Public Library for the Performing Arts, Nan McGlohon, Dan Morgenstern and Vic Pelote of the Institute of Jazz Studies, Rutgers University, Helen Nash, Portia Nelson, David Newell and "Mr. Roger's Neighborhood," Father Peter O'Brien, Paul Padgette, Ray Peters, Lewis Porter, Willard Pratt, Rex Reed, the Ronald Reagan Library, Evelyn Sasko, my agents Susan Schulman and Christine Morin, Bobby Short, the late Frank Sinatra, the Directors of the Mabel Mercer Foundation, Father Lee Smith, David Rae Smith, William Stowe, Ernest Urvater, Marlene VerPlanck, Adde Wallin-Beach, Ronny Whyte, Welsa Whitfield, Margaret Whiting, Faith Winthrop, William Woods, and Marian Zailian. For design and technical support I thank Radomir and Mary Perica, Trish and Peter Wright, Jim Glenn, and Michael and Pamela Noble.

I am especially grateful to the Schomburg Center for Research in Black Culture of the New York Public Library for its excellent resources on Mabel Mercer, Bricktop, and other artists of their era. On my first visit to the Library I was thrilled to see a display of two National Medals of Freedom—one awarded to Langston Hughes and the other to Mabel Mercer.

M.C.—2000

Chapter 1
Affairs of the Heart

In her long Sunday searches of the New York country-side for a bit of God's earth to call her own, Mabel Mercer almost despaired. It was 1950 and the entertainer was the same age as the twentieth century. At least, she reflected, returning to her crazily overcrowded Manhattan apartment with country greens still shimmering behind her eyes, at least they did not burn crosses on 110th Street, which was actually borderline Harlem, or Central Park North as she preferred to call it.

To the uninitiated, entering Mabel's apartment was a challenge. It was not easy to navigate through pathways and tunnels to the little clearings that remained after her many years of collecting and stockpiling the material consolations of life. Though she might laugh and call herself a "demented squirrel," she never stopped cramming her home with broken and cast-off furniture. She kept collecting; somehow it helped fill an old emptiness.

Harry Beard was only the most recent manifestation of the problem. After their last blow-up, he had gone to Chicago to work for a mortgage company. Mabel did not know if she would see him again, or even wanted to. The thought of living without Harry was impossible, yet the hope of ever living with him was purely farcical. He was a Jew, married, with children; she a colored Catholic, still married in the eyes of the Holy Roman Church. Laughable.

Mabel addressed that final word to the chastising cats who rushed to greet her—all, that is, except Winkle, whom the jealous others knew to be crouched in his prime yellow mixing bowl on the highest bookshelf. Mabel would pretend to search for him amid the jungle of furniture. Finally, like slowly rising bread dough, Winkle would deign to lift his great golden head and yeowl at her as if to say, "Where the hell have you been?" causing the singer to exclaim with mock surprise and delight.

The courtesies and rituals having been observed, she would steam up the apartment by showering her many plants, then herself. Putting on her favorite satin pumps and an elegant street outfit, she launched her old Buick with haphazard abandon toward the club on West 52nd Street. There, where even strangers knew her as Mabel, all but her intimates and colleagues addressed her as Miss Mercer. Occasionally she glanced out a front window at limousines disgorging the unforgivably rich, the splendid, the titled, the rajas and rakes and royals. She would whisper to Bart Howard or her accompanist Sam Hamilton, "Who *are* all these chichi people?"

How, indeed, did this small, unostentatious woman attract such determined throngs? More than mere admiration, it was almost a form of worship. Nor was it just older entertainers who vied for her favor and friendship, but people of all ages and walks of life. Once they had found her, they seemed to fall under a spell.

On any given night in the smoky, overcrowded nightclub, regulars might see her chatting with the Archbishop of

New York or the Secretary-General of the United Nations. Always a young and adoring priest would be hovering somewhere in her sphere, usually trying to seem invisible. Sometimes Harry Beard was there. The tall good-looking Philadelphian, his eyes discreetly swimming all over "Madame" as he called her, would finally settle into his private corner, his forehead tilted into laced fingers, a sign that he was not to be disturbed.

Composer and arranger Loonis McGlohon recalled with awe that everyone who encountered Mabel Mercer seemed immediately to recognize her gentleness, the aura of goodness about her. "When she was in public," he said, "her fans treated her with a kind of reverence. ... Every chair she sat in became a throne. No one ever grabbed her or tried to get her attention by loudness." He remembered one night at a theater when several people spotted her, came over, and knelt beside her aisle seat. If anyone touched her at all, it was only with light fingers on her hand. People always spoke so quietly. And generally it was to say something like, "I love you, Miss Mercer."

Yet Mabel Mercer was the last person in the world to invite worship. It embarrassed her. She did not even like to be addressed in public as "Madame." People who had met her in other contexts often knew her for years without suspecting that she was famous, or even an entertainer. Mabel was simply and indisputably Mabel, no matter where or when. In her private life, she believed that doors were made to be closed.

Although neither physically beautiful in the classical sense, nor even fashionable, she exuded a charism, especially on stage. In conversation she radiated a warmth that helped

17

people find new and surprising things to admire in themselves. Although she was often described as America's most influential singer, her greatest gift was surely her ability to enrich the spirits of those who met her or heard her sing.

William Livingstone, the scholarly editor and columnist of *Stereo Review,* speculated that part of her enigma lay in her gift for true friendship, as opposed to mere acquaintance. He asked, "How does one recognize a kindred spirit and how much of one's inner being is one willing to share with another person? Not everyone has the gift of sharing. We know how difficult it is to really express what is closest to our hearts or minds. Some people have a talent for eliciting confidences or communion with another's soul. Despite her reticence— her famous discretion—Mabel had the gift of making people feel that they could put down their defenses and reveal their true vulnerable selves."

Of course, it was partly Mabel's famous discretion that encouraged so many to confide in her. Since she refused to talk, for example, about her rumored acquaintance with Queen Elizabeth, American friends were sure the two women must be close.

Mabel disliked being called on to analyze her own musical style. Artists who sing, play, paint, write, or fly through the air are usually impelled by inchoate emotions, and they themselves often wonder whence the creative urge and what it might mean. Mabel, who was to vocalists what Louis Armstrong was to horn-blowers, found it all but impossible to explain. Her response to those seeking critical analysis was usually, "It's all in the songs, dear, all in the songs." Once, perhaps feeling near the end of her tether, she was heard to say, "It's all in the punctuation."

But she was able to describe the kinds of music she

loved, and the problems of singing to a small group, and how she felt when others began to tailor their styles to hers. She attracted admirers of extremely wide-ranging and diverse talents. She said of them, "It's wonderful that they say these things, and it makes me very happy, but you know, I've never had a pupil or coached another singer. I can't think of anyone specifically who influenced me as a singer. The Americans, when I first came, all sang so differently. I admired them a lot but I felt theirs was a style I could never acquire. I never thought I was good enough to do anything anyway, and as long as I could sing and get by and get the rent, I'd be happy."

Her humility was no put-on, nor was her fear of want. As she sipped tea one day with William Livingstone and Donald Smith, the men smiled to see her casually dropping a few sugar cubes into her pocket, presumably against the next world famine. Yet it was this same self-effacing woman who inspired the megastars of song.

"If you have any *listening* ability," she said, "you naturally learn from watching others perform. Mostly you see their mistakes and think of ways to avoid them yourself. First you have to learn how to stand and what to do with your hands." She described a young woman she had heard sing in the Bahamas. "She had a beautiful voice and she just came out and sang. Dead still. Never moved…not even her hands. And I said, 'Of course, that's it. Don't make any unnecessary movements!' I've never forgotten her composure."

As to the tricks of singing to intimate cabaret groups, "You have to learn to sing for them and somehow sing at them, but not sing to them in a way that embarrasses them. So I tried singing at them, but ignoring them, and they'd suddenly relax and become engaged in each other if they were lovers…and not in me, but in what I was singing and how they could apply it to themselves. That's how it started, and I became very comfortable with it."

Mabel added, "I look at the audience, of course, but individuals don't know whether I'm seeing them." Still, she admitted being pleased when someone told her, as they often did, "I felt that you were singing particularly to me." What that meant, she concluded, "is that they were able to apply the lines of the songs to their own experiences."

A mutual love of cats drew her and William Livingstone together. "Mabel was very fond of cats," he said. "She told me how much it upset her whenever one of her cats died…. Afterwards, she said, it was like being stabbed in the heart if she came across a snapshot of one of her departed cats." Mabel usually performed "Chase Me, Charlie," a little-known Noel Coward song about two cats, whenever she spotted Livingstone in the audience.

Big-band singer and Broadway star Thelma Carpenter said that Mabel always reminded her of a cat. "She walked like a dancer, or a cat." Thelma described her "bluest-blue" eyes, like those of a Siamese, and said that Mabel had a cat's watchful indirection and subtlety.

Carpenter confessed that she knew Mabel (who was English, Welsh, and African-American) for five years before she even realized the singer had blue eyes. "She sort of looked at you through her eyelashes. We were on the train one day going to see summer stock with Joel McCrea and his future wife. I was sitting across from Mabel when the sun suddenly struck her face and I said, 'My God, you got blue eyes!' She said, 'But of course, dear.'" Thelma remembered that she was always "cracked up" by Mabel's high-society air and her "dishy little *hah-hah-hah* laugh. She was so *good* at it."

Mabel's rapport with audiences extended especially to her following of gays. Perhaps it was her irreverence toward the stuffy and proper, or her quiet, non-judgmental nature that endeared her to those who were then living outside the norms of society.

As to self-analysis, Mabel was as puzzled as anyone. The orphan child in her ultimately began to give way to the knowledge that she embodied a real and precious link with the universal family of life. "I sing in a nightclub," she said in her later years, "and it seems to me I can reach people through the songs. And even though my voice is practically gone..., people all tell me they get great feeling from me. People come and say such nice things to me—personal things about themselves—and what effect I seem to have had upon them and this comes not from me, but from Someone else. I feel that's when the Spirit is around. You give solace to this one or that one; this is the gift that has been given me to make use of."

She went on, "I have great faith.... When I'm troubled, I go out and sit in the country and look around, and I feel a great presence and a sense of wonder and amazement continuously—just the beauty of the earth and things that grow, and this is what gives me peace of mind. It's like being in the middle of a stormy day and suddenly the sun shines through; it's like someone saying, 'I'm here, I'm here all the time.' Well, I just hope I can pass on that feeling to other people when I'm performing."

In truth, Mabel never understood her effect on her audiences. "I often think, how can anybody sit and listen so quietly? People seem to turn inward and see within themselves things aroused by my performance —I mean spiritual things for them. I get so many letters, and I say, 'Good God, I didn't realize I would have such an effect on this person or that. Certainly, it's something other than me.... The listener gets something through me but it's not me at all...."

It pleased her to reflect that she and her audiences had grown up together, learned together, and aged together, like a family. "I've got to know very many people because they come to see me—continuously. And they have grown up in those years, and so have I.... You become a link with everybody.... I don't understand what it is. They come to me and say I made them think about things that probably they didn't want to think about. You ask me if music expresses the spirit.... I think everything around us expresses that."

The goodness that so many people felt and were drawn to as Mabel aged was probably best explained by her certainty that everything in nature possesses spirituality; one need only be receptive. Her own human antennae had been finely tuned over the years by "affairs of the heart." For beneath the coffee-and-cream complexion of this talented and sensitive artist dwelt the most human of qualities—pain, sorrow, loneliness and doubt.

Chapter 2
Princess of Serendip

Tiny, childlike Emily Wadham was barely fourteen years old when she rushed to a midwife's house after her last set on a music hall stage at Burton-Upon-Trent in Staffordshire, England. It was February 3, 1900, near the end of the reign of Queen Victoria.

The young Anglo-Welsh mother had been born in the booming waterfront city of Liverpool to a family of singers, dancers, musicians, and painters. Her birthplace was significant. People of western England cheerfully modeled their leisure pursuits not on those advocated by fusty royalty, but on more imaginative entertainments. Local entrepreneurs and impresarios created their own versions of London musical theatre, newspapers, concert halls, pleasure gardens, and walks. The most prominent British actors joined touring companies, strutting the boards off-season in the "Empresses" and "Palaces" of Liverpool.

No doubt something about the city's busy docks, its salt air, and the prevalence of low dives encouraged such blithe behavior. Liverpool had originally soared ahead of its neighboring cities on the strength of a colonial trade in slaves and tobacco. It then reached eastward with a far-sighted string of canals and horse-drawn barges into Lancashire cotton. The merchant oligarchs, who ran Liverpool like a family store, thoughtfully diverted some of their trove into libraries, alms-houses, and charity schools. In the great tradition of *noblesse oblige*, the arts and artists of the port city flourished through the decades, even down to a mid-20th century event revered in living memory as the debut of the Beatles.

As for Emily Wadham, she had escaped from her family in Liverpool and was living temporarily in an actors' boarding house in Manchester, a sprawling industrial town proudly known as the cotton milling jewel in Britain's textile crown. There it was rumored that even the clergy talked of nothing but trade. Manchester was also a place of public houses and inns, music halls, cockpits, factories, Irish-immigrant shanties, capitalist mansions, churches, convents, smugglers, tooth-drawers, and houses of prostitution. Emily was pretty, five-feet-one-inch-tall, with intense blue eyes and a fair complexion. She was stage-struck and possibly also in love again. She had become a small but popular hit with the Liverpool sporting crowd. And now she was having a child.

The unusual baby was delivered by a competent midwife in a chamber perfumed with lye soap, rather like the Florence Nightingale school of fearful competence. The tiny red ears of the emerging newborn still echoed to the whoops and whistles of Emily's fans, to which the embryo must have grown accustomed during its final bouncing trimester. Now suddenly that enthusiastic applause was replaced with the mother's birthing screams, to which the baby added her own indignant squalls. The midwife took one look at the wet, wiry black frizz on the infant's head, gasped, and began blotting it with a towel as if to expunge it.

Then, just as suddenly, she stopped and crossed herself. The skin coloring was off too. It must be a *lusus naturae*, she thought, a sport or freak of nature, an ugly duckling that with God's blessing might turn into a swan. She hastily cleaned and wrapped the tiny creature, then placed it beside the blond mother, who lay groggy with chloroform.

The assistance of a midwife in the patient's own home would have been more common, but young Emily Wadham was, as usual, on the road. Moreover, she correctly suspected that even in the bosom of a family as bohemian as hers, her lying-in would have been imprudent. She managed a peek at the baby. *Cor!* It would be enough of a shock anyway. She herself had been in a state of such vigorous denial and so unprepared for this arrival that she had not even consulted the midwife in advance.

Needless to say, Emily had also not consulted *The Young Wife's Advice Book*, an ominous looking volume she found on her bedside table, chock full of know-it-all lore. With mild interest she noted the recommendations for the infant's first *layette*: vests, bootees, matinee coats, bonnets ("for use in east wind"), gloves, Turkish napkins, Harrington or muslin napkins, long-sleeved jerseys, binders, barracoats, and pilches ("...not needed until the baby is shortened...."). Emily paused, lifted the receiving blanket, and peered down at the child. A smile touched her face. This one looked as if she had already been shortened quite enough.

Although the young mother considered herself a worldly sophisticate, she would not have known a barracoat from a barracuda, and her interest in a pilch was certainly zilch. As she read on, her blue eyes widened in outrage. "One must not allow rooks in the pilches." What did they take her for? Emily was originally a country girl who knew rooks, and she knew that rooks built their nests in chimneys. Still, she yawned, it might be rather sweet to take the baby to her first show wearing a little matinee coat. She thought of Ben Mercer, whom she had not seen for more than half a year. Examining the tiny moist shriveled face again very carefully, she sighed and fell into a weary postpartum sleep.

Emily Wadham's nickname was Mame. Her stage name at the time was Mabel LaBlanche, which she later changed to Emily or Mame Ling, when she became the shorter half of a popular vaudeville act billed as "Ling and Long." Emily registered her new baby as Mabel Alice Wadham out of fondness for her own stage name (she was rather reluctant, however, to part with the LaBlanche).

Finally mustering her courage, she introduced the infant to the rest of the family at her mother's cottage in rural north Wales. The baby would be raised for the first six years of her life by Grandmother Wadham (who was born a Bacon), in a house frequently resounding with the combative spirits of talented aunts and uncles, not to mention those of Grandpa Wadham himself.* Em, at intervals between her gigs in the provincial music halls of the Midlands, would dash home to cuddle her unusual child.

The baby born on February third in the first year of the twentieth century had soft blue eyes like her mother's, but they were fringed with dark lashes beneath strong arching black brows. Her complexion was a golden compromise of her northern and southern genes, with a sprinkling of tiny freckles. The mouth and nose were beautifully shaped, the hands and feet delicate. Perhaps best of all, her disposition was as sunny as the sky of Wales on a good day in spring.

---

* Unfortunately, the full names of Mabel's grandparents, and even the name of their village, have vanished.

The baby's hair, however, was then and remained forever after a comical black frizz. The adults in the Wadham family, worldly as they were, had seldom seen any African-Americans or other people of color, let alone a mixed-race infant.

Staring down at the new arrival, they were perplexed but fascinated—except for Uncle Phil (his true name mercifully forgotten), who turned his favorite color, cadmium white. He threw down his brushes and stamped from the room, slamming the door. Grandmother Wadham tried unsuccessfully to conceal her delight as she picked up and cuddled the warm, wiggling bundle. To the others, the newcomer seemed blessedly good-tempered and designed for play, much like an eager and intelligent puppy.

"Per'aps," cracked Grandpa Wadham, who was English, "if we keep a 'at on 'er 'ead...." The young aunts thought she might wear a blond wig, since she was likely to go on the stage. No one really minded the baby, as it turned out, except Uncle Phil. He never got over the disgrace of being related to such a child, holding it personally against her.

The child's biological father (his name unknown to Mabel for many years) was an adventurous black entertainer from the United States, 24-year-old Benjamin Mercer, born in 1876 to Joseph and Mary Mercer in Yonkers, New York. His parents were probably ex-slaves who had been smuggled north through the underground railroad or arrived later, after being freed by the Emancipation Proclamation. There is no record.

Their troubles did not end, of course, when they reached the North, where blacks were generally resented. They may have experienced the horrors of the New York City draft riots in July of 1863, in which hundreds of citizens, mainly people of color, were hanged by the mobs.

Benjamin Mercer grew up short, dark, agile, and bright. By the time he was an adult, he was thoroughly enlightened about the racial customs of his native country. He therefore worked his way across the Atlantic ocean on a merchant ship, arriving in England with six other nimble young men in a tumbling act known as the Jiminy Crickets. Their ship docked on the Mersey river near Liverpool in late 1898, where Ben Mercer was fated to meet a tiny blond teenaged entertainer who called herself Mabel LaBlanche.

The Jiminy Crickets, who were acrobatic dancers, were usually billed with musicians, mimes, palm-readers, singing parrots, and other performers. The romance between Emily and Ben was brief, however fruitful. Ben Mercer knew that the English girl was pregnant with his child in the winter of 1899, and the members of his troupe also knew, being both scared and impressed. So far as is known, marriage was never considered. The troupe remained together, and soon the agile gymnasts moved on to greener fields on the Continent.

Little Mabel knew nothing of her father's identity for many years. She did not realize that she was colored; she didn't even know the meaning of the word. The continuing antipathy of Uncle Phil remained baffling and hurtful to the lonely little girl.

For almost her entire life she would be, for practical purposes, both fatherless and motherless. But when she grew old enough to enter show business in the family tradition and had at last traced the secret of her African-American heritage, she unhesitatingly chose Mabel Mercer as her own stage name. It was alliterative. It sounded right to her and was not an affected Gallicism. Most important, if her father should see the name of Mabel Mercer on a showbill or the-

28

ater marquee and want to find her, he would know exactly where to look. He would find Mabel Mercer, the granddaughter of American slaves, who had been on the stage before she was born.

The Wadham family with whom the little girl spent the formative years of her life included a number of uncles and her grandfather, all of whom reputedly were painters. The women—Grandma Wadham, at least two aunts, and Mabel's mother—were music hall singers and dancers. In that family, singing and dancing were not things you were taught; they were what you did. You also played the piano.

Her earliest memories of the cottage in north Wales were redolent with the mingled fumes of turpentine, linseed oil, oil paint, and greasepaint. She remembered days of perpetual fiddling, clogging, declaiming, and general crashing about by adults in exotic costumes, as family members prepared for a gig. Added to the general bedlam were the screams of a parrot and a monkey, both Liverpool imports. The resident music critics also included a couple of dogs who howled and a cat that arched his back at the high notes. With the whole raucous crowd at home, the very roof seemed ready to explode. It was a little like the night of the toddler's birth, with everyone an audience and everyone a performer, yelling their lungs out for a share of the limelight. How could she ever forget that cottage in Wales!

Those early years, before she became aware of the family tensions that seemed to focus on her in particular, held many happy moments. Much later, as an entertainer, she would thank God that no one in the family had been stuffy and repressive—if one could forget the strangely cold uncle. Mabel would remember only brief times when she did not yearn for her mother and later, for the authentication of having a real father. There was a hollowness in her that was never filled, and an ache that became so familiar it seemed almost like a secret relative. She may have thought that her feelings of worthlessness were normal for a small girl. No matter how often she choked back her sadness, it became a permanent presence, a scar on her heart.

The successful act known as Ling and Long kept Em and her partner, Tom Long, on the road during most of Mabel's childhood. One unforgettably thrilling night in 1907, before they left on a world tour from which they never returned, they took the child to a local music hall to watch them perform. She remembered it as a fairyland routine in which they tossed luminous clubs back and forth across a net on a darkened stage. Her stepfather, slim and tall, and Mum, short and pretty, sprang about like acrobats in their white tennis costumes. "My stepfather had invented the luminous clubs," Mabel would recall many years later. "You'd see these squashy balls of light drifting back and forth through the dark, and it was a beautiful spectacle."

She never got over her first view of the footlights, any more than she recovered from what those footlights had taken from her. Not that she ever consciously begrudged her glamorous mother's freedom. To Mabel, the graceful Emily seemed a creature from a dream world. There were wonderful occasions when Emily popped in unannounced to cluck and cuddle and croon to the child, only to fly away again. She left Mabel fantasizing that she would one day grow her own set of gossamer wings. Then she would do something splendid to win her mother's love, and would be taken to live with her.

But until the age of eight, she had no idea why her mother

did not wish to be her mother or why she had no real father, and could only suppose it meant she was a bad girl. Uncle Phil seemed to hate her. Some days, no matter how perfect she tried to be, only Grandma and the old short-tailed cat were decent to her.

Eventually, Emily and Tom, who were deeply in love, went on their world tour as the original "Ling and Long." The names of the countries on the postcards arriving in Wales sounded completely alien to Mabel, making the couple seem even more remote. When the "European War" broke out in 1914, the talented twosome, now married for a year, settled permanently in the United States.

They entered through the port of San Francisco under the names of Emily and Thomas Long. Tom then assumed what may have been his real surname, Stonehouse, and Em was vouched for as a U.S. immigrant by one Mamie Stonehouse, an American relative. After traveling about the country, the young couple settled permanently in 1918 into an insular village in upstate New York where the charming Emily Wadham Long Stonehouse passed as a childless woman. They became active in the life of the community and were well liked and respected by neighbors.

Whenever a future occasion required Emily to recognize her mulatto child, she would pose as little Mabel's English aunt. She did this not from a lack of affection for her daughter, but because of priorities: a fear of racial reprisals from the townspeople, and her desire never to embarrass Tom. As Mabel's aunt, Emily apparently felt herself one step removed from guilt.

In later years, Mabel pretended to feel only gratitude for the heap of misfortunes that led her to seek consolation in

31

God. As she grew up, she even learned to look back on her childhood in Wales as happy and carefree. To white friends she made a practice of speaking only of the good things. And maybe it *had* been a happy time, all things being relative—including relatives.

She remembered toddling through the country lanes with Em or her beloved Grandma Wadham, gathering handfuls of spring flowers for daisy chains. "I looked like Ophelia all done up in flowers," she once recalled. "We were taught in school how to grow mustard grass and other flowers. Each year we'd watch for the crocuses. We were *implanted* with a love for the earth." She was also implanted with a lasting impulse of kindness to animals.

From Emily she had inherited a passion for poetry and music, flowers, the earth, the weeds and trees and wild creatures. In the early years when Em came to visit and they went for little rambles, her mother always carried a pair of scissors in her pocket to snip flowers trailing over the stone walls, which she would then take home and root in glasses of water. This habit of her mother's once led little Mabel astray. Having concluded that flowers belonged to God and all His creatures, she was spied one day by her grandmother raiding the neighbor's blooms with her trowel. The error, although fixed in her memory by a rare spanking, did not change her mind about the true ownership of nature and growing things.

Another, more pleasant recollection was of her grandmother's kitchen—the warm, vital heart of the family. On baking days, Mabel was allowed to stand on her highchair and plunge her arms into the spongy bread dough. She helped stir batter for scones, trifles, and tarts, and she licked the spoons. The fragrance that emanated from her grandmother's old chipped-enamel and cast-iron range proclaimed the kitchen's importance as the source of treacly delights. Mabel laughed at the belching hot-water "geezer" near the stove that created a snug haven for dressing on icy mornings and warmth for her weekly bath. From her grandmother, in fact, she learned most of the homely wisdom that girls are supposed to acquire from their mothers: to measure flour intuitively by so many handfuls, milk by a drizzle, sugar by a dollop, and salt by the pinch. Why, she giggled, did Grandma want to pinch the poor salt? She learned to cook by memory and taste, rather than by recipes.

Regional dialects in the nearby villages changed every few kilometers. Even when she was tiny, Mabel picked them up easily and democratically, including the "Mersey Sound," also known as "Scouse." This had woven its colorful way into the idiom via a flood of Irish workers during the industrial revolution. From there Scouse fanned out into the great world, sailed to Australia on the convict ships and, much later, was imported to America by various entertainers. To the bewilderment of Mabel's American friends years later, she could sing out a greeting in lilting Welsh upon encountering a traveler from Wales, or rattle off a wonderfully foreign-sounding patois if she happened to meet someone from Lancashire. "Ee, but th'art a gormless lad!" she once exclaimed to an American interviewer during a conversation in which they had been speaking French.

In Mabel's childhood, this talent for slang and weird regionalisms must have appalled her stage-struck mother. Em, when she thought of it, was determined that Mabel should learn RP (Received Pronunciation) or the King's English, the standardized speech encouraged in British schools. RP was

33

an English child's only hope of gaining access to the educated classes. Carried to public-school extremes, one could
be considered *fraffly* well-spoken by the simple device of not
dropping *aitches*, by saying *chahnce* for chance and *evenchalleh*
for eventually; by remembering that a *bison* was not the thing
you washed your *fice* in, and that one did not win gold stars
for standing around *oidle*. None of this was too intricate for
Mabel, however, with her natural ear for nuance.

   An American friend, the composer Bart Howard, once
said he was perplexed by the fact that she insisted on saying
swimmin' pool for swimming pool, considering her famous
diction. But as one authority has written, "it is an irony of
English speech distinctions that the 'assured' upper and 'in-
different' lower classes should share the casual 'in,' in sharp
contrast to the careful 'ing' articulation of the ever-anxious
middle classes." By mastering such mysterious but infallible
distinctions, the fatherless mulatto child became the regal lady,
Mabel Mercer.

   One early morning in north Wales, before leaving on
her world tour, Emily arrived unexpectedly for Mabel. She
took the child downtown to a vacant, barnlike music hall.
Leading her onto the stage, Em told her to stand there while
she climbed to the highest balcony, a vastness inhabited by
bats, cobwebs, and the ghosts of departed thespians. When
the little girl could barely find her mother in the vault of the
building, Em yelled down, "Now sing! And I want to understand every word!"

   Mabel, speechless and dry-mouthed, her knees banging
and her lips trembling, wanted more than anything to please
her mother. From the distant darkness, Em's voice echoed
forth again. "I can't hear you!"

Mabel struggled with the terrible gripping stage fright, an affliction from which she would never be free. At last she sucked in a deep breath and found her childish soprano treble.

She and her mother left the theater only after she had sung, as loudly as she could, the expected song. Her mother heard every word, and Mabel never forgot.

Chapter 3
"Golliwog"

Until she was nearly eight years of age Mabel was not aware that she was different from other children. That innocence ended abruptly when her mother delivered her to a boarding school in Manchester operated by the Italian nuns of a Catholic order. From that time on she would see Grandmother Wadham only during holidays, and her traveling mother never again in childhood.

From the green valleys of northern Wales and the security of her grandmother's kitchen to the blackened pall of the industrial metropolis was change enough for a lifetime, but it was only the beginning. The nuns at Blakely Convent School spoke with foreign accents. Shrouded from head to toe in black habits and black high-button shoes, they reminded the small girl of so many swooping black bats. God had dropped Blakely into the sprawl of Manchester, not far from the soot-darkened iron and coal fields, and then He had dropped the scared orphan into Blakely. The convent was really, and more appropriately, named Blackley, but in her later years Mabel always spelled it the other way.

The students she first saw through her tears were of uniformly fair English complexions and normal size for their ages. Some had blond locks like her mother's. No one there, including the nuns, had ever seen a child like Mabel. The children stared, slowly circling her on the playground. Her bonnet had been knocked off in the trauma of learning that her mother was leaving forever. Her manner of speaking seemed strange enough, but oh, the hair! What could God have been thinking? One little girl pointed and said, "It's a golliwog, Sister." Some of the others said, "Ooooh!" in a don't-touch-it tone of voice she had never heard before. While Mabel could not understand the word they had called her, it seemed unfriendly. The tears rolled slowly from her blue eyes and down her round beige cheeks, engraving the experience forever in her memory.

One of the nuns comforted her, explaining that the girls were referring to a grinning pigtailed little Negro doll that was sold in London shops. Mabel still did not understand, for the word Negro was also foreign. When the nun explained to her that she was half white and half black, Mabel looked at her skin in shock. It was still just a warm all-over écru shade, almost like the the eggs laid by Grandma's pillowy red hens. Was she the only person in the world who looked like this? A golliwog. Why had Mum and Grandma never talked about it? Was that why Uncle Phil—? She must be very ugly.

The nun took her hand, led her to a dormitory, assigned her a cot, and told her that God, who moved in mysterious ways, had made her special for His own reasons. God, said the nun, would never desert her, and the other children did not mean to be cruel. They meant it in a kind way, as if she were the school mascot. "What is that?" she asked with dread, and the answer failed to reassure her until many years later.

The golliwog part was bad enough, but the little girl was also gammy-handed, as they said in those days. Left handedness was considered a serious moral flaw, to be overcome only by penance. When the nuns first saw her crossing herself with her left hand, they were aghast, shaking their black-wimpled heads. Child, what will God think, they asked her. Mabel tried to imagine how God looked when He saw her being stupid, but all she could see was Uncle Phil's grimace of revulsion. She wanted to run and hide her shame.

Morning and night, Mabel prayed to God, who was reputed to love and forgive little children. Before each meal, she stood behind her chair and thanked Him for her food and her many blessings. She became the proverbial seven-year-old Catholic-for-life. The distress of being laughed at by the other children and constantly criticized as gammy-handed brought on the further problem of bed-wetting, which she quickly learned was another major defect of character. Although the nuns felt sorry for the little girl, they believed that firmness was God's love, His way of helping her to be better.

In those still Dickensian times, a bedwetter was required to take the wet sheet off her bed in the morning and sit under it in a corner of the dormitory while the other girls dressed for chapel and breakfast. Huddling under the humiliating tent, Mabel heard them giggle as they stampeded past, heard the nuns shush them, and wondered if there would be anything left for her to eat. Her stomach was never full. She sobbed, longing for Grandma Wadham's soft, comforting arms and for one of her thick scones drizzled in treacle.

One classmate suggested that Mabel might have to wear a nappy, which was a diaper—and they also teased her about having "nappy" hair. It was all so confusing. How could God ever manage to love such a wash-out? She despaired.

In time, however, she managed to cross herself with her right hand, which put her in better standing with the sisters and the Mother Superior. Later on, as a professional dancer, she would even claim to feel grateful to them as she mentally crossed herself with her right hand before taking the first step with the correct foot. God's help in converting a handicap into both a religious and secular triumph undoubtedly reinforced her faith.

The nuns also drilled her in the duties of a good girl: learn to sew, cook, mend, clean, and study; be gentle, patient, and kind; avoid idleness and gossip, respect old age, hold her tongue, keep the dormitory and her smocks tidy, control her temper, help the weak and sick, dust away cobwebs; and above all, mind her religious gratitude. Gradually life became easier for her at Blakely Convent School, but Mabel had one flaw that she wisely never recanted. That pertained to the large fussy category described as woman's work. Cleaning and dusting she detested and always would.

She gradually won over the other children, who sometimes called her an African princess, which she found mystifying but vaguely pleasant. Her real forte was demonstrated at night in the dorm when the weary nuns were asleep. Then Mabel entertained her roommates with a precocious repertoire of the vaudeville and music hall numbers she had learned at home. She taught them clogging and shuffles and a wicked routine called the shim-sham-shimmy, to the tunes of "Bye Bye Blackbird" and "Alexander's Ragtime Band."

Her hair, which never grew long, remained the bane of her life. Mabel took various creative steps to make it look long and swishy, like the gorgeous flaxen mop of Queenie Vail, who sat next to her in the refectory and whose name and blond mane she would never forget.

In a moment of candor at the age of seventy-five, Miss

Mercer told editor William Livingstone how indelible these early impressions had been. "I remember one little girl said to me, 'Oh, you'll never get married.' And I said, 'Why?' 'Your hair's too frizzy,' she answered. 'No man will ever marry you.' And another kid said, 'We'll turn you upside down and sweep the floor with you.' And I got terribly upset because I had golliwog hair."

Being nothing if not creative, Mabel collectèd bright tag-ends of yarn which she laboriously tied to a band around her stubborn black frizz. Now she too had something to swish. Queenie Vail called her a "jolliwog," and her other school-mates were envious. Funny and clever, shy but sly, she won her way into their hearts.

The fact remained, however, that being singled out as an orphan, a golliwog, a gammy-hand, a mascot, and a ragmop at a tender age was deeply scarring to her self-esteem. She learned to look for strength to survive mainly in the school's religious teachings. When the first bell rang in the morning, she actually looked forward to jumping out of bed in the aching cold, splashing water on her face, hurrying to Mass through the dark corridors, and sinking to her knees. The chapel was cozy and mysterious, smelling of candlewax and incense. In prayer, she felt warm and secure. She knew that God loved everyone, including the stray cat that hung around the convent's back door and with whom she felt a special rapport.

She was not without criticism, however, of the Blakely path to piety: since the kingdom of God was supposed to be within her, Mabel felt that the nuns might feed it more generously rather than on a menu obviously designed to inspire martyrdom. Sparse helpings of gruel, potatoes, beetroot, cabbage, or Brussel sprouts, with spaghetti for a Sunday treat, did not measure up to Grandma Wadham's starchy artistry in the kitchen. She was certain the Italian cook considered sugar venial. If she could only get into the convent kitchen, she could teach those nuns how to turn out decent scones, how to make oat cakes, cinnamon buns, and that heavenly junket a la Grandma. During the years at Blakely she was nearly always hungry and acquired a permanent sweet tooth.

Mabel, although she was the only mixed-race child in the convent school, was probably not the only orphan. Every metropolis in both Europe and America then had its plague of the homeless, tubercular, and starving, the displaced masses of the industrial revolution. It was not at all unusual for poor people to die of cold and neglect in the streets. On the train going home through Manchester for holidays, Mabel was stricken by the sight of little children sent forward to beg by their mothers. The desperation in their hollow eyes frightened her and would always haunt her.

At home, she noticed that Grandma Wadham was herself growing frail and anxious. Aware that Mabel's chances of marriage were not good, the grandmother warned her of the tragic and picturesque fates of little girls who did not study hard in school. She must learn how to "bring home the bacon," said Grandma Wadham, who was a Bacon, making her favorite pun. In only a few years, at age fourteen, she would finish convent schooling. To become what? A nun? A chorus girl? Granny Wadham, studying the eager little face, saw it framed not by a wimple but by fringes and beads and bangles. The child was too beautiful. She asked Mabel what she would like to become.

"An engineer," said Mabel.

41

The grandmother laughed, but not unkindly, as she explained how it was with God. God, for reasons even she did not understand, needed women for dusting. Another pun that Grandmother Wadham made was part of a homily, "What you want and what you get are two little pigs that never met!"

"But I am not a pig," said Mabel. She had already learned from the nuns that her family's talent for singing and dancing was not considered a respectable calling. This she found deeply disappointing. How could anyone not love the footlights and music, the shimmering ascent of curtains, and the marvelous costumes and music and dancing? Although her own small talents had helped to make her schoolmates happy, apparently laughter was somehow sinful. It was a great puzzle. Grandma Wadham, to Mabel's frustration, often said, "Ask me no questions, I'll tell you no lies." Then she would sing a sweet Welsh lullaby.

Mabel, being very bright, found in time that her precociously proper way of speaking seemed to awe the other children. Recognizing this as a good thing, she began to speak more and more properly until she finally sounded rather like an elderly lady. People often thought Mabel was older than she really was. But despite this protective gift, she continued to suffer in school from the paralyzing effects of stage fright.

She could not even stand up to recite a poem without trembling and stammering like a fool. Fear so possessed her that her own words seemed to come from another dry mouth a great distance away. She was even unsure when she had come to the end of her piece and should sit down. When she realized she had recited the same line several times, she would rush to her seat at last and bury her head in her arms. Years later, she confided to a friend, "I still don't know how I ever became an entertainer. I would blush and my lips trembled and I could scarcely say the words. There I was, the child of performers, and I couldn't get over it. Horrible, horrible."

Despite God and the nuns and her fright, however, she knew in her heart that she was destined for a life on the stage. She learned not to talk about it. Then she worried about what would happen to her when she got as old and wrinkly as Grandma, which apparently even children did, *evenchalleh*. Once her grandmother suggested that she might marry a man who would love and care for her. "No, Grandma," she said, choosing not to explain for fear of making her grand-mother sad. "I cannot."

Anxiety about the future moved into her stomach and sank among the undigested curds of longing for Emily's love. Mabel began to steal lumps of sugar at every opportunity and hide them in the box beneath her cot. Most of her early confessions of venial sin related directly to the purloining and hoarding of sweets.

The long days at Blakely dragged on. She watched the dark-eyed foreign nuns scurrying to and fro in their black habits and wimples, from first bell until long after nightfall, always grave and stern, forever telling their beads, crossing themselves, bobbing up and down in prayer, shushing the little girls and assigning acts of repentance. Increasingly she knew that the nuns' life was not for her. From her high-spirited mother and black tumbler father, of whom she was still ignorant, she had inherited a special imp-in-residence that cried out for happiness of the flesh, for the sensuous love of people and music, dancing, color, and laughter. She longed for flowers, good food, poetry, perfume, painting, pretty clothes, romance, wildness, and other joys and excitements. As the years passed, Mabel's physical hunger for freedom, like her longing for her mother and her real father, sometimes overwhelmed her, leaving her fearful of the powerful anger of a righteous God. She would always be close to God, she decided, but from outside the convent walls.

Mabel's family had always evaded questions about her father. From the speculations of her sexually curious schoolmates, she deduced that she must be yet another strange and unfriendly word—illegitimate. An illegitimate golliwog. She went to her favorite nun, who was kind and honest enough to explain that Mabel's parents had never been married. The sister assured her, however, that she was a good girl whom God loved. Still, the nun did not explain the colored connection and, since Mabel had never seen a person of African origin, it did not occur to her to ask. She continued to feel as if it were some kind of an infection.

Worse news lay ahead. During her second year at Blakely the Mother Superior summoned her into the office and gravely explained that she would not be returning to her grandmother's cottage in Wales for future holidays. Indeed, she was never to see her Grandmother Wadham again.

Chapter 4
Epiphany

Mabel fled to her cot, sobbing wildly, and refused to leave it. The sisters prayed for her grandmother's soul in heaven. Queenie Vail, when they were alone, put her arms around Mabel and spread her sheaf of blond hair over her wet face. Their blue eyes met, eyelashes tickling. After a long time Queenie coaxed a smile from her again. The other girls washed her face, retied her ribbons, and begged her to come back and teach them a new dance called Walking the Dog. At last she had to blow her nose and consider the changed world that confronted her.

By the age of nine she knew that, aside from these friends and the nuns, she was truly alone. Blakely Convent School had become home.

Christmas drew near, the other children were leaving, and her stomach hurt all the time. She had no reason to believe that this worst of times would ever get better. To her surprise, however, she was picked up by Aunt Sadie, Em's sister, and taken to the Manchester home of Aunt Rhoda Ring, who was also a vaudeville entertainer. Aunt Rhoda's stage name was sometimes Mademoiselle DuRoche. The child found a little consolation in the sudden attention of these glamorous aunts. There were also an uncle and some male cousins, all of whom were performing artists.

Mother Emily and Tom Long, when last heard from, had written from a strange planet called Australia. Although the Manchester relatives tried to make up for her grandmother's loss, Mabel found herself looking forward, on the day after Christmas, to getting back to the nuns who really loved her.

She was determined that as soon as she got out of Blakely she would learn the name of her father and search for him. The problem remained, however, that even if she did find him, he might not want to see her. Did he even know he had a daughter? One wretched little schoolmate speculated that her real father lived in an African jungle where he smeared his body with ashes and paint, wore feathers, and danced around, wolfing human flesh. Possibly, this tormenter laughed, he ate Catholic missionaries after boiling them in a big pot. In a rare outburst, Mabel kicked her on the shins, which led unfairly to another penance.

In the spring of 1914 Mabel Wadham, chronological twin of the 20th century, graduated from the Blakely Convent School that had been her home. Leaving her schoolmates and the sisters and stepping off into the real world, she found herself struggling with the familiar orphan's dread of loss that any changes in life had thus far taught her to expect. She could not help reflecting that she was now older than her mother Emily had been when she was born.

Perhaps she had not actually loved the old convent school, but its solemn tones of black and gray, the monotonous separation of the days by clanging bells, the whisper and clatter of the girls in their drab uniforms, the dreary penances, predictable food, antiseptic smells, and most of all the warm security of the chapel had somehow given her a

46

core of strength. The nuns had done their personal best for
her. She would ever afterward feel a sense of gratitude to
Blakely. For years, the caring nuns and her classmates were
the nearest thing she had to a family. Decades later, in America,
Mabel would name her beloved farm for the convent, spell-
ing it her way, and christened more than a few of her dogs
and cats in its honor. Her entertainer friends often sent her
match books sentimentally printed with the name Blakely.

The adolescent Mabel, an omnivorous if undisciplined
reader, had emerged surprisingly well educated, considering
the formal limitations of her studies. She was to learn a great
deal more, and very quickly, in the graduate school of the
streets. There she met many older entertainers, developing
her skills as a singer and dancer as well as her natural intu-
itiveness and curiosity. Her most valuable talents at the time,
she sensed, were her ease with the English language and her
rather awesome dignity. She still suffered as a teenager from
her old psychological wounds. The short woolly hair would
always be with her, but she was a delightfully attractive girl.
The smooth café-creme complexion accentuated her eyes—
blue-green or bluest-blue or soft-blue, depending on the
viewer. Rearing her frizzy head on her elegant neck she could
attain a full five feet in height. She could glide across a room
as gracefully as a dancer, or move with the sedate and regal
bearing of an aging monarch. Subjected to insults from street
oafs or coworkers, she learned to shrink them with a look of
sincere, almost papal compassion or, on rare occasions, to
lay them low with a deadly cut. Such armaments seemed almost ludicrous to those who knew her shyness, insecurity,
and genuine humility.

She impressed strangers, then and later, with a quality

47

of simplicity, accepting everyone she met with open, non-judgmental pleasure. Mabel really liked people and felt no need to demonstrate superiority, if indeed she felt any at that point in her life. Whether God, nature or nurture could claim credit for this rare attribute, everyone recognized its sincerity.

Before leaving Blakely she had become acutely aware that her body was maturing. Heaven knew, the nuns had warned her about the awful consequences of being attractive, their cautions maddeningly lacking in specificity yet somehow concerned with boys. Schoolmates having convinced her that no one would wish to marry her, she had good reason to fear becoming pregnant. She continued to struggle diligently with conflicts of the spirit. Although sometimes, while growing up, the blows to her self-esteem had seemed almost too much to bear, she had found succor in religion and friendships. If those let her down, she turned inward to her tough alter ego, the Wadham imp. That mischievous sprite had concluded at an early age that love and laughter were far more desirable than tears, and that nature was good. If perchance she strayed, was it not God's job to forgive? From practical experience, Mabel learned never to look back unless the view was one she really cared to see again.

From the imp she inherited the creative Wadham talent for dissimulation. She learned, for example, a survival trick to use when her mouth was too dry to speak or sing and all her nerves screamed out to run and hide: start with a clumsy gesture that would cause the audience to laugh sympathetically, and then begin. People seemed desperate for laughter, and that was a lesson in itself. Mabel noticed, however, that they preferred to laugh at someone other than themselves. That, she soon discovered, was what made the black minstrel shows from America so enormously popular.

She took genuine pride in being a British subject which, after all, was not so different from being a Catholic. Both offered disciplined ritual, showmanship, the comfort of identity, and a demand for uncritical faith. Perhaps it was only chance and the proximity of a convent boarding school that had led her to lifelong Catholicism rather than becoming a member of His Majesty's Anglican Church, but more than fate held her there. The Mass was to her an exciting artistic performance, and on leaving Blakely she promised the nuns that she would go every day. Because they had been so keen on humility, it remained a part of her simple but sacred armor. No matter what dreadful things anyone might do or say to her, she would turn the other cheek—most of the time.

Practical considerations centered immediately on her desperate need for a job of any kind. She heard that chorus girls were being auditioned at an out-of-town music hall and, after practicing a routine with two white girls of modest talents, she went with them for tryouts. They were hired, but Mabel, the better dancer, was rejected. It seemed as if the old problem of her hair would never stop plaguing her.

She bought a package of henna dye, went to her boarding house, and soaked her short wiry mop in the preparation. The result was a depressing mess, most of which she scrubbed out before returning for another try. This time, however, the manager saw her, grimaced like a gargoyle on a drain spout, covered his eyes with one hand and waved her away with the other, urging her to seek another line of work. Penniless and in tears, she went to consult Aunt Rhoda.

"Mademoiselle DuRoche" and Monsieur, her handsome old husband, together with their sons, agreed to make room for the unusual looking teenager in their performing company, "The Five Rings," as they toured the Moss and Stoll circuit. Since the other family members were of fair complexion, her boy cousins threatened teasingly to hold Mabel under a tap and give her a good scrubbing. Biting back tears, she drew herself up and in her most majestic tone said, "I should jolly well not try it if I were you, darlings." Watching the boys back off was an unforgettably energizing experience.

Mabel felt an instinctive familiarity with the Manchester music halls, even though she had seldom visited such places except prenatally and in her dreams of a life with Emily. As for going on the road, she soon found that it held none of the glamour implied by her mother's stories. The cousins had learned singing and dancing from their parents as they played in the many music halls that flourished throughout the provinces. There was little they did not know about a vaudevillian's life. They delighted in regaling Mabel with tales of hardships and their own cleverness in circumventing them.

The provincial music halls were little more than drafty warehouses where the smoke and grime grew thicker from year to year. Little care was paid to accommodations for the actors, who were treated like hired hands unless, like Aunt Rhoda and Monsieur, they were professionals who knew the ropes. As for the audiences, most were ordinary miners and factory workers with a penchant for devouring heavy snacks between curtains and expressing their enthusiasm exuberantly. They could be unrestrained in shouting their opinions of entertainers they did not fancy, but contrariwise, were also extremely warm, funny, and generous.

In mining towns, the troupe would present a matinee at 10:30 in the morning to accommodate the coal miners coming off the night shift. The fast rhythmic clatter of clog-dancing was a major part of the troupe's act. Mabel would remember how "the judges sat below the stage and reached their decision from what they heard. I was a pretty bad dancer, but somehow I got away with it." Almost everything about her new life thrilled her. Compared to the secure and pious monotony of her recent past, this was real and grown-up. Every day brought surprises, new faces, strange experiences.

Her first performance with the troupe was an act that her boy cousins had taught her. "I learned from them what was called step dancing rather than today's tap dancing," she reminisced. "We were on stage together until they were called into the first World War...."

An important part of the thrill was being able to earn money, not that she was spoiled with luxury. Music hall managers were rarely noted for excessive generosity. The family DuRoche, however, rented a private railroad car with their own billboards on the outside. They moved on Sundays by train from one town to another, playing two houses a night. Mabel learned to expect that at any time they could be fired or their act canceled. The manager might just abscond; the theater might burn down. They could be stranded on a siding in their rented car, miles from home, in midwinter. When the worst happened, a stiff upper lip was the rule, an exemplary experience for a budding entertainer. Often the DuRoches would perform impromptu shows on the train platform, hoping for an audience to appear out of the night and help them recoup their losses.

Loving the serendipity of each new day, Mabel soon adjusted. She could fall asleep sitting straight up in the train as it banged and jerked through the countryside. On long trips, their bones ached with fatigue, yet the show must go on. "Another gig, another tuppence," Uncle Monsieur would boom heartily as they hit the boards in another strange town. She became a night-owl who could awaken wide-eyed and bright after only a few hours of sleep, a talent that impressed her friends in later years. Even the vast draining ugliness of the factory cities she passed through acquired a certain calm in the morning light. Among her other new talents, Mabel prided herself on holding firmly to a boiling teapot as the train hurtled through a tunnel or shrieked around a curve. Serving tea in one's own private car seemed to her the ultimate sophistication.

She remembered from this period that she and her adolescent cousins were always ravenous, always wondering if they would never eat again. As a team, the Five Rings got along reasonably well, practicing new lines as they jolted and swayed toward their next curtain call. The cousins kept Mabel amused with outlandish vaudeville jabber. The troupe always tried to incorporate fragments of local dialects into their acts, sometimes with hilarious inadvertence, and were pleased with Mabel's linguistic quickness.

They even decided that they could accommodate her dark hair and golden complexion by renaming themselves "The Five Romanies," and becoming a gypsy song and dance group. Now they would burst onto the stage, leaping wildly about in a clatter of tambourines and screech of fiddles. This was more like it! Mabel, in her bangles, a kerchief, and layers of petticoats, could not help laughing as she flashed about the stage, wishing the nuns and her old schoolmates could see her. She often wondered how many of these new found pleasures she ought to relate in confession. The advice of the Wadham imp, she suspected, should not be relied on.

On one exciting evening, Aunt Rhoda (who sometimes also played Robin Hood) handed her niece the baton and sent her into the pit to direct the musicians. The troupe was playing at the Theatre Royal at Didsbury. Although the stunned teenager could play the piano a little, she knew nothing about conducting, but she recovered from shock and threw herself into the challenge. When they moved on to the Palace Theatre at Chorlton-cum-Hardy, she was again called upon to play the piano and conduct the orchestra. She had begun plastering back her willful hair and she wore a shiny old tail coat and white tie. Just as the teenager was beginning to enjoy a surge of confidence, however, her cousins were drafted into WW I and the family act abruptly dissolved.

No longer part of a family act and looking for work again, Mabel reexperienced the horrible orphan sense of parting and loss. "I had to go out on my own," she told a friend many years later. But this time would be truly different. She would experience an epiphany, a manifestation of stunning importance to her future artistic career.

"I thought I knew how to sing well enough and dance well enough to get by, so I joined a troupe of girl dancers," she recalled. "When we played Manchester, the home of the 'Tiller Girls'—they were like the Rockettes—I asked for an audition and they said I could go into one of their smaller troupes. So I joined the Tiller Girls, that is, until the head man saw me, and said, 'Oh, out with her, she's not right in the line.' I was so different, you see, with my woolly head, rather like … the Afro.

"But I joined another troupe and in time met up with a coloured show. Now that was a first experience! I had never known any coloured people, never met any. Isn't that funny? My family never discussed anything, and I was the only one at school, so I just took it for granted that I was one of a kind. Finding these others was like a dream.

"I was delighted. We were all different shades but all the same."

Chapter 5
Welcome To The World

Having learned finally, in her early teens, that she was not and never had been the only colored person on the planet, Mabel embraced the true passion of her life with a verve that led her, during the next two decades, into almost every aspect of the performing arts. She played in minstrel shows and circuses, in multi-lingual cabaret, theatricals, revues, opera, and early cinema. She did male impersonations and even conducted an orchestra. Such versatility, unbeknownst to her and unlikely as it may seem, was bread-and-butter preparation for becoming one of the world's most influential popular singers.

The first black entertainers she worked with, around 1915, were a minstrel show called "Spades and Diamonds." That year she also met the Bouchers, a multiracial family some of whose members became her lifelong friends. Mabel was the dancing star of the minstrel group, and she also sang in a trembly treble whatever numbers the audience asked for, including "That Coal-Black Mammy of Mine."

During England's WWI blackouts and bombing raids, the girl from the convent school and her fellow performers joined hands each predawn in a human chain to grope their way home through darkened streets. The wistful adolescent was later to claim that her life had been shaped by wars. World

War I introduced her to the camaraderie of black entertainers and a life that was both exhausting and thrilling. Mabel would never forget Harvey White, a handsome African-American boy in the group, a cut-up and clown who took advantage of their going-home to link hands with her, making sure they were always at the end of the line. One night he kissed her. When she said that she must not kiss him because she could never get married and told him why, he laughed and kissed her again. Just as she was trying to decide whether to confess to the local priest, that show too came to an end and Harvey went on his way. It seemed like another final curtain in the theatre of the orphan.

Minstrel shows led in turn to her finding a home and lasting friendships in London with the generous extended family of Bouchers. Mr. Boucher was black. Mrs. Boucher, who was white, felt that Mabel was too young to be on her own in the city, and insisted that she move into their boarding house. The two Boucher "daughters" were like Mabel's sisters. They formed a trio that kept in touch with each other ever afterward. Ena Boucher, who was light-skinned, was a chorus girl who later became a nurse. She and Madeline Graden, known as Dicky, were thought by most who knew them to be sisters although they were unrelated. Dicky was very dark and quiet. She eventually married and her daughter, Joan McPherson, became Mabel's goddaughter.

Having a family and a warm kitchen again was almost as close to heaven as Mabel hoped to get. She taught Ena and Dicky how to make Welsh muffins and they introduced her to a crusty pie-like marmalade tart. It was the first of Mabel's mutually sustaining culinary relationships. Good food was always sustenance for her soul and a blessing she shared eagerly with the other wandering minstrels of the world.

She quickly felt at home in the Boucher household with its high-decibel mix of Cockney, Lancashire, and Caribbean dialects. She picked up the street songs and dances of London blacks, a melding of West Indies and African-American imports with Old English, Welsh, Scottish, and Irish folk music. With the Boucher adolescents, Mabel belatedly discovered the meaning of a normal girlhood: the "sisters" gabbled and giggled about boys, sewed frocks, smudged their eyebrows with charcoal, blotted their cheeks with wet pink crepe paper, used acne remedies and Vaseline hair straighteners, and found outlets for the superstitions of show business. Mabel began saving coins and playing the lottery, a habit that would happily pay off in the future. With Ena and Dicky, she pored hungrily over horoscopes for hours on end. Like them she began sprinkling her speech with dears and darlings, which they all felt lent an aura of grown-up celebrity. When their favorite astrologist reported seeing a cloud over Mabel's stars, all three girls worried.

America's most popular contribution to 19th century theatre was the plantation minstrel show, a forerunner of 20th century musical comedy. By the time minstrel shows reached and captivated Europe, however, they were usually performed by white artists in blackface, and their humor lay in ridiculing what they assumed to be African-American culture. Until then, popular music had consisted of English parlor songs, Scottish and Irish ballads, and Italian street opera. The advent of American plantation minstrel shows was soon followed by ragtime music, spirituals, blues shouting and finally jazz, all expressions of black creativity born in and of oppression.

When Mabel spoke of her life as having been shaped by wars, she intuitively recognized the earlier influence of slavery and the American Civil War on the music of the black people she met in London. It was unlike anything she had ever encountered. Black religious music, as Edwin Rogers Embree wrote vividly, portrayed:

"the peculiar cadence and imagery of escape from an intolerable world into a lovely and gorgeous heaven.... It grew out of the toil and torment of the race's position during its entire history in America. The case is similar in the realm of profane music, with jazz and the blues, one a syncopated staccato of frustration and rebellion, and the other syncopated moaning. This troubled, jumpy, neurotic music expresses so poignantly the bafflement not only of Negroes but of all human beings in the stress and strain of industrial and urban life, that jazz and the jazz age have come to be regarded as belonging to America generally and to the whole world of western industrialism."

Embree also noted that the rhythmic contributions of Negroes were gifts to America, which was otherwise remarkably barren of folk music.

The great black dancer William Henry Lang, known as Juba, was already famous throughout Europe before the American minstrels caught on, as were other fine black entertainers and family troupes. Mabel, behind her convent school walls, had been isolated from any knowledge of their existence. Discovering that all this was part of her own heritage, she felt reborn. In her religion there simply had to be room for both the sacred and the profane. There had to be room for dancing the cakewalk from West Africa, had to be a place for the whole crazy mix-up. Even the minstrel shows, humiliating though they were, contained a valuable lesson: they introduced her to a singing style in which the communication of words was more important than the tune. She began learning to mesh the spoken and the sung in her rhythms, attitudes, and high-stepping body language. This combination of elements originated with minstrelsy. Mabel had no way of gauging its importance to herself and to the evolution of popular music.

Although minstrel shows had been co-opted by whites, African-Americans were never content with handed-down "blackface" songs. At every chance they stubbornly reintroduced their own jokes, music, and exuberance into the shows. As a result, black dramatists and composers began for the first time to see their work produced, along with that of gifted choreographers. Billy Kersand introduced the soft shoe dance long before Al Jolson sang "Mammy" to U.S. movie audiences. Ma Rainey, Mamie Smith, Bessie Smith, Joe Turner, Scatman Crothers, and dozens of other black entertainers were drawing enormous audiences with their own brand of humor and blues. They barnstormed their way from Memphis to Mobile, from New Orleans to Kansas City to Chicago, and on to New York, Paris, London, and the world.

Baring their souls, the classical blues singers bemoaned every pratfall of life, from faithless no-good ramblin' lovers to sickness, death, salvation, and sex (straight, gay, "pork chop," or lesbian), from lying preachers to cheating grocers and heartless landlords. Just as a pianist could not play jazz, it was said, if he could read music, classic blues could not be sung "without a full heart and a troubled spirit." At first this was considered "whorehouse music," and shunned by middle-class Negroes.

Sophisticated vaudeville arrived early in Mabel Mercer's career. Photos of the time show her as a jaunty, attractive young woman with a flair for comedy. The public had begun to prefer the sentimental ballads being introduced with revues, and she was happy to give them whatever they requested. One favorite was "Daddy, Won't You Please Come Home," which Mabel no doubt sang from the heart.

Torch songs were catching fire in every large western city, fanning out from New York's Tin Pan Alley. Almost in lock-step came the popularization of the microphone, phonograph, movie camera, and radio; then the juke box, and finally television, which heralded the arrival of one of the world's largest—and still growing—industries, entertainment. Everything new pushed aside the old and, just as cities tended to reinvent themselves over time, so did the arts.

After "Spades and Diamonds," Mabel met her first group of "real American musicians." She felt on top of the world. "Oh, this is the ultimate," she said. "If I could just perform like that! In those days I was just trying to do a few shuffles and sing ballads. But I danced for them, and they engaged me. They must have thought I was the funniest thing they ever saw, because they were Americans and I was still doing it all in my English way. But they were nice fellows and I was young, and we had good times."

The show was run by an African-American director whose name, unfortunately, has been lost. "He had collected a few Africans," said Mabel, "and a lot of artists of mixed blood in England and put together a fine show. It was called Coloured Society, I think, a very good singing and dancing show, with comedians, a regular revue. The boss was an excellent lyric tenor, we had a big fellow from Africa with a gorgeous bass, and there were a lot of fine voices in the group. The first scene was from an American show, *In Dahomey*, and we were all Zulus, running around and saying, 'Woo, woo, woo.' Then we'd each do our different things and we'd wind up, believe it or not, singing the sextet from *Lucia* (in Italian). I sang the soprano part.

"It was so unexpected," she laughed, "all those Zulus singing *Lucia*. I loved it. I never realized the incongruity until I was grown up and looked back and wondered, what must people have thought!"

Mabel would later tell distinguished music arranger and composer Loonis McGlohon that the Coloured Society producer had probably never seen an American minstrel show, judging by his uninhibited mixture of cultural effects. "The costumes were Polynesian, American Indian, and African—grass skirts and flowers and so forth. The opening scene was a dance. There were six blacks and I was the youngest. I'm not sure how many had come from Africa, but there were several very well-trained opera singers who had studied in Italy."

She described the first scene as a jungle set, "with vines hanging around the stage and tom-toms in the orchestra, which played an African beat." After the woo-wooing, the piano played a bell tone. The wild dancing stopped abruptly, the dancers formed a straight line and began to sing the sextet from the famous Italian opera. Accustomed to singing opera and making dramatic segues, they never understood why the audience at that point always gasped.

Mabel, too, found nothing unusual about this until one night, as the players were going out the stage door, she overheard a critic comment, "Isn't it marvelous how this director has trained these savages phonetically to sing Italian."

The future song stylist realized then that no matter how splendid their music, she and her newfound people would always be judged by the shades of their skin. She stayed with that show until the end of the War and the Spanish flu pandemic of 1918. "That was terrible," she recalled. "Our conductor had such a bad case of it that he couldn't work and my boss sent me in in his place, as a pianist/conductor down in the pit. I'd rush up on stage for my title part in Lucia.

"The conductor never rejoined us, and I continued as pianist/conductor as we traveled about, until we got to London and were to play in a theatre with an orchestra of fifteen or sixteen men. Here I wasn't to sit at the piano but to stand and conduct, and when we went to the first rehearsal I was scared to death. One of the graybeards in the orchestra looked at me [Mabel was then eighteen years of age and five feet tall] and said, 'What can she do?' and my boss spoke up very strong, 'She can do exactly what I want her to do.'"

He took Mabel to a tailor who rigged her out in a stiff-bosom shirt, white tie, and tails. Her barber, to her delight, clipped her hair close to her scalp and greased it flat. Her small breasts were flattened with a girdle. A photograph of the artist from that period shows a marked transformation, not just interestingly androgenous, but with a new glow of humor and self-assurance.

"I thought I was *it!* Entertainers used to have what we called cigarette cards, their photographs with their names on them; and when we got to Bristol, I had my picture taken in my white tie and tails—and a monocle, if you please—and someone put a cigarette in my hand. That was me as a con-

ductor. And I had 'Musical Director' printed on my card."
Mabel enjoyed the charade immensely but it became trickier
when the manager said, "You can't talk, Mabel. I'm telling
the orchestra that you are a very eccentric temperamental
African conductor—volatile. If they ask you anything, just
sort of grunt."

Loonis McGlohon, a Southern raconteur by nature, re-
counts what followed: "She said that she got through the
first night, the second night, the third night. After the third
performance, on the fourth morning, they were having breakfast. The guys knew who she was. When Mabel said, 'You
know, I think it's a miracle that I've passed so far,' one of the
guys said, 'No, you haven't, Mabel, not exactly. Last night
after the show, my girl friend said, 'You know, I've seen a lot
of conductors, but that's the first Chinese fag I've ever seen.'

"It's not the kind of story that Mabel told very often,"
McGlohon recalled. "She was so ladylike and didn't like pro-
fanity or anything risqué. I was surprised that she told the
story, really. But you know, she had that lovely gold-colored
skin and very high cheekbones."

Mabel later confided to composer Bart Howard that an
admirer in the audience made a date with the conductor one
night, showed up to meet "him" at the stage door, saw Mabel in a gown and fled.

For the young entertainer, the experiences with Coloured
Society were seminal. She told Whitney Balliett of *The New
Yorker*, "We sang everything, *a capella* and with piano accom-
paniment; lieder, Negro spirituals, French songs, 'Yes, We
Have No Bananas,' 'Carolina In The Morning.'"

In the general miscegenation of musical modes then
taking place all over Europe, one was the adaptation of Ne-

gro spirituals to concert music. A member of her group who had been a choirmaster detected her potential and urged Mabel to study voice. She began taking lessons in the hope of disciplining her velvet soprano and becoming a mezzo-soprano concert singer. But to pay for her lessons, she had to continue working in clubs and revues; and that, she later said, "is no way to become a classical singer."

Mabel matured in an artistic atmosphere that opened her to broad experimentation, both in unusual kinds of songs and in modes of rendition. Neither she nor her friends suspected, as she slowly found her own style, that she was to become one of the great innovators of popular song.

Her English tour lasted through the rest of the war. In 1919, when travel restrictions were lifted on the Continent, she was offered a job in a huge nightclub in Brussels. Needing a passport, she was forced to write her mother about the painful details of her birth. Emily at last responded, "Go to Somerset House, Vital Statistics Division, and find your birth certificate. Then forget everything you read there...."

Mabel looked up her records and read: "Father: Benjamin Mercer. Nationality: U.S., Race: Negro." The young performer, far from forgetting, changed her name at once to Mabel Mercer. It not only rang true as a stage name, but her father, she believed, would be sure to recognize it when it appeared in lights on theatre marquees.

After learning the identity of her father, assuming his surname and obtaining her British passport, the reborn Mabel Mercer joined forces with a Cockney girl named Kay to go on tour to Brussels, Belgium. As Kay and Mercer they erupted on cue in song and dance in a huge three-story music hall that offered varied adult entertainment. After each act, men were supposed to toss tips onto the tables to attract the entertainers. Because Mabel was so shy, the more soft-hearted hostesses would call her to a table. She quickly learned to smile and duck while deftly scooping up coins or catching them in her modest cleavage. She also plucked up enough courage to begin asking strangers if they knew or had known her father, Benjamin Mercer. She had no photograph to show them nor even a memory to describe. Nobody had heard of him. She and Kay went on to Ostend.

In her travels about the world she never stopped searching for her father, who had become an almost mythic figure. Did he look like the tall and often very black Americans who were bringing jazz to Europe, or would he be short like herself? When she first met Paul Robeson, she could not help hoping that her father resembled him. One story has it that Mabel eventually found her father playing with a musical group in the south of France; that she watched and listened to him for a time, and went away without identifying herself.

Wherever they could find jobs in clubs and hotels on the Continent, the giddy team of Kay and Mercer performed. If their dancing did not seem to please an audience, they sang—alone or together. Sometimes Mabel donned a tuxedo and did male impersonations, a form of entertainment with an ancient tradition in Europe and one that was enjoying a revival in French and German cabarets. Mabel's solos usually consisted of popular ballads or Irving Berlin songs. Hard as her life was, she could not have been more thrilled as African-American music and dance galvanized Europe, creating in the early twenties what became the Jazz Age.

Now twenty years of age, she worked with a group known as "The Southern Trio," starring the team of Lord and Cabot. She also continued to work with her old partner Kay. In Amsterdam they sang in the circus ring, between trapeze artists and dancing elephants. In Germany they performed with a three-ring circus called the Heidelbach while roustabouts changed the sawdust in the rings.

"This was a great experience!" she recalled. She also appeared in a Negro variety act featuring the comic dancing of Williams and Taylor, one of whom was short, the other tall, in a routine inspired by the popular black American team of Fluornoy Miller and Aubrey Lyles. Mabel developed a crush on Williams, the shorter and sweeter of the pair, but their romance never stood a chance because of her conviction that she could not marry. The only man she really longed for was still her father.

As "The Chocolate Kiddies," wearing blond beehive wigs, she and Kay appeared in nightclubs in Constantinople, Cairo, and Alexandria. Four of the tunes on their program, "Jim Dandy," "Jig Walk," "With You," and "Love Is Just A Wish For You," had been written for the Kiddies in the U.S. by a twenty-six-year-old unknown named Edward Kennedy (Duke) Ellington. He claimed to have written all four in a single night, for $500. Once again Mabel's travels were illuminating. The Sphinx was then being excavated in Egypt, and she went to the Pyramids whenever she could to hear the rhythmic chanting of Arab workers passing buckets of mortar in the torrid sun. The rhythms of ragtime, blues, and jazz connected with race memories of an alien world, incorporating the hypnotic chants of laborers and chain gangs and gandy-dancers in the American South.

In later years she would tell a joke on herself that occurred during the Mideastern junket. While she and Kay were

66

in Cairo, a passionate Turk from Ankara wooed Mabel. Telling her that he was going home to prepare his family for their marriage, he begged her to wait for him. Before he left Cairo he sent her a romantic letter. While the address on the envelope was Miss Mercer's, the letter within was meant for another woman, to whom he had also proposed. Apparently the other potential bride got Mabel's proposal. As Mabel told an American friend many years later, "And that's why you don't have to go see me in Ankara these days."

Throughout the twenties and thirties, she continued to travel between the Continent and England. Her first performance in Paris was as a replacement for a tenor with the John Payne and Roseman Trio, known for performing Negro spirituals. She found work in the choruses of a few famous musical revues, including Lew Leslie's *Blackbirds of 1926-1927*, which played in both London and Paris. The star was Harlem's own beloved Florence Mills. Mabel understudied her in a show called *Silver Rose*.

Florence was known for her birdlike voice and, as a hard-eyed manager once said, "She ought to be able to sing—she has legs like a canary." On stage, however, the audience forgot about legs when the Dresden China doll turned into a stick of dynamite. The resemblance between Florence and Mabel was not just in their pure sweet soprano voices; both singers projected ingenuous and lovable qualities that endeared them to audiences, as witnessed by no less an authority than Broadway star Noble Sissle. Mabel's shapely legs, however, could never have been considered birdlike. Florence Mills had left Sissle and Blake's popular show, *Shuffle Along*, for international stardom in a show called *Plantation Revue*, and in doing so strained her delicate health. If Mabel could have continued as Florence's understudy, she might have followed quite a different path in musical theater, to which she always aspired. But Florence died suddenly in her early thirties of appendicitis, throwing all of Harlem into mourning. She was said to have been the most loved performer of her race.

Mabel had other early brushes with fame, perhaps the most thrilling being her performance in the chorus when her idol, Paul Robeson, starred as Joe in *Show Boat*, in the 1927 Theatre Royal production on London's Drury Lane. The American blues singer and composer, Alberta Hunter, played the role of Queenie, Mabel always longed to play the poignant role of Julie in *Show Boat*. But she returned to Paris and resumed singing in clubs, and that was ultimately where her stardom lay.

She once told her friend, composer Alec Wilder, about an imperishable lesson she learned: "A very great Negro act, called Layton and Johnston, came to England. When I was singing in Paris I got to know them, for they came over sometimes on weekends. I was singing then at the Chez Florence, and the customers were talking loudly. It disheartened me so much that nobody seemed to be listening. Mr. Johnston called me over and said, 'Mabel, I've got to tell you something. I was listening to you, and a lot of other people were listening. Don't feel so bad if people talk while you perform. Ignore them! Do what you have to do to the best of your ability and go off the stage satisfied with yourself. Always remember that, no matter what the noise, what the crowd, there's always somebody listening to you alone.' Well, I've kept that in mind…. I'm sure lots of young singers have and will continue to experience this. They come off practically in tears and fear going back on the stage…. You must learn to ignore...." The lesson influenced far more than Mabel's sing-ing style.

It should be noted, however, that when Miss Mercer acquired age, authority, and panache (literally, feathers in a warrior's helmet), she learned to stop singing and wait quietly until a loud or disrespectful audience settled down.

In the early twenties Mabel met Louis Mitchell, the American drummer, who had formed his own band in Paris, Mitchell's Jazz Kings. His enthusiastic reception by the French was a boon for the careers of a number of fellow entertain-ers who hung out after hours in his Montmartre café. Florence Embry Jones, the wife of pianist Palmer Jones, with whom Mabel had worked in Ostend, was managing a tiny club called Le Grand Duc, on Rue Pigalle. At first, she and Mabel were the only black women in the Parisian entertain-ment world. Bobby Short wrote that "Madame Florence dazzled her clients with a splendid wardrobe and her own particular way with a song, until drugs and alcohol cut short what might have been a brilliant career." Florence left to open her own place in Montmartre, the Chez Florence, while Ma-bel briefly stepped into her old spot as performer and man-ager of Le Grand Duc.

The owner, African-American war hero Eugene J. Bullard, wanted a more aggressive manager, however, and realized that Mabel's talents did not lie in that direction. Bullard had run away from Mississippi at eight years of age. His fa-ther had told him that in France there was equality for all. "After too many KKK encounters, little Eugene set out for France," says writer Alex Simmons. "... He made it by the time he was fourteen and for several years fought in the French Army and Air Force...." He had been a decorated pilot.

Having acquired Le Grand Duc, Bullard wrote to Harlem in May 1924 to recruit an experienced cabaret hand named Ada Smith. A smart, red-haired, half-Irish mulatto born thirty years earlier in Detroit, Ada was said to be 100 percent TNT and the opposite of shy. She was sexy-looking, resembling Mabel in the disarming sprinkle of freckles on a luscious café-au-lait complexion. Ada, or Bricktop, as she became known, sang a little, danced a little, had an amusing and sophisticated line of patter, a keen sense of cash flow, good legs, and perhaps most important, a talent for taking charge. This future owner of Paris's fabled Bricktop's Cabaret was in almost every way complementary to Mabel. Brick quickly appreciated that the latter's style and warmth would appeal to the insecure millionaires and playboy royalty she hoped to attract as soon as she got a club of her own. Meanwhile, she performed capably as the hostess/manager of Le Grand Duc and Mabel stayed on as a fill-in vocalist. It was the seedtime of their legendary partnership.

Mabel was beginning to develop her own unique and idiosyncratic repertoire of songs from black revues. Brick, writes biographer James Haskins, "was the sort of woman who, when Ernest Hemingway or Scott Fitzgerald walked in, would yell across the room, 'Mabel, look who's here!'" Despite the fact that Mabel cringed at such advertisement, she understood the nightclub patron's universal hunger, whether wealthy or poor, for a place where somebody (and preferably everybody) knew his name. Mabel and Brick may have been the shrewdest psychologists in Pigalle.

A longtime friend of Mabel's, American jazz singer Marlene VerPlanck, recalls that Mabel once told her of an unforgettable incident that happened while she was greeting

70

guests at Le Grand Duc. "I heard the most glorious music," Mabel said in a hushed voice, "and could not help turning around. There, seated at the piano, was a strange man who was introduced to me as the American composer, Cole Porter." This was the stuff of legends. Mabel herself was to become one of his favorite interpreters of his songs.

Had Paris not been jumping with jazz and rich Americans and bluestocking women and morose intellectuals (the "Lost Generation"), and had it not been for the fever of the times, Mabel at this point in her life might have become seriously involved with her old partner Harvey White, who had returned from New York as a successful musician and comedian. She loved Harvey, who was working at the Chez Florence in 1931 when Mabel moved to Bricktop's. He advised her to ask for an upscale 200 francs a week, which she did, and to her surprise, got it.

But Harvey had vanished again with someone else, and Mabel held her elegant head a little higher. Few of her friends knew how deeply she was hurt by the end of the romance. It might have been nice to settle down in a little cottage in Lancashire and raise six children with kinky hair. Nice. But exciting? The Bible spoke of "a time for all things."

Mabel was still taking voice lessons but had lowered her sights from concert singing. Like Marlene Dietrich, the plump young German siren who was just beginning to create a sensation in Continental cabaret, Mabel continued to put on her old tuxedo and do male impersonations whenever an opportunity arose. Bricktop later said, "Around town there was the feeling that Mabel wasn't going anywhere. No one sold her talents short—it was just that they felt she didn't have the personal aggressiveness to put it over."

The expatriates who came to Paris between the World Wars tended to orbit in small, warily concentric circles, close enough to observe each other but seldom touching. Aside from the English nobility and Cole Porter, all of whom could afford to winter in Paris and summer in the South of France, there were the Left Bank entertainers like Mabel, Josephine Baker, Bricktop, and the American jazz musicians; and the Right Bank circle of society writers, heiresses, and social climbers, like Edith Wharton, Winaretta Singer, Anne Morgan, Elsie De Wolfe, Mabel Dodge, and Elsa Maxwell. There were clever native novelists and designers from working class backgrounds like Colette and Coco Chanel, whose commercial success allowed them to move from Left to Right. Also on the scene were such lesbian intellectuals as Gertrude Stein, Natalie Barney, Janet Flanner and ever so many more, who seldom consorted with the heiresses and social climbers.

In a category of their own were the French bookstore owners (Monnier and Beach) who subsidized impoverished writers (Joyce and Pound); and of course, the gifted native writers like Proust, Cocteau, and Gide, who vied for their share of the pie and, one suspects, resented all alien circles. Few of these figures among whom Mabel Mercer's reputation developed were well known at the time, but they would later be recognized by their surnames alone.

Black jazz musicians gyrated in their own macho circle, admitting few whites, and fussing about how hard it was to find an under-educated pianist. Meanwhile, Mabel sang and shimmied her way into this celestial sphere: "We were all young together." Few of the artists she knew got special attention.

When whites appeared in the French cabarets, it was usually as patrons. Blacks were the entertainment. In America, segregation prevailed even at the Cotton Club in Harlem. Sooner or later, Mabel met all the black stars who made a name for themselves in Europe, such as Ethel Waters, Bert Williams, Bill Robinson, Valaida Snow (Queen of the Trumpet), Josephine Baker, Duke Ellington, and Louis Armstrong; and she took pride in their musical successes. For those few precious years in Paris, African-Americans were *Le Rage*, the new royalty.

Mabel's little apartment at nearby 59 Rue Pigalle was her most treasured possession, a retreat where she could practice her music, paint, read books, adopt needy cats, and from which she went each morning to one of the beautiful nearby churches. She bought fresh flowers at the wholesale market, relished her breakfast of onion soup with the fishmongers, picked up lottery tickets, chuckled over horoscopes, and when she could afford it, cooked rich food for her friends. She loved the street scenes and gregarious nightlife of Paris.

Walking home one evening in the early thirties, she was struck by the strikingly passionate voice of a pale young waif on a Montmartre street corner, and would remember: "She had tiny legs. They were like fingers, and so were her wrists. But what a powerful voice!" Not many people then knew the name of Edith Piaf, the arthritic street urchin also known as the Little Sparrow.

The first summer Mabel worked with Bricktop at Le Grand Duc, wrote James Haskins, they were ignorant of the annual exodus of wealthy patrons in August. The hot summer months found them sitting around with Gene Bullard and a busboy who became famous as the writer Langston Hughes, worrying and waiting for their bluebirds of happiness to fly back from the Cote d'Azur.

Even that winter as Brick and Mabel sat around Le Grand Duc, practicing their song and dance routines, few came in. One who patronized them was the tall, gloomy, but observant writer Herbert Jacoby, who counted customers with them and would later turn in his pen to develop two of the most famous supper clubs in Paris and New York. Sometimes he was joined by another French writer, Louis Aragon, and by American musicians who were usually looking for work. Bricktop, who had a healthy self-perception, claimed that they all sat and looked at her for hours. Time passed.

Mabel sought and found a few one-night stands in other clubs. Brick noticed that while people found her charming and her appearance striking, she seemed unlikely to become a sensation. She left for a time to work at Chez Florence, where Harvey was still engaged. Her old dancing partner seemed to be doing well for himself. "He ain't the marrying type," Brick warned her. Mabel blushed and bit her tongue.

"I learned a lot from Brick," she later said, "not how to sing, but everything about night clubs, how to meet and talk to people." She was also learning to cope with the Americanized racial and sexual jibes that invaded Europe with black music. "Yaller gal," she discovered, was both a racial and sexual insult, yet one that African-Americans might also use good-humoredly among themselves. She herself was labelled "high yaller," which could be good or bad, depending on the speaker and the circumstances. The designation "black" was then a dangerously derogatory term that could lead to violence. No one used African as a hyphenated word. The singer Ethel Waters, who was the same age as Mabel but had grown up in an American slum, once dosed her light-skinned foster child with black pepper for calling a negro man "black." She did it so that the child would remember that there were places in the world where she might be killed for such a lapse. The Wadham imp was strongly attracted to the flashy, ebony-toned young Americans and felt surprisingly at home with them, as if she had always known them.

Meanwhile Mabel went each day to church. Among other things she continued to pray that God would help her become the daughter that Ben Mercer would be proud to come forward and meet.

Chapter 6
The Champagne Age

Bricktop, in those lean years, often remembered her swinging nights back in Harlem, and the gangsters with their generous tips. Then one evening in 1925 composer Cole Porter dropped in at Le Grand Duc and Paris nightlife began to change. He caught Brick performing one of his songs. Young and well-to-do, he was already famous for his clever lyrics and risqué fraternity songs, his Broadway flops, and his alleged wartime exploits in the French Foreign Legion.

Porter, who reserved a table year-round whether he was in Europe or not, begged her not to shout forth his arrival. It was not Bricktop's singing that interested him, but her "talking feet and legs." He wanted someone to teach him and his guests how to do the Charleston at private parties.

All the new dances of the period were greeted with "unaccountable outbursts" of enthusiasm. In the case of the Charleston, an unresolved war over its origins continues even today. Many British and American whites felt better after they traced the dance to an adaptation of the old Sailors' Hornpipe, thus removing the curse of its being a negro import. Pianist James P. Johnson actually wrote the song for a black revue. Unwary dancers were warned of physical danger from adjacent kickers. The Prince of Wales was said to be practicing the "tricky steps" instead of going to his gym.

The elite circle opening to Bricktop through dance instruction was gratifying, and one to which she soon introduced the under-employed Mabel. As new dance fads preoccupied the idle rich, the two women began to enjoy a welcome rise in their earnings. Sexism had not yet become a noun and the most popular song of the day in London was, "I Wish I'd Bought My Missus On The Hire-Purchase Plan," followed warmly by "Hottentot Totsy" as sung by the Hottenham Totspurs.

The chic designer Elsie De Wolfe, by marriage the international socialite Lady Mendl, had been awarded the *Croix de Guerre* for her brave work as a military nurse during the War. Now she was more than ready to give all her attention to frivolity again. She joined forces with New York party giver Elsa Maxwell and joy was reborn, generously financed by treasure flowing from the wartime fortunes of American bankers, manufacturers, and munitions makers.

When Mabel applied for her license to work in a cabaret, she was unpleasantly surprised by the racism she encountered in bureaucratic Paris. She asked the attending clerk what to write in the "race" blank on the form, explaining logically that she was half white and half black. He replied, *"Noir."* Mabel said, "But—." The clerk said, *"Vous etes noir."*

Since she felt strong loyalty to her mother and had no idea how she might feel toward her father, she bit back an angry retort. She would always feel outraged when officials and their pernicious forms cornered her, forcing her to confront this arbitrary decision. She realized, from her conversations with Bricktop and other American blacks that France offered relative freedom compared to what she might expect to find in the racist United States. Not that she intended to find out in person.

The Harlem writer and editor Jessie Fauset presumably spoke for many of her race when she wrote simply, "I like Paris because I find something here, something of integrity, which I seem to have strangely lost in my own country. It is simplest of all to say that I like to live among people and surroundings where I am not always conscious of 'thou shalt not.' I am colored and wish to be known as colored, but sometimes I have felt that my growth as a writer has been hampered in my own country. And so——but only temporarily——I have fled from it."

Bricktop—smart, ambitious capitalist that she was—not only danced at every millionaire's party to which she was invited, but also saved her money. She and Mabel began to meet many socially and politically prominent citizens of the world. "Everybody came to Paris," Mabel later reminisced, "the Prince of Wales, Prince George, the Duke of Kent, and Princess Marina, they were our constant patrons.... And the American families like the Singers and the Cranes (not the bathtub Cranes, the cash register ones). Every year it was like meeting old friends—the Indian princes, the Maharanee of Cooch Behar, and this one and that one. I knew them all and they were all very nice.

"When you went to a party, you never knew who would be there, and we were constantly being invited to parties. Brick was very strict about that. You can go to a party but you don't sing; if you go to a party and sing, you get paid for it."

The elite were charmed by Mabel and amused by Bricktop. Into their tiny, convivial boite squeezed celebrities and climbers, counts and countesses, toffee noses, nobs and royals, nouveaux riche, old money, showgirls and playboys. Le Grand Duc soon carried a marquee sign that read

BRICKTOP. Brick and Mabel were in business now, the former literally, the latter figuratively.

Le Jazz Hot was for Mabel another epiphany, an art that was always evolving, as fluid and exultant as life itself. When the first Victrola records arrived in Paris the young entertainer saved her francs to buy them. Her sweet soprano voice and graceful dancing were beginning to be known in Left Bank cabarets, as well as the after-hours spots where American musicians gathered for jam sessions. Despite the number of black musicians in France, a Black or mulatto female was rare and much in demand. Mabel, always a happy captive of the after hours, loving the new sounds and rhythms from America, seldom retired before dawn.

Scholarly looking Noble Sissle wrote to his partner, ragtime pianist and song-writer Eubie Blake in New York: "Jim [Europe] and I have Paris by the balls in a bigger way than anyone you know...." Jim Europe was leader of the military band, the "Hellfighters," a part of the New York Negro regiment assigned to France that had jazzified Allied soldiers and even German prisoners of war. He told of their entering a tiny village and beginning to jam one day when, to everyone's surprise, an elderly French woman began dancing "Walking the Dog." He knew then, he said, that American music was destined to become the world's music.

Josephine Baker, a sensational vision of long legs, beige flesh, and crimson lips, her body encircled with peacock plumes and bananas, arrived in Paris in the mid-twenties. She was seventeen and the essence of nubility when she first appeared with *La Revue Negre*. It was *La Rage*.

Mabel, who was no prude, may nevertheless have been shocked at the dancer's candid display of her wares, and

79

Josephine may have sensed it. The convent graduate presumably had only learned to bathe in the nude since leaving Blakely at age fourteen. It was reported, perhaps maliciously, that Josephine later studied Mabel's style and tried in vain to emulate it. Such a take-off, if true, could only have been satirical. Whatever the case, they did not become friends. This was unusual in Mabel's experience if she genuinely liked someone. Neither woman discussed the matter.

Mabel still both hoped for and feared a night when her blue eyes, cautiously sweeping the audience, might brush across the face of a middle-aged tumbler, the black acrobatic dancer Ben Mercer. While searching every room through lowered lashes, she always wondered whether he might already have seen her and turned away, or had heard someone speak of her and not responded. What woman was dear to him now? Had he another daughter, perhaps a "real" one?

As to jazz, Ben Mercer's lost child was excited by the American players' exuberance and the raw emotionalism of their music. It was said that Mabel never sang jazz, yet later in life she would often be invited to sing on programs with the finest jazz groups in both Europe and America. She had the feel of jazz if not the rendition. Denis Baggi, a European jazz scholar, commented on how "special" she was: "She did not sing with the emotion of a jazz singer," he wrote. She had "a special emphasis, somewhat like pathos, which makes the difference, a clarity of line, almost an abstract, perfect quality, which is what must have influenced Frank Sinatra."

As always when she was caught up in a popular fever, Mabel continued to feel her way along her special path. In the early years, rather like her phantom father, she maintained an elusive style. Wishing to please, she tried to sing everything the patrons wanted, within her own firm concepts of decency. She was still and always haunted by an almost genetic fear of becoming, as she put it, a "down and out" entertainer, and continued to hoard precious commodities like sugar. Beneath the surface of her smile lurked all the old rejections for being born, for disgracing her family, for being the girl that only a grandmother and a stray cat and God and the kind-hearted nuns could love.

Finding her first apartment in Paris, she decorated it with a security wall of broken chairs and ruptured sofas. She suffered from the opposite of claustrophobia, and felt safest in small enclosures. Few would have guessed that this timid entertainer was bound for fame.

At thirty-one years of age (1931), she felt especially lucky to be in Europe. Following the great stock-market crash of 1929, jobs in the United States were vanishing to the point of panic, but no one would have guessed it from the high living of the "lost ones" still in Paris.

That year, Bricktop announced that she was preparing to open a newer, roomier, and more splendid cabaret at 66 Rue Pigalle. Rejoicing echoed from Harry's Bar at the Ritz Hotel across the Atlantic Ocean to the New York Yacht Club and back again to Windsor Castle, where a crash of drums could be heard from the upper dormer of a young prince named David whose monogram was a simple W. Wan young intellectuals browsing at the Shakespeare & Co. bookstore on the Seine smiled as they quietly marked their places. In a back room, James Joyce pleaded with Adrienne Monnier to smuggle a few copies of *Ulysses* into Boston Harbor. And Mabel, like the Little Match Girl, dreamed of wearing a gown by Schiaparelli to Bricktop's opening night. In fact, she did wear a brand-new Schiaparelli gown to opening night. It was either a gift from a wealthy admirer or lent by the couturier. Greeting the tall suave men in evening black and women with pale chic shoulders, she made them feel like guests in Brick's own home, contributing admirably to the ambiance.

An old receipt discloses that the singer had attended auctions at the *Salles de Ventes de Montmartre*, where she purchased several chaises for the new Bricktop's and a sable (for Brick?) for a total cost of 13,000 francs, giving as her reference Madame DuCongé. The latter name signified another important change in Brick's life, her recent marriage to the American musician, Peter DuCongé.

The new Bricktop's was conceived and executed in high style, providing the international set with soft music, the latest American show tunes, and the excellent champagne that refined tastes craved. black jazz musicians did not hang out there for after-hours jamming. As Brick noted, they wouldn't have been "right" with her clientele; she knew they would be much more comfortable at Louis Mitchell's club. Nor were unescorted females admitted to the cabaret. The room's spectacular glass dance floor was illuminated from below. It was framed by patent leather curtains and other dramatic touches, the dominant colors of the tables and banquettes being red and black. As elite guests moved around the floor they could admire their own long shadows, courtesy of lighting by the designer Hoyningen-Huené, and survey each other's gowns, created by the leading dressmakers of Paris and London.

Mabel's charm and genuineness in this smart setting melted even the most jaded millionaires, whose jokes she laughed at unless they were off-color (in which event she would float away on a ripple of noncommittal sound). She sometimes sipped champagne with the guests but was careful not to play favorites. Sometimes, late at night, Cole Porter would sit down at the piano to run over a new song with her. Her theme song at Bricktop's, and one she eventually popularized, was the wryly amusing "Just One Of Those Things." Porter was easily offended by the way singers treated his work, and claimed that Mabel's rendition of it was the finest he ever heard. When he requested that she alone sing his songs in his presence, she felt a well deserved surge of confidence.

Mabel was supposed to begin singing at midnight in the large new room with the band, but always delayed her appearance as long as Bricktop allowed. Most patrons, she protested, were well along in their cups by midnight and unlikely to be eager to "hear a soprano screeching." Microphones were not then available, and she would never enjoy using them. To solve the problem of her soft voice in the large room, and at Brick's suggestion, she began moving from table to table and sitting down to sing for intimate moments, a technique that became popular with a generation of cabaret performers. At times she also used a small wooden megaphone to reach the larger audience.

Gradually Mabel learned that by an extreme effort of concentration she could draw upon the power of higher intervention to overcome her stage fright. Prayer could and did help her gain control of the trauma before each performance.

Difficult as it is to mark the crucial turning points in an artist's development, Bricktop's café was certainly one for Mabel. Developing an original, adventurous, and rule-breaking style of phrasing and diction, she began linking together thoughts and lingering on notes with special enunciation. The effect produced a fresh sound that thrilled cabaret audiences and delighted composers. No singer before had ever paid such disciplined respect to their lyrics.

Grateful composers in turn brought her songs that no one else in Paris had heard. She began to build up an unusual repertoire. Some of the songs had been cut from American musicals. If Mabel liked them and they were not well-known, she made sure that they became so at Bricktop's. One rather mediocre song she tried to popularize for a young composer led to her "arrest" by a gendarme one night, to the amusement of Cole Porter and his friends. He had warned her that if she sang "Thank You for the Flowers" one more time, he would have her handcuffed and bodily removed. She sang the song and Porter carried out the practical joke.

It must be noted that not all listeners were enthralled the first time they heard Mabel sing, and a few never were. She became known as an "acquired taste," like caviar or a cucumber stirrup cup. As time went on, she sometimes philosophically described herself as a barnacle that grew on people, or contrariwise, did not.

But at Bricktop's, moving from table to table with cat-like grace, approaching strangers from other lands and offering to perform their requests, she almost invariably began to weave them ever so gently into a spell. Mabel evoked moods described in languages ranging from Arabic to Zulu as bewitching, alluring, magical, delicious, delectable, *ad infinitum.* As silence fell in a crowded room, she became aware for the first time of a gift that seemed to come both from within and beyond herself.

"When I was young," Mabel recalled a long time afterward, "the thing was to come out and show your smile. That was 'personality'—get out there on the stage and give it all

84

you've got… Later I used to rebel at that—you don't sing about heartbreak and parting with a grin that goes from one ear to the other."

Her emotive power emanated from a hunger that could only be filled by the expression of her genuine love of people. As the poet Marianne Moore observed, "The world's an orphan's home." At Bricktop's Mabel first began to notice the phenomenon that all singers pray for. Before her performances, the room grew expectantly hushed.

Even more thrilling, perhaps, was the entreé she gained there to camaraderie: meeting the rich, the famous, and the talented; singing with early jazz composers and instrumentalists such as gypsy guitarist Django Reinhardt, European jazz violinist Stéphane Grappelli, and the distinguished American jazz orchestra director and violinist Eddie South. She had no idea that destiny would someday take her to the birthplace of jazz with all its connotations, both good and bad.

Chapter 7
"Love for Sale"

The word shocking was seldom applied to songs that Mabel sang—until, that is, she performed a 1930 Cole Porter tune that had been banned on radio in the United States. It was not even played in U.S. theatres until its show, *The New Yorkers,* acquired a black cast and its venue was moved to Harlem. Mabel wanted to sing "Love For Sale," she said, because she liked the sadness of the lyrics.

Even tourists gasped when, standing erect and quiet onstage at Bricktop's, she began one night without introduction to sing:

"...Let the poets pipe of love
In their childish way,
I know ev'ry type of love
Better far than they.
If you want the thrill of love,
I've been through the mill of love,
Old love, new love,
Ev'ry love but true love.
Love for sale,
Appetizing young love for sale.
If you want to buy my wares
Follow me and climb the stairs,
Love for sale."

She recorded the song only later in America. Among the hundreds of romantic ballads she helped popularize in Paris are dozens still considered immortal: Rodgers and Hart's "Dancing on the Ceiling," "My Funny Valentine," and "Little Girl Blue;" Kern and Caldwell's "Once In A Blue Moon," Berlin's "How Deep Is The Ocean," McHugh and Fields' "I Can't Give You Anything But Love," Green and Heyman's "Hello, My Lover, Goodbye," Heyward and Gershwin's "Summertime," and Porter's "It's DeLovely," among many. Of older songs, she resurrected the forgotten "Wait till You See Her." Composer and arranger Loonis McGlohon said of Mabel, "When she believed in a song, it became one of her missions in life to make sure it had longevity."

One winter night in Paris in the mid-thirties, Mabel stayed home with an inflamed throat. Unable to miss more than a night of work, she returned too soon and strained her vocal cords. Her voice when she sang emerged from a tentative croak to a low and sexy contralto that the audience adored. Although her old voice soon returned, she found that she could still reach the lower, sexier registers. An alert journalist noted, "She began working on a new class of songs with her new voice."

She sang in French, German, English, and sometimes Italian, and the international nightclub world took notice. New York, Berlin, Rome, and London talked of this singer who conveyed an emotional kaleidoscope of almost indefinable nuances, from bittersweet and hauntingly vulnerable to intimate and half-mocking, funny and sad, gauche and ultrasophisticated and worldly-wise. Mabel explained to a friend in words remindful of Mehitabel the Cat's, "Well, I've been through a lot, and I know what I'm talking about."

Her reserves of energy and her ability to sleep only a few hours a night remained extraordinary. "There was a curious law in Paris at the time," she recalled. "The bistros had to be closed for two hours around midnight. So we'd go to work around seven in the evening, get two hours off after midnight, and then go back to work until any time. People stayed up all night in those days.... Nights were wonderful and exciting then. Dawn in Paris...nobody thought there was anything odd about about visiting the flower market and having breakfast at dawn."

People were carefree. There was time for fun and practical jokes. It was not unusual, she said, to see Louis Armstrong with his trumpet and Django Reinhardt with his guitar, jamming together in a small café all morning long. (Mabel's memory may have erred; another source reported that Django was snubbed by Armstrong, who only granted him an audience once, and listened impatiently.)

Duke Ellington's arrival in Paris with his classy orchestra was a major event. Mabel, according to singer Thelma Carpenter, thought him "the most gorgeous man in the world." Few of Mabel's white friends, according to Carpenter, realized that she preferred very black men and that the light-skinned Ellington was an exception. Josephine Baker also performed with Ellington at Bricktop's club.

Many patrons of Bricktop's were now coming especially to hear Mabel, because, truth to tell, they sometimes found the flamboyant personality of the cabaret owner tiring. A jealous woman by nature, Brick had no intention of letting Mabel usurp her place, and Mabel had no intention of allowing it to happen. They maintained their partnership in delicate balance through the anxious times that lay ahead.

Despite the problems brewing in Europe, Edward, Prince of Wales, continued to frequent the international nightclub circuit. He had himself a ball at Bricktop's. Mabel remained a personal friend of the (later) Duke of Windsor and his American duchess Wallis Warfield Simpson Windsor, even after he abdicated his throne, though she also continued to hold the British monarchy in highest esteem. Chris Goddard writes in *Jazz Away From Home* that the Prince's "royal seal of approval" enhanced the popularity and importance of jazz. "Many of the stories about the Prince of Wales' drumming are no doubt exaggerated, but he certainly seems to have sat in with enough bands...." He would arrive with a party and get stoned, according to jazz musician Leo Vauchant: "Then he wanted to play drums. He just kept time. He was with us or he wasn't.... He'd just come up to the band and say, 'I'd like to sit in.' And we'd say okay. We'd play some tune, and the people would applaud, and we'd play the same tune again."

Another observer said, "There might have been worse drummers! But he was very popular, you know."

Mabel and Brick had many stories to tell about the royals, but they were always discreet. When they went to Biarritz in the summer of 1932 and temporarily opened a club called the Merry Sol (to keep their clientele who went South for the summer from being lonely), the Prince of Wales came faithfully every night. "Everyone" at the time was said to be titillated by his scandalous affair with Lady Thelma Furness. One rainy day Brick and Mabel sat on the floor of their club with another young prince, George, the future King of England, playing with a wet dog and drinking champagne.

Both women enjoyed the lavish parties to which they were invited when "everyone" went back to Paris for the winter. The age of elegance would vanish all too soon, but for the moment the wealthy lived in the same luxury they had indulged in before World War I. Mabel noted that they still left their gold and diamond cigarette cases strewn on the tables as they were dancing. The city continued to churn with creativity and extravagance, determined to ignore the flu statistics of 20 million dead and the threat of another war.

The rampant inflation in Germany, however, soon spilled into France. Mabel noticed that the Lost Generation of writers were beginning to rediscover themselves, along with unpleasant cash-flow problems that kept them out of Bricktop's. Two by two, or three by three, the famous and those who were not began drifting homeward. The fabulous era was winding down.

New Yorker journalist Janet Flanner wrote acerbically, "The recent unpleasantness in Wall Street has had its effect here. In the *Rue de la Paix* the jewelers are reported to be losing fortunes in sudden cancellations of orders, and at the Ritz bar the pretty ladies are having to pay for the first ten rounds themselves." She added that little firms living exclusively on the American tourist trade had not sold one Chanel knock-off in a fortnight.

The thirties also brought, via wireless, press, and newsreel, the genocidal ravings of Adolf Hitler, new chancellor of the German Reich. All art, entertainment, and writings by Jews, including those in the avant-garde German film industry, were being systematically banned or distorted to serve fascist propaganda.

Mabel's new German friend, Marlene Dietrich, had made it emphatically clear that she would not bend to the new fashion. She was not a Jew, but the daughter of a former German officer, and already an international celebrity for her portrayal of Lola Lola, the alley-cat cabaret siren in the German film, *The Blue Angel*. Dietrich drew a firm line against the Nazi regime, and for a short time she lived in Hollywood where the power, the money, and the fleeing directors had gone.

Marlene and Mabel, who were almost the same age, had met at a party on the Riviera during one of Bricktop's summer forays in pursuit of the rich and famous. Their respective climbs out of music halls to fame on the Continent had been somewhat similar, although they had very different personalities. Marlene, as a teenager, for example, had been fired while clutching between her legs the musical saw she was engaged to play as the only female member of a traveling theatrical orchestra. There were double-standard accusations of sexual distraction. She was ravishingly beautiful, teutonically ambitious, and noted for her prodigious sexual liaisons. She was also courageous and, in her fashion, highly moral.

Despite the German siren's cheerful vulgarity and Mabel's innate good taste, the two liked each other. Marlene was captivated by Mabel's fresh way with a lyric, and the latter could see, even in silent pictures, that the rather plump German actress packed an explosive promise of greatness. Each had a flair for comedy and dance and had shared the knockabout experiences of vaudeville; each had loved prancing around in a top hat and tuxedo as a male impersonator. Marlene, however, shocked her admirers of both sexes by kissing pretty girls on the lips.

In the South of France in 1936, Marlene arranged for the first recording of one of Mabel's most haunting love songs, "You Better Go Now" (with "The Folks Who Live On The Hill"). She made it partly so that she could study it on her phonograph during her stay in Hollywood.

Meanwhile, in depressed New York, black musicians and singers were finding it almost impossible to get work of any kind. Even white entertainers, playwrights, poets, and artists competed for street-sweeping jobs, while important publishers were surreptitiously stuffing cardboard in their shoes.

The economic deterioration of all the Great Powers—isolationist America, recklessly aggressive Germany, cynical France, and Blimpish Britain, not to mention the unknowable Communists—was in retrospect the preface to another global conflict. Everyone believed that everyone else was lying about the prospect of war.

In her late thirties, Mabel realized with shock that if she now had to fill out a form regarding her age, the bureaucracy would require that she list herself as a black "Spinster." The recent years had been almost dreamlike. During occasional get-togethers in London with her old friends the Boucher "sisters," Ena and Dickie, she could tell from their searching questions that they were worried about her, and mainly about whether she still had "time to find happiness." Although they may have envied her artistic success, they shared a bourgeois conviction about the indispensibility of marriage. Secretly Ena and Dickie felt that Mabel was too vulnerable to survive on her own. They were also aware of the marital skittishness of black men, especially entertainers.

They worried because single women making their living in cabarets were all too likely to be stigmatized as burlesque dancers or prostitutes. Mabel had seen enough of sexist and racial discrimination, not just in England and France but during her travels to the Middle East, the Balkans, and other regions, to open her blue eyes. In fact, it had been as much for their own self-protection as for pandering to the patriarchal set that Brick had always banned unescorted women from her cabaret. Mabel apparently disliked this policy, however, as her later concern to make singles feel welcome at her performances would indicate.

Brick's marriage was on the rocks (she had separated from Peter DuCongé) and so was her famous nightclub. In the autumn of 1936 she turned off the lights and cancelled the champagne orders forever for the legendary Bricktop's. She and Mabel found work at a club owned by Jimmy Mussolini on Montparnasse, where it was understood that they would receive a share of the profits.

This was only fair, because the British royalty who were still in France followed the pair, as did the international "nobility" including Cole Porter, Lady Mendl, Miss Maxwell, and their flocks. Business picked up and the new place soon became known as Bricktop's. Mussolini, however, made the mistake of refusing to split the profits as agreed. Brick and Mabel soon walked out, with their retinues.

Next they led their loyal royals to a club called the Big Apple, in honor of a new and swinging dance in New York City. Once again everyone called the place Bricktop's, although it was owned by musical-theatre star Adelaide Hall (who had introduced "I Can't Give You Anything But Love") and her husband. In mere months at this club, Mabel expanded into jazz and blues singing, more likely to build an audience, along with her usual ballads. The group that challenged her to stand on stage and deliver was the wildly popular, talented, and eccentric *Quintette Du Hot Club De France*. Mabel, Django Reinhardt, and Stéphane Grappelli made a curious trio indeed. Unfortunately, no recordings exist of Mabel singing with this group, although jazz violinist Grappelli for years afterward recalled the period in which he accompanied her, usually at the piano, as one of the most beautiful in his memory. Among the many instrumental pieces he and Django composed and recorded, the two titled "Mabel" and "Bricktop" were dedicated to their favorites. During Mabel's final months in Paris she would also sing and tour with Eddie South, the "black angel" of the jazz violin, and his fine orchestra of white and colored musicians from America.

The musical partnership of Grappelli and Reinhardt was incredible enough, including as it did two other guitars and a bass in contrast to the usual trumpets and saxophones of the Americans they admired. The Quintet is sometimes credited with inventing "chamber music" jazz, a phrase that fails to capture their breadth, versatility, and imagination. They created a sensation in France that soon attracted musicians the world over.

Both men had been self-taught in the streets of Paris, although Grappelli may have had brief classical training. The son of a poor Italian professor of philosophy, he also played piano, saxophone, and even the accordion. He claimed to have learned jazz violin by listening to the recordings of Eddie South.

As for the volatile Belgian gypsy Django Reinhardt, he had triumphed over a crippling injury to the fingers of his left hand in a caravan fire, going on to infuse early jazz with his distinctive folk rhythms of song and dance. It is said that his "freewheeling and inspired improvisations" were probably the most inventive jazz sound ever to come out of Europe. As a virtuoso guitar soloist and composer, he joined with Grappelli and their group to make dozens of recordings that are still popular today.

94

Grappelli described 1937 as "the last perfect year in Europe," and Bricktop's club as its essence. He played piano while Mabel sang the "St. Louis Blues," with Lady Mendl, the King of Italy, and the King of Belgium in the audience. Every night Grappelli asked Mabel to sing Porter's, "I've Got You Under My Skin." "It drive me mad the way she do it," he said. "It give me goose pimples. All these memories bring back *tristesse*—sadness."

One of Mabel's tasks at first was to make sure that Django showed up to play, frequently a difficult responsibility when he was distracted by a nearby billiard parlor. But when a celebrity like James Roosevelt, the American President's son, showed up especially to hear the absent guitarist, Bricktop's temper flared. Sometimes Django simply went fishing or retired to his gypsy caravan parked near the flea market, giving Mabel a long way to walk. But she rehearsed her own songs as she threaded her way through the back streets, and noticed that people smiled, thinking she was talking to herself. On occasion Django and his gypsy relatives impulsively departed *en caravane* for the Cote d'Azur, where the family tended to block the main entrance to the club where he had a gig, and where presumably Mabel could not pursue him. Once the famous guitarist vanished from a luxury hotel and was ultimately found fishing on the banks of a stream near his caravan. He complained that deep carpets hurt his feet.

On another occasion, Grappelli had arranged a contract for them with an English manager that included first-class travel. But the illiterate Django stabbed his finger at the hard-won travel clause and said, "I object to this!" Grappelli, mustering a laugh, hastened to explain that it was just Django's odd sense of humor and that he always acted like that.

An almost eerie consonance of style and harmony can sometimes be detected between Grappelli's celestial violin and Mabel's voice—on separate recordings, made with different accompaniment, at different times and places in the world. A case in point is Cole Porter's sophisticated song, "It's All Right With Me," which joyously opens both a Mercer LP by Atlantic and a CD featuring Grappelli and other musicians. It is as though voice and violin somehow floated off and found each other in space.

Mabel's mother,
teenage
music-hall
entertainer
Emily Wadham,
circa 1900.
(Donald Smith
Collection)

Right and Bottom: Mabel as a teenager on the English music-hall stage, circa 1915.
(Donald Smith Collection)

Below: In conductor's tie and tails, London music-hall, circa 1917.
(Donald Smith Collection)

Mabel with the jazz orchestra of Eddie South, the "Dark Angel of the Violin; Tuschinsky Theatre, Amsterdam, 1937. (Donald Smith Collection)

Mabel with Bricktop and guests, circa 1935. Donald Smith Collection)

The famous Bricktop's restaurant and club, Paris, circa 1936. (Schomburg Center for Research in Black Culture)

*Famous friends
at Bricktop's:
Back row, center,
author Louis Bromfiel[d]
Front row, L to R,
Jack Hawkins, Brickto[p]
Marjorie Ulrichs
(Mrs. Eddie Duchin),
and Mabel Mercer;
circa 1932*
(Photo by Tony Delano,
Schomburg Center
for Research in
Black Culture.)

*Left: Mabel with GIs
and other entertainers,
Bricktop's, circa 1936.*
(Donald Smith Collection.)

*Above: In 1937,
when Bricktop's
closed, Brick and
Mabel moved across
the street to work
with with Django
Reinhardt and
Stephane Grappelli.*

*Left: Legends
Stephane Grappelli,
Bricktop, Joseph
Reinhardt, Mabel
Mercer, Django
Reinhardt, Louis
Vola, Roger Chaput.*
(Donald Smith
Collection)

Below: William Engvick, who composed "While We're Young" and other hits; circa 1954. (Photo by Frances A. Miller)

Above: Portrait of Mabel in a turban, probably in the early forties. (Schomburg Center for Research in Black Culture)

Right: With singer Jimmy Daniels, circa 1940. (Schomburg Center for Research in Black Culture)

Below: Joe Carstairs' "Whale Cay" mansion in the Bahamas. (Pearl Lemert Collection)

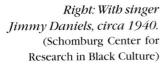

Right: Mabel as poster girl, 1940s. (Mabel Mercer Foundation)

Above: A trio of musical geniuses: Duke Ellington, Mabel Mercer, and Ethel Waters, with unidentified couple. (Collection of Fr. Peter O'Brien)

Above: Mabel with friends in her Manhattan apartment. (Schomburg Center for Research in Black Culture)

Mabel with composer Bart Howard at Hamilton College in the late 1940s. (Schomburg Center for Research in Black Culture)

Confident and calm in her fifties, Mabel is seldom without her St. Genesius medal. (Collections of Adde Wallin-Beach and Donald Smith.)

Lower Left: Mabel approving sketches by artist Lisa Rhana. (Photo by Fred Bornet)

Lower Right: The famous Lisa Rhana portrait of Mabel made in 1946; later destroyed by fire. (Donald Smith Collection)

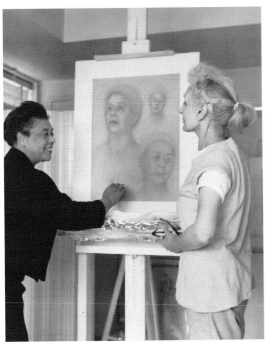

Right: Mabel with Harry Beard, circa 1960. (Schomburg Center for Research in Black Culture)

Right: The Mabel Mercer "Romantic Sincerity Test for Suitors." View from behind Mabel's head, at Chicago Playboy Club. (Schomburg Center for Research in Black Culture)

Right: Playboy Club brochure, 1960. (Photo by Avery Willard.)

Left: Portrait of Mabel in her seventies by author/photographer Carl Van Vechten. (Used by permission of estate of Carl Van Vechten, Joseph Solomon, executor)

Below: Mabel at a theatrical with Bricktop and Jimmie Daniels in New York. (Donald Smith Collection)

Below: Sharing a good joke—Loonis McGlohon, Thelma Carpenter, and Alec Wilder. (Loonis McGlohon Collection)

Right: Character study— Mabel at cards with a friend. (Schomburg Center for Research in Black Culture)

Right:
Donald Smith and
William Livingstone
accompanying
Mabel to receive her
honorary doctorate
from Berklee College
of Music, 1975.
(Donald Smith
Collection)

Below:
Mabel with actor
Alec McGowan.
(Donald Smith
Collection)

Above:
Gathered for NPR series
"The American Song."
Top row—Alec Wilder
and Loonis McGlohon.
Singers, L to R—Marlene
VerPlanck, Barbara Lea,
Teddi King, Mabel Mercer,
Johnny Hartman, and
Thelma Carpenter.
(Camera 1, Loonis
McGlohon Collection)

Left: Mabel in the snow, feeding the birds. (Schomburg Center for Research in Black Culture)

Above: Mabel's beloved farmhouse and retreat in East Chatham, NY. (Author's collection)

Left: A proud Mabel celebrates springtime. (Donald Smith Collection)

Right: Mabel, Father Peter O'Brien, and Mary Lou Willliams at his ordination, 1971, Fordham University.
(Fr. Peter O'Brien Collection)

Below: Stereo Review edition announcing annual Mabel Mercer Award, 75th birthday celebration.
(William Livingstone Collection)

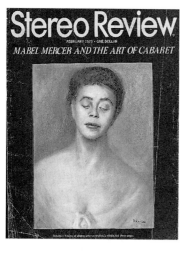

Right: Mabel and musical pioneer Eubie Blake.
(Donald Smith Collection)

Below: "The Kissiest" 75th birthday party. St. Regis Hotel.
(Donald Smith Collection)

Right: At Cleo's, New York, in the seventies.
(Donald Smith Collection)

Right:"Mabel Mercer Madness," in Los Angeles, with Jack Nicholson and Warren Beatty.

(All photos this page from the Donald Smith Collection)

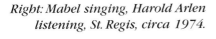
Above: Mabel with Donald Smith, her manager.

Above right: Mabel during an interview with the BBC, 1970s.

Right: Mabel singing, Harold Arlen listening, St. Regis, circa 1974.

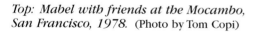

Top: Mabel with friends at the Mocambo, San Francisco, 1978. (Photo by Tom Copi)

Above: Mabel and Lena Horne.
(Donald Smith Collection)

Above right: Eileen Farrell and Loonis McGlohon with Mabel coaching, in 1982.
Photo by Ken Howard
(Loonis McGlohon Collection)

Right: Andrea Marcovicci, one of "Mabel's Babies." (Photo by Richard Dunkley, from Donald Smith Collection)

*Above: President Ronald
Reagan presenting Mabel
Mercer with the National
Medal of Freedom, with
playwright Clare Boothe
Luce looking on.*
(Courtesy Ronald Reagan Library)

*Left: Frank Sinatra's
"Love Letter to Mabel."*
(Donald Smith Collection)

love Mabel

"That's What I'll Say..."
Mabel Mercer, 1982.
(Photo by Margaret Miller)

Chapter 8
Farewell

Mabel's final years in Europe, despite the encroaching war, were a whirl of creative experiences. She returned to London in 1937 for her first and only cinematic appearance in *Everything Is Rhythm*, with Harry Roy's big band. In a full-bodied mezzo-soprano she shouted out, atypically, "Black Minnie's Got The Blues," with a grand supporting chorus and a tattoo of tapdancers. For her it was a step into the Harlem jazz and revue tradition. But that was not the path she would take.

During this period, she also made rare recordings of other notable theatrical tunes including Gershwin's "I Love You, Porgy," and a haunting rendition of "Summertime." These bravura performances proved that she was capable of musical theatre. Years later she commented without bitterness that the "timing" had not been right—meaning, perhaps, that white actresses in dark makeup were usually cast in those important roles.

One of her versatile young admirers, entertainer Julius Monk, described her mezzo-soprano rendition of "Summertime" as "a perfectly charming and enchanting voice…." The tall twentyish American southerner was a pianist, writer, and producer of comic revues, but his sense of the absurd especially endeared him to Mabel. He explained better than anyone else, perhaps, how gay men felt about her. "I would absolutely scale boroughs, arrondissements," Monk told James Haskins, "to get over to Bricky's to hear Mabel do, 'How Deep Is The Ocean?' We were like spawning salmon." He once told Mabel that she was the equivalent of a breast-feeding. Every gay man (and woman) seemed to have a mama fixation on Mabel's apple-shaped breasts and small flowing body. They saw her as the Mother Earth and Mother Courage of their world. Monk, who died in 1995 after a famous career in New York, had worked for a time at Bricktop's, as well as being the artistic director of the Paris Ruban Bleu.

Mabel gave up her apartment for a smaller one at 63 rue Pigalle, no doubt to economize. Sometimes she performed duets with a new boyfriend, Opal Cooper, a banjo player and vocalist who had come to France originally during the First World War.

In February 1938 she went to Amsterdam with Eddie South and his American orchestra, where they performed at the Tushinski Theatre. At the time it was unusual for different races to play together, even in Europe. Unfortunately no recording is available of this rare performance.

Mabel left Paris again for an undisclosed destination, and Brick noted in her diary, on July 7, "Mabel flew back. Started *Boeuf*." She had agreed to go to work for the morose intellectual, Herbert Jacoby, who had founded two smart clubs in the city, both named *Le Boeuf sur le Toit*. Jacoby sensed what was coming in Europe and was leaving for greener concrete in New York, to open yet a third cabaret of the same name. Many of Mabel's friends worked at the Paris *Boeufs*, including Jimmy Daniels, who would become her accompanist in New York, Jean Sablon, Charles Trenet, and the Incomparable Hildegarde (never seen in public without elbow-length gloves). Mabel's headliner role at *Le Boeuf* was credited with giving the club a brief new lease on life. The rumble of German tanks across the Low Countries toward France sent Jews, gypsies, and persons of color fleeing Europe, but Mabel did not wish to hear. She remained in a state of denial, having seen the havoc of Europe after World War One and thinking nothing so terrible could ever happen again.

Her group enjoyed one more halcyon summer. Monk and his friends went to the fishing village of St. Tropez and "got two pianos from Marseilles for which we were almost banished as witches by the natives, who had never seen any before." They rented a 17th century house and opened Chez Julius, an open-air terrace where "we made a killing by serving corn-on-the-cob, corned-beef hash, and hot dogs at 15 francs a throw to such clientele as Prince Philippe of Greece, the Duke and Duchess of Kent, and Marlene Dietrich." The season's peak was a contest to find the most amusing sandals, and the judges were Marlene and Noel Coward.

Mabel went south to join her playmates at summer's end, where she made a lifelong friend. The well-muscled British-born heiress, Marion Barbara Carstairs, was known as Joe and sometimes "the Pirate" to her friends. Among other things, she was a speedboat racing champion, a yachtswoman, a philanthropist, and an irritant to the proper English. The granddaughter of a major shareholder in Standard Oil of New Jersey, Joe Carstairs owned an island in the Bahamas from which she imperiously sailed forth at intervals to befriend the hungry actors, musicians, and pretty ladies who wandered into her maritime web. The Carstairs philanthropy also extended to putting poor young men through college or, if they seemed very talented and very poor, providing them with life trusts. In appearance she was trim, tanned, tattooed, handsomely mannish, and given to dramatic arrivals and departures in her black yacht.

Joe was introduced to Mabel, who was singing at a private party near Cannes, by Marlene Dietrich. All three were the same age. The oil heiress was much impressed by the English singer. "...I thought she was a very great lady and had a marvelous voice. She was very proper, you know, just the opposite of me. She always seemed much older than me. She didn't behave young at all." While Joe and Mabel became "like sisters," Joe and Marlene Dietrich were lovers.

Mabel could only marvel at the political and sexual agendas of her famous friend Marlene, who had recently acquired U.S. citizenship, insulted Hitler, and incurred his undying hatred by declaring she would never return to Germany. She also found time for an abortive effort to dissuade the Duke of Windsor from marrying Mrs. Simpson. Now the actress was dividing her amorous attentions among author Erich Maria Remarque, director Josef von Sternberg, Max Colpet, and her German husband Rudolf Sieber. Marlene was also commiserating on the state of the world with Greta Garbo's erstwhile lover, Mercedes de Acosta, for whom the Mercedes automobile was named. And just as she was being called upon to judge the funniest-sandals contest, who should sail into port but the lean and lusty Joe Carstairs!

History provides various accounts of their meeting, the least amiable being in the biography written by Marlene's daughter, Maria Riva. As luck would have it, Ambassador Joseph Kennedy and his family were then Riviera neighbors, and Maria's playmates included the future President of the

United States and his little brother, Teddy. After her mother vanished into the Carstairs yacht, Maria saw a lot of the Kennedy kids. Carstairs tempted Marlene with the offer of a palace and court of her very own in the Bahamas, and with troops of ladies-in-waiting. But sadly, according to Steven Bach's biography, *Marlene Dietrich*, the German actress felt herself spread too thin for a sustained nautical caper, even for someone with her prodigious appetites. She therefore added Ambassador Kennedy to her Riviera A List and then, Bach claims, stayed rather firmly anchored to the Hotel du Cap. He quotes Marlene later, however, saying at one of director Billy Wilder's Hollywood parties, "Women are better, but you can't live with a woman."

Mabel, presumably a mere observer in this fast-and-loosely assorted group, felt old beyond her thirty-eight years yet still an innocent among hedonists. She must have regressed at times to the bewildered childhood feeling of being a kind of mascot. She seemed to have been catapulted by popular demand from Victorian adolescence and a firm Catholic grounding in guilt into a role of faux maternity.

Having had few normal associations with men except for the brief period on the road with her male cousins and her mostly fleeting romances with other entertainers, Mabel's sole source of nurturing love appears to have been women, nuns, and girls. The conditions of her early life were in fact a breeding-ground for same-sex attractions. The many lesbian and gay friends drawn to her throughout her life were evidence of her unusual empathy and understanding. Yet in the opinions of those who knew her best, such as Bart Howard, Thelma Carpenter, and Adde Wallin-Beach, Mabel was not bisexual. Carpenter sometimes referred to her as the Mother

Superior, but never within Mabel's hearing. In Howard's view, her friendships with such colorful lesbians as Joe and Marlene were just that. They were simply part of the crowd in which she found herself. It was true that both Elsa Maxwell and Lady Mendl gave her expensive gowns, and that neither of them was noted for flaming heterosexuality; yet Mabel was just an entertainer whom they liked very much and who needed the clothes. Howard said, "I do not know if Mabel was in love with anybody, but she absolutely was not gay. She just liked people, all kinds of people."

Still, few of her best friends ever guessed the degree to which she compartmentalized her life. Like Duke Ellington, whom Mabel adored, and whose sister Ruth said of him, "he wore veil upon veil upon veil," Mabel Mercer kept her life (and even her death) a model of privacy and sanitized records. Clearly she allowed the vital statistics of her parentage to be known in her lifetime, but not completely. With respect to her mother's cruel ambivalence, no one ever heard her betray bitterness about that. It was life, not a rose garden, she would have said. People were always surprised to detect no malice in her toward anyone. Joe Carstairs confided, however, that Mabel often seethed inwardly from the limitations imposed on her by bigotry. But that developed later in her story.

The war was definitely coming. Her friends in Paris were urging her to leave. The only place where nightlife now offered her a chance of making a living was America; but, much as she liked Americans, she could not bear to leave her little apartment and the city where she had found such great happiness. There was also the matter of Winkie, her little cat.

Though she tried to cling to the past, she was forced to face the future. An article she read in *Time* magazine was a cruel reminder of her "golliwog" days. It noted that the few remaining Jewish children in German schools were being used as object lessons. A teacher called a little Jewish girl to the front of the class and asked the other pupils, "What do you see in this face?" Obediently, they answered, "A gigantic nose, negroid lips, inferior frizzy hair." The teacher added, "Also you see a cowardly and disloyal facial expression." Clearly, the time had come to leave Europe.

Mabel had only her English passport. Bricktop, who had an American passport, was also reluctant to leave Paris. In this period of indecision, Mabel thought often of her mother and stepfather in America. For all her searching and hoping, she had never located Ben Mercer. She felt sure he must have heard of her, if he were alive and in Europe. Her mother, who still lived in New York State, was apparently not well. She wrote to Mabel that, if she came to New York, she would try to meet her. Period.

Her dearest neighbor in Paris, Edith Rankin, urged her to leave as soon as possible, saying in effect, I will take care of your cat and buy your lottery tickets, and send your horoscopes in French. Her "sisters," Dickie and Ena, wrote from London that they would miss her but urged her to leave at once. Joe Carstairs, who nagged Mabel to get a U.S. visa and sent her a steamship ticket, recalled, "It got iffy. I mean it got pretty bloody awful. But I finally got her to leave. She came on the old Queen Mary, and it was the day before they took the lights off the shipping across the Atlantic."

Bricktop finally took over the apartment as well as Winkie the cat (Mabel expected to be back soon), and noted in her diary that Mabel had left her tax papers in the spoon drawer.

It is impossible to guess at Mabel Mercer's feelings as

she arrived in New York City, along with the U.S. ambassador to Italy, a viscount and viscountess, a lord, and a baroness. Unlike them, she was not mentioned in the shipping news of November 17, 1938. She was attractively dressed in a couturier outfit outgrown by a society friend. Her two suitcases contained a Molyneux gown, a coat, and a raincoat contributed by Lady Mendl. Around her neck she wore the medal of St. Genesius, the actors' saint and a Roman martyr.

Leaving U.S. Customs, she was met by a young man who introduced himself as Tim Brooke, Joe Carstairs' secretary. He arrived just in time to see an older woman of about Mabel's height leaving rapidly. The singer's mother had kept her promise, but on seeing Brooke, Emily Long Stonehouse neé Wadham averted her face and vanished into the crowd.

Brooke was embarrassed when Mabel turned to him with the kohl surrounding her blue eyes streaked and wet. She appeared disoriented at first, but apologized and produced the famous smile.

Chapter 9
America!

Joe Carstairs' limousine whisked Mabel and Brooke to the Hotel Pierre, thus sparing her possible racist rebuffs from New York taxi drivers. A group waiting on the thirty-second floor of the hotel had spent the morning considering strategies for getting her into the elevator without a struggle.

Among those waiting to greet her was Bart Howard, a twenty-three-year-old song writer from Iowa who had lately joined the golden boys "adopted" by Carstairs. In those days he was lean, eager, unknown, and looking for a good vocalist to introduce his work. He became a prominent composer of American popular songs ("One of the best," said William Engvick, who himself is among the finest of lyricists). "Fly Me To The Moon" is Howard's best-known song, although it was not his favorite.

On that autumn morning in New York, Howard had been briefed by Joe and her court on Mabel's uniqueness both as a vocalist and as a regal British lady. Like the others, he found it disgusting that the gentle foreigner would encounter discrimination right after her first view of the Statue of Liberty. Howard recalled her as freckled and rather pale. Her blue eyes were a little teary. She was well-dressed, looked very smart and not heavy ("but you could tell she would be").

"In England and Paris," he said, "she had mixed with all

kinds and colors of people. It was different when she came to the U.S. But Joe Carstairs said she was coming up on the elevator to the thirty-second floor, and that was that."

Other huskily-built members of the welcoming committee were sitting behind newspapers in the hotel lobby. On Mabel's arrival, they sprang up and formed a protective circle, sweeping her into the elevator before the security guard realized what was happening. In the Carstairs suite she was greeted with relief and celebration by old friends and new.

"The first day she was a guest of Joe Carstairs, who had helped her come over, but that night she had to go to Harlem to sleep," recalled Howard. Various possibilities for her in the black neighborhood were explored. A temporary room was found for her that night, followed by an apartment she would share with a woman named Sadie at 2040 Seventh Avenue in Harlem.

That first day, Mabel felt a natural empathy for the witty and talented Howard. He was to become her closest friend in a long line of gay men. He would write songs for her, accompany her at the piano, and be a brother to her. Among the other welcomers was Marlene Dietrich, who was in excellent form and spirits despite certain occupational travail. Having become an early sensation in Hollywood, thanks to movies like *Morocco* and *The Blue Angel*, she had quarreled with the studio powers and was momentarily in disrepute. She was on her way back to Europe to look for work, and to persuade her mother and sister to leave Germany.

Bart Howard had heard Mabel's 1936 French recording of "You Better Go Now," by Graham and Reichner. "Mabel, when I first met her," he said, "sang in a pure high soprano. Later she put me to work, and we lived together as brother and sister, and we bought an old LaSalle together."

That first day Marlene urged Mabel to introduce Bart's new song, "When You Leave Paris." She had the music with her, but Mabel felt very unsure about ever being able to sing again of her beloved city. In any event, she had no stage.

Depressed America was coming back to life, throbbing and chattering to the rivets of an awakening wartime economy preparing to supply materiel for another of Europe's "bloody messes" (an ocean away, as most people hoped). Bankers, shipbuilders, and aircraft and munition makers were beginning to feel optimistic. Joy was spreading, as it is wont to do, from Wall Street by way of private wealth to city neighborhoods and thence to places of nocturnal pleasure. Broadway and 52nd Street (or Swing Street) in New York now attracted the richest pool of musical and theatrical talent in the world, providing relief for people newly liberated from Prohibition. The gifted and prolific composer Alec Wilder, a permanent resident of the Algonquin Hotel, compared 52nd street to a perpetual block party where everyone knew your name and nobody seemed to sleep.

Mabel perked up as she learned that the city was enjoying an explosion of the arts similar to that of Paris in the twenties. On 52nd and 56th streets and in Greenwich Village, old brownstone speakeasies were being converted into saloons or smart supper clubs that offered literally every possible kind of entertainment. Although loving the perpetual block party, she felt at first overwhelmed by the concrete city with its monolithic towers which, she said, reminded her of gravestones for giants. Despite the constant routine bigotry she encountered downtown in buses, taxis, stores, restaurants, and hotels, white admirers often said that they knew her for a long time without even realizing she was colored. Blacks, on the other hand, knew at once that she was one of them, but few had ever encountered anyone quite like her. (God forbid she might be trying to "pass" with that phony accent.) Some of her fellow white entertainers assumed that the accent was just a put-on, a part of show business. In any event, she soon found a brighter side to the picture. There were jobs to be had.

About two weeks after arriving in America, she opened at Le Ruban Bleu at 4 East 56th Street. Conquering a feeling of dread, she managed to introduce Manhattanites to Bart Howard's nostalgic "If You Leave Paris," performed with particular sincerity. Helping her get through it was her loyal cheering section, Howard, Dietrich, Tim Brooke, Clifton Webb, and Carstairs among them.

The club had been started by her old friend Herbert Jacoby, who intended it as a replica of *Le Boeuf sur le Toit* in Paris. Mabel was one of his first performers, along with such other elegant imports as Lotte Lenya and the beloved Viennese singer Greta Keller. Lenya performed songs composed by her husband Kurt Weill and by the American Marc Blitzstein. New York's intimate nightspots included Le Pavillon, the Vanguard, the Blue Angel, and Café Society, all of which served as training grounds for young talent. Their graduates would soon become familiar names in musical theater and Hollywood.

Recalling that first evening, Mabel remembered Elsie Houston: "She had a beautiful voice, not really a classical voice, but it had great tenderness, and when she sang those fados she was marvelous. Greta Keller came that year. And there was a wonderful couple who were in *Sillman's New Faces*.

She was a very dark girl with a smile that lit up the room.... She used to sing, 'I'm The Prettiest Piece in Greece,' so you know they were good songs!"

Asked what she thought of New York at the time, Mabel replied, "With all due respect, I thought it was frightfully strange. It didn't begin to grow on me for about six months. I could never get over the fact that I couldn't go here or couldn't go there. I couldn't understand why not."

For patrons, nightclubs were a bargain. Female and ethnic employees were discriminated against even by the labor unions, and entertainers were underpaid as a matter of course. Often there was no cover charge to hear the finest singers, comedians, jazz groups, cocktail pianists, diseuses (professional reciters of songs, usually with dances), and classical guitarists. For the price of a beer, one could be amused by bird imitations, whistlers, mimes, puppets, ventriloquists, tumblers, and trained dogs and monkeys. Almost any talent found a home somewhere, but not much of a living. Mabel still could not pass a billboard featuring acrobats without stopping to study their names. She sensed that her father was near.

Later the taste for elegance succumbed to wartime conditions as the clubs catered to thousands of free-spending defense workers, soldiers, and sailors. The new demand was for less urbane humor than in the little revues, and for fresh-faced blond pin-up girls. Mabel reflected that she should have kept the blond beehive wig from her Chocolate Kiddie days.

Jazz aficianados had many small clubs like Bon Soir, the Onyx Room, Kelly's Stable, the Little Club, and Spivy's Roof. Often they were just tiny rooms with a bar, a make-do stage, and a piano. If business was good, the owners might cram in a few small tables and hire a singer.

Mabel's timing was auspicious in the sense that a few white club owners had begun to rebel against the color bar, even when it cost them customers and criticism. Barney Josephson, the son of a bankrupt Latvian shoe merchant from Trenton, New Jersey, courageously founded the first completely desegregated clubs in the U.S.—Café Society in 1938 and Café Society Uptown in 1940. If guests complained about the presence of negroes in his club, Josephson gave back their money and showed them the door.

He invited mixed audiences to Café Society in Greenwich Village, and no less an artist than blues singer Billie Holiday greeted black patrons on the first bill. She was soon followed by such popular entertainers as pianists Hazel Scott, Meade Lux Lewis, and Albert Ammons, and later the young Lena Horne, among an endless line of great artists—all of whom brought their friends. Josephson considered it outrageous that African-Americans were barred from other clubs, saying, "The only unique thing we possessed culturally in this country was the music that black people gave us."

Julius Monk took over Le Ruban Bleu and ran it for many years, then started the Downstairs, and the Upstairs at the Downstairs. Discrimination, sorry as it was, seldom kept the toughest and most talented entertainers down. Ella Fitzgerald, whose early life on the streets might have doomed to failure anyone less talented, was destined to become the great lady of jazz. The teenager had talked her way into an amateur contest at the Apollo Theatre in Harlem in 1930, and won immediate recognition with an exuberant rendition of "The Object Of My Affection." Like Mabel, Fitzgerald inspired generations of instrumentalists and fellow vocalists with her own distinctive style.

Mabel, after singing at Le Ruban Bleu well into May 1939, found herself again unemployed. Although she got short engagements, she was often hard-pressed to earn the rent for her little apartment on Seventh Avenue. By now, however, she had many new friends, some of whom helped when she was in need, among them singer Jimmy Daniels and the ever reliable Joe Carstairs. She herself passed on such favors when she was able, but nevertheless it was humiliating to rely on the kindness of friends. Bart Howard said that although it was years before he earned enough money to help her, he was always an eager escort.

On March 30, 1939, Joe Carstairs' New York attorney, Francis L. Robbins, Jr., transmitted a draft of 2,000 francs in a letter from Mabel to her dear friend Edith Rankin in Paris, perhaps to pay the rent on the apartment to which she still hoped to return.

Another well-known refugee arrived in New York in late November, also looking for work. Bricktop had finally given up hope of outlasting Hitler. Although Mabel was glad to see her old partner, she was unable to lend her money since she herself was barely surviving. Brick was quickly disabused of opening a new club in New York: the places that "her" crowd patronized, like the Stork Club, "21," the Colony, and El Morocco, were expensive and discriminating in both senses of the word. When her friend Cole Porter threw a welcoming party for her at his Waldorf Towers apartment, she too encountered the color bar.

With wartime tastes running to the blond Betty Grable, even the ambitious Bricktop found only short-term jobs. First she worked at Jimmy Savini's club on 56th Street, where the manager got mad at her for buying drinks for "her" custom

111

ers. From there she moved on to a "signature" room at the Coq Rouge. Again, the fickle patrons did not understand her type of showmanship. The hard times continued.

In that cheerless winter of 1939, Mabel was stricken with one of the illnesses that singers most dread. Her old problem of tonsillitis recurred and this time she was told she must have a tonsillectomy. The doctor would make no guesses about her musical future. By coincidence or perhaps a fit of Freudian rivalry, Bart Howard got tonsillitis at the same time, and the ever-resourceful Joe Carstairs took care of them both.

Their tonsils were removed at a local hospital, and she brought them to recuperate at her Pierre Hotel suite, color bar be damned. If the management objected, they did not dare to raise the matter. "I was very overpowering," Ms. Carstairs told Jim Haskins, "I said she's going to stay here and that's that. After all, you don't stand for any of that shit."

For two weeks Mabel and Bart were pampered with cold drinks and ice cream, while Mabel agonized about her future. Close to tears, she thought often of Paris and especially of the little cat, Winkie. Letters arrived occasionally from her friend Edie on Rue Pigalle, and from "sisters" Ena and Dickie, who were still in England. Edie always supplied details of Winkie's condition, but life was hard for all of them. The clubs in Paris were dead, supplies were short, and the wartime atmosphere cheerless and dull.

Then one day, with the entire Carstairs ménage in nervous attendance, Mabel mustered her courage and tried her voice again. After moments of pitiful croaking, she was able to coax forth the old magic. From then on she was able to camouflage any limitations of resonance and range with a newer version of her husky mezzo and what critics described with continued awe as her parlando, or talking song. She could become a thespian of cabaret and continue to earn a living in the life she loved.

But where? Joe Carstairs, who was preparing to weigh anchor for the lambent skies and seascapes of Whale Cove, her private walled island in the Bahamas, once again came to the rescue. She invited Mabel to recuperate in the Great House she had built there, partially clearing the island of swamps and local fauna and flora with the help of local workers. The island had been a base for rum-runners during Prohibition in the U.S., but the original buildings quickly fell into total disrepair in the tropical climate. The Cay lay thirty miles northwest of Nassau and a ninety-mile sail from Miami.

Moreover, Joe was an amusing hostess who enjoyed giving parties and masquerades. In England, according to biographer Kate Summerscale, her delight in "dressing up" as a frowsy woman instead of in her usual masculine attire had been a bit much for the British. They were not unhappy, apparently, when she became a colonial and sailed away to "do agriculture," as she put it, for HRH (the Duke of Windsor). King George had appointed him governor of the Bahamas in a scheme to remove him and his Duchess as far as possible from England, as well as from his suspect relationships in Nazi Germany.

Mabel was excited by the chance to get her hands into "God's earth." Whale Cay, Joe told her, even offered a lovely little church on a hill where native "Fifth Day Adventists" worshipped, and where another sect she called "Jumpers" bounced around and made a lot of noise. But she assured Mabel that they were broadminded about papists and would be happy to allow her to pray in their chapel. The singer found her first brief experience in the Bahamas highly enjoyable; she did a lot of exploring in the wild terrain, planting trees and other vegetation. "She used to walk around with a basket over her head and a shovel," Joe said. "She was very strong, you know. We all worked jolly hard."

After returning to New York late in 1939, Bart Howard and Mabel went back to the Bahamas in 1940 to perform for a season in a Nassau nightclub. Joe Carstairs, then ensconced at the Pierre, gave a rousing two-day party for their departure, and revelers reported that the steamship journey was a continuation of the wassail. Although Mabel only sipped champagne, the partying may have distracted her from seeing to a vital matter that would later cause a great deal of pain. She had neglected to get a re-entry permit, and she was not a U.S. citizen. By December of 1941 the United States was at war, and Mabel was a refugee again.

Chapter 10
A Very Bad Year

Sometime before returning to the Bahamas in 1940, Mabel slipped away for a meeting with her mother, a fact that emerged only years later. Despite her mother's fear of receiving her at their home in upstate New York, several letters show that Mabel managed somehow to remain close to her mother and her stepfather, Tom Stonehouse.

Mabel talked about what must have been a deeply emotional and almost clandestine reunion only when she herself was an old woman, during an interview with an *Oakland Tribune* reporter in, of all places, the Southern Pacific Railway Depot at Oakland, California. She began speaking generally, as she often did, of the eternal beauty and bounty of nature: "When I first came to this country my mother and I drove to upstate New York to see the changing leaves. I couldn't believe what I was looking at. I was almost in tears. It's probably best they change once a year. If they lasted too long, people wouldn't appreciate them."

For the time being, she was delighted to be returning to the Bahamas where she could trudge the tropical beaches wearing pedal-pushers, with a basket for a sun hat, contentment on her face, and a few extra pounds on her five-foot, one-inch frame. She had treasured such idyllic moments all her life. And to top it off, she and Bart Howard had jobs.

"We worked at a club in the negro section of Nassau and we lived together like brother and sister," recalled the eternally boyish Howard. In Paris, Mabel had known the sensational Harlem entertainers, Paul Meeres, the "brown Valentino," and his white wife, dancer Poppy Meeres. Paul and Poppy at the *Folies Bergere*, in trio with Josephine Baker, had excited audiences with the undulating pigmentation of their brown, black-ocher, and white nudity. In Nassau, Mabel and Bart took two rooms on the Meeres' floor of the hotel, where the foursome lived much like a theatrical family.

There was little time for sleeping that winter. Mabel and Bart did a midnight show, then opened at two a.m. in an adjoining bar. There they sang and played piano until the sun burst over the harbor. After a few hours' catnap, Mabel would be out and about again, absorbing the colorful island life. She was the first black singer in Nassau, it was said, whose charms and talent were enough to lure the white colony across the tracks. In 1940, she and her accompanist were a refreshingly welcome addition to local entertainment, and Bart was inspired to write more songs for Mabel to perform.

Sometimes she appeared on the same bill with Paul and Poppy at another club in Nassau, but she firmly drew the line at the near-nude dancing for which the two were popular.

At other times Joe Carstairs would send a boat to fetch them to Whale Cay for rest and recuperation. When they were not booked in Nassau, they planted flowers all over her lush estate. At Joe's they ate well, slept well, practiced their musical arrangements, and were treated like honored guests.

Occasionally, Mabel's old friends the Duke and Duchess of Windsor invited them to Government House, where they were very popular with the British. Mabel was glad for

116

opportunities to sing at various charitable functions, such as the annual Red Cross fundraiser. They adored the extremes of her performances. She would belt out, "Mandy, Mandy, make up your mind!" then break their hearts with a ballad of bittersweet love, closing perhaps with a hilarious version of "Dear Dorothy Dix, I'm In An Awful Fix."

She wrote to her mother and stepfather, suggesting that it would be safe for them to come to Nassau for a vacation, since the islanders seemed friendly. No one back home, she said, need know about their relationship. That was when she first learned that her mother was gravely ill with high blood pressure. Mabel decided that if they could not come to Nassau, she must go at once to see her mother. She applied for a reentry visa to the United States and discovered with shock that she was, in effect, a woman exiled.

Having little money, no job awaiting her in New York, and no relatives willing to take her in, she was brusquely told by the U.S. consul that he had no idea when, or even if, she might get U.S. papers again. A long line of European war refugees was ahead of her. Mabel, even with her old fear of being down and out, had always been able to summon the strength she needed in a crisis. The sudden loss of personal control of her life landed like a hammer blow. She was forty years of age, forced to rely on friends and strangers, and stuck in a place where she could see little professional future.

The mother for whom Mabel had grieved since childhood seemed ever farther away. Emily might even die and she would not know of it. She experienced flashbacks to her early trauma, the tragic time when the Blakely nuns had brought the news that her only real family, her beloved Grandma Wadham, had died.

After absorbing the bombshell from the U.S. consul, she had little heart for singing. Her anxiety as she waited for news of her visa showed in the cheap promotional photos she had taken during this period. They were unflattering, the strong inner glow gone from her eyes. Misery made her seem older than her years, and even in an odd way ashamed. She was terrified of losing the direction in her life that she had worked so hard to find.

Bricktop came to Nassau briefly, hoping to find club engagements for herself, and Mabel was glad to see her. But Brick was now middle-aged, overweight, and ill-tempered. Little comfort to Mabel in their mutual woes, she could yet lord it over her with her freedom as a U.S. citizen. She could and soon did go back to New York.

Mabel's mother wrote from the U.S. several times that year, referring to the "terrible war," and saying, "I hope the Club is doing well and that you are coming out okay…." They were long, loving letters that included news from the family in England, with Tom Stonehouse usually joining in.

Finally, on June 8, 1940, Emily wrote to Mabel confirming that she had signed a paper to assist with her re-entry documentation. Her mother had obviously been stalling and tried to make a joke of it:

> "… you see, Mabel, all the lawyers in the world could not get you in until I made it possible. Everyone puts too much faith in the other person, instead of God…. I realize my fear regarding your entry into my life, but all things will work for good to those who love good. Write soon, and may God bless you. We shall soon meet again.
>
> Yours lovingly, Em."

In a postscript she expressed ambivalent optimism that the Duke and Duchess of Windsor would "start the ball rolling there. Wish I could see you for a couple of weeks but it is impossible now."

Although neither woman knew it, this was the last letter Mabel would receive from her mother.

Spring of 1940 brought devastating news from abroad. In April the Germans, within a few short hours, took Dunkirk and skirted that great bastion, the Maginot Line. In June, German tanks rolled into Paris, and the French Vichy government signed a pact with the Nazi invaders. It was all over for France and for Mabel's precious City of Light. For a time she had no news of her friends in London and Paris. It seemed like the world, Mabel's in particular, was ending.

Then Edie Rankin wrote shiveringly of a "war front" that remained unreal in its remoteness, more like what they had come to regard as the "phony war." Night after night, Londoners and Parisians scanned the empty skies, some almost relieved when air attacks ruptured the boredom of civilian life, its rationing and tedious blackout precautions. Black markets appeared; soldiers marked time by digging ditches. Edie wrote that Mabel's old flat had been rented, and that she had heard on the BBC "...your old friend Marlene broadcasting from a record, falling in love again.... This girl Billy Sparrow from the Boeuf [Piaf?] was broadcasting on a French wave. I like her voice." Edie also reported that some of their musician friends had been jailed or fled to Belgium. She herself planned to get war work and feared Mabel might have to wait years for her papers, since the U.S. immigration quota was said to be five years behind.

She reported on Mabel's lottery tickets, and sent her a

bill for 1,643 francs owed for rent, gas, and insurance. Brick, she explained, had not paid for them, so the electricity and gas had been turned off. Winkie the cat, who was pining for Mabel, had been allowed to get thin.

"Mabel, I still have 29 francs of yours in the old. oak chest. I will get you some lottery tickets and send them in the next mail. What a BRRR winter we have had. Thanks so much Mabel for offering me your flat; it is very sweet of you. Madame [the landlady] is terrified that you won't have any money for your old age! ...All my love, Edie."

French patriots joined the underground. Hitler's buzz bombs started crossing the English Channel. During the Blitz, people fought literally with their bare hands to put out the fires from nightly air raids. Mabel sat helplessly in Nassau reading newspaper reports of the terrible incendiary attacks on London. Every morning and evening she included in her prayers the nuns at Blakely convent school and her relatives and friends in England.

The Bahamian colonials gathered nightly around the wireless to hear the BBC with Edward R. Murrow and Eric Severeid, seeking togetherness in their clubs to weep or cheer over pink gins. She waited in dread for news of her "sisters" and other intimates.

Another distressing message arrived from Edie:

"I know darling you must be very upset about Winkie's death. Mabel if I had been here when he died I would of bought him a little grave. I am be-ginning to understand your last year's horoscope when it said, 'overshadowing influences.' I think you had a few over-shadows...."

In America, influential figures had begun rallying to pull strings for Mabel with the U.S. State Department. Helen Cutting wrote from Gladstone, N.J., that she was asking Ambassador William Bullitt to intercede on her reentry permit. In Nassau, Mrs. Cutting had once asked Mabel to sing at a private party, and wrote, "Bring your bathing suit and swim." Madel attended but would not accept payment. In the Mercer ethic, one could not be both a guest and a paid entertainer. Former New York Mayor James J. Walker, a familiar face from the Paris days, also tried to help by referring Mabel's case to New York lawyers. Nothing seemed to work.

A brave New Year's letter arrived from Ena Boucher. It conveyed the spirit of British courage in response to the treacherous bombings:

"I really thought Christmas would see lights up, but we are still groping about in the dark, dodging rockets. One consolation, these rockets travel faster than sound, so you are hit before you know; and if you hear it, you were not hit, so we don't pay any attention to them.

From your sister, XXX."

Help came eventually from an unlikely place. While she was still in the United States, and perhaps with the idea of applying for U.S. citizenship, she had finally gotten in touch with relatives of her father, Benjamin Mercer. While this avenue, which must have been pursued by her mother, resulted in no contact with the father, a sister of his was found living in the Bronx. The long-lost aunt tried to help. Audry Mercer Brooks of 45D Grand Concourse, the Bronx, N.Y., had sent a "To Whom it may Concern" letter dated June 30, 1939. It stated: "Benjamin Mercer, born in Yonkers, N.Y. in 1876, the son of Joseph and Mary Mercer, is my brother. I was born in New York in 1895 to the same parents. Benjamin Mercer went to England sometime in 1898. He became the father of Mabel Wadham who is known as Mabel Mercer, and who is my niece."

Thus the singer was able to establish beyond any doubt that she was half American by birth. By then her father would have been sixty-three years of age. Mabel never misplaced this important scrap of paper; she reread and refolded it many times. But she continued to refuse to discuss her parentage with strangers, once saying to a persistent reporter, "I've been misquoted too many times."

As promised, her mother had also signed a certificate to help her return to the United States, falsely identifying herself as Mabel's "aunt." In this sad, strange, and ambivalent document issued in the State of New York, County of Orange, Emily had assumed responsibility for Mabel while at the same time distancing herself. She declared, "I, Emily Stonehouse, depose that I was born in England in 1886 and have now lived on Edgemere Avenue, Greenwood Lake, N.Y. since 1923. I own a building and lot worth $8,000." She also reported that her husband, Thomas Stonehouse, had a net worth of about $2,400. "I am the aunt of Mabel Wadham, who is gifted, and will be able to support herself. We assume responsibility for her."

No wonder, Mabel may have reflected, that whole nations felt chary about having her as a resident, considering how her parents regarded her birth. Even with her abundant natural resilience, humor, and faith, she could not help being depressed by this long period in limbo with what amounted to the family skeletons. But if there were scars on her soul, she did not bare them. Friends of longstanding knew little of her private life, or that discretion had been her guiding principle. Fortunately during the Nassau period, she turned her sadness, which seemed to be a rather homey pool she shared with most of humanity, to catharsis and creativity.

What happened next crucially affected her future. A well-educated, talented, and attractive young black singer from Florida named Kelsey Pharr, II, who was little more than half Mabel's age, offered to share his U.S. citizenship through a proposal of marriage. They had become good friends while singing together. And she, like countless other stranded nationals the world over, accepted his offer of a "paper" marriage. And although she and Pharr were married, she was still forced to remain in the Bahamas for several more months. A revised Act of Congress in 1922 had repealed the statute by which foreign-born women automatically acquired citizenship through marriage.

For Catholics, a marriage performed under civil law rather than in the church, as in Mabel and Kelsey's case, was no marriage at all. According to the rules of the church, the newly married couple were living in sin. And of course this was very disturbing to Mabel. It was as if she were accepting voluntarily the sentence pronounced upon her so long ago by the children in the convent school. But then, what choice did she have? Perhaps the greatest irony was that the handsome Kelsey Pharr was gay.

Joe Carstairs and other friends tried to distract Mabel from her unusual depression by bringing her new music. Someone provided the recorded compositions of the versatile and eccentric Alec Wilder, a native of Rochester, N.Y. Wilder was becoming well known in Manhattan, perhaps less for his truly prodigious musical talents than for his unpredictable behavior. When Mabel first heard his "Octets from America" she said, "I must meet this man."

Wilder was a shy and moody young man, guilt-ridden about his family's wealth and determined to drink his way through his patrimony as soon as possible. He usually lived at the Algonquin Hotel, but was known to take impulsive cross-country train trips to anywhere—or nowhere. Tall, thin, erudite, and acidulous, Wilder also was given to playing elaborate practical jokes. He always spoke in a very loud "outdoor" voice that his more understanding friends believed was a way of compensating for shyness.

The Wilder Octets were curious little instrumental pieces combining jazz influences with classical formality and structure. Only a few minutes long, they were written as chamber music, and usually left untitled. If the composer were pressed to come up with a name, it was usually something like "Mama Never Dug This Scene," or even, as his longtime collaborator, William Engvick, noted, something less printable.

He became one of America's most prolific popular and classical composers, producing ballet and movie scores and writing definitive books on popular music. He also arranged music for such eminent vocalists as his good (and equally tormented) buddy, Frank Sinatra, for Mildred Bailey, Peggy Lee, Perry Como, Judy Garland, Lee Wiley, Eileen Farrell, and Jack Jones. Mabel and Wilder soon developed a special relationship that was both professional and personal.

During the bleak months of exile, Mabel lived by begging and borrowing music. She dug out old folk songs and orphaned show tunes, and as always, studied their lyrics intensively to get at their true meaning. Her repertoire had always contained an unusual mixture of ballads and poetry. In Nassau she worked to perfect the austere dramatic delivery that for the rest of her life was uniquely Mabel Mercer. It was a time of significant artistic growth. But, to paraphrase a song title, "The Worst Was Yet To Come."

Tom Stonehouse wired her the news in February 1941, the month of her birth. Her mother, the little music-hall entertainer from England who for years had lived in dread of racial ostracism, had died at Greenwood Lake. "She did not see the doctor. She had a stroke. We were 29 years married. I cannot sleep in the house without my only love. Please excuse more, darling, yours lovingly, Tom."

He followed the wire with a letter: "Emily was talking of you just three days before the passing." He added, as if writing the obituary his wife would have wanted to read: "Emily was loved by everyone in the Village, and how they miss her. All my fondest love to you dear, until I see you, your loving stepfather."

A vital part of Mabel's life and youth had vanished. Although she had never been close to Emily since early childhood, she had always kept that dream alive. There would be no more hope of celebrating a birthday with her glamorous blond mother, or hearing her stories of family life in Wales. A chunk of her center shorn away, she retreated into her small hotel room. For a time her friends did not see her and she felt no desire to live.

Chapter 11
Every Maiden's Dream

Mabel Mercer Pharr was readmitted to the United States on January 21, 1941, to find that she had not been forgotten, either personally or professionally. A show business pal in need of cash and consolation, having broken up with his gentleman friend, wrote asking to borrow fifty dollars. Bundles of V-mail letters from servicemen who had heard her sing in New York and Paris finally caught up with her. Manhattan agent Irving Rose felt sure he could get her a club engagement at $180 a week, and a photographer was eager to make new promotional photos.

Best of all, her new husband had rented a large two-bedroom apartment for them in a nice if segregated address on 110th Street between Lenox and Seventh Avenue, with windows on Central Park. Seventh Avenue in the heyday of the Harlem Renaissance was like Broadway, where "everyone" promenaded on Sundays after attending the Abyssinian Baptist Church. Although the grand era had ended before Mabel and Kelsey arrived, she was enchanted by the cherished old wardrobes of men in white spats, checkered suits, striped pants, French lisle hand-clocked socks, black custom made brogues, velvet-collared overcoats, and mahogany walking sticks like J. P. Morgan's. Women still sported gay parasols, monkey-fur collars on their coats, georgette dresses with lace, hats with egret feathers, and tan shoes styled with "bull-dog toes." Thanks to the installment plan and discount buying, before the depression struck even maids and waiters could afford to be fashionable. Blacks of the time categorized each other with fifteen or twenty highly descriptive terms for skin color including "mustard seed" and "inky dink," which must have puzzled Mabel.

She kept the apartment for decades and at once began cramming it with plants, emergency refrigerators and pianos, cast-off furniture, and enough food and spices for a hungry army. She also began to rescue homeless dogs and cats.

Kelsey, who had toured Europe as a jazz singer with the popular Delta Rhythm Boys and had sung with Count Basie's Orchestra, now seriously considered a new career. With Mabel back in New York, he even contemplated getting a steady job at the post office in the hope that they could make a real marriage. But soon he was off on a new gig, first to Chicago to play a resident of Catfish Row in *Porgy & Bess*, then on to other major cities. The genuine fondness between him and Mabel, as evidenced by their letters, might have surprised their intimates. She kept his room closed to her own company when he was touring, which was most of the time. Irreverent friends speculated that the door was shut mainly from fear of starting an avalanche of Mabel's own collectibles.

On November 25, 1941, Kelsey cabled to congratulate her on a new engagement at the smart supper club, Le Ruban Bleu, where she sang for six months and proved, to her own surprise, that she was a hot attraction. The intimacy of cabaret was her métier. Critics raved about her. Robert Connolly, after an evening of Mabel, wrote: "On a good night when both artist and audience are relaxed and responsive, it can be unforgettable—a musical high no drug can produce."

The singer's procedure when she discovered a new song was to read it through first with her pianist. "I have to find a key I can sing it in, listen to the song, learn it phrase by phrase," she told a music critic. "Then I have to think about what I'm saying. When I'm learning a new song, it stays in my mind. I go through it when I'm asleep and then when I'm awake. I'll be walking down the street and people will say, 'She's talking to herself.' But that's not it at all, I'm rehearsing. At home I sing to my cats. If I sing a high note, one cat will jump up and put his paws to my face, as if to say, 'Where does it hurt you?'"

At Le Ruban Bleu she first heard and was attracted to the well-known pianist Cy Walters, who shared with her a love for early show tunes and obscure but timeless ballads, and whose understated sense of humor was much like her own. Cy played at the Algonquin and then moved on to Tony's Club. According to Brick, Mabel "had a thing" going with him and ran back and forth between Le Ruban Bleu and Tony's to catch his sets.

After Le Ruban Bleu, she joined Bricktop again for a brief billing at a club called the Three Deuces on West 52nd Street. With Brick acting as manager, the two tried to recreate the Paris Bricktop's of old. But within a short time, a dispute among the club's owners ended that dream. Mabel and Brick moved on to the Onyx Club at 52 West 52nd Street, followed by a growing and ever more captivated troop of Mabel Mercer admirers. She received another congratulatory (but cautionary) wire from Kelsey: "Remember have more fun loads of love, Your Husband."

Although Kelsey seldom wrote letters, when he did so they were long, neatly scripted, and full of affection and humor. Presumably Mabel responded, although her letters have vanished. Whenever Kelsey's group returned to New York, he made directly for the Central Park North apartment and the Kelsey Room that was off limits to visitors. After one such reunion, he wrote, "Gretchen said you cried at the station....That's sweet. My favorite wife." Generous in praise of his fellow cast members, he wrote from Buffalo about Eddie Matthews as Porgy: "It was his evening.... The show was really terrific... and I just felt I had to write you and tell you about it."

Like other entertainers, he recoiled at the high cost of hotels in wartime and the special difficulty blacks had in finding vacancies. "Fortunately I was lucky enough to hit the numbers this week because these hotels really stand one up."

Mabel and Brick, together again, opened a third incarnation of the famous Onyx Club. The hot-jazz spot was located in a formerly elegant brownstone house that had served as a speakeasy during Prohibition. It was one of a number of popular gay bars that thrived only with official mob pay-offs, or operated to launder Mafia money. A friend of Mabel's once quoted her as saying, "I'm the only person in the place who gets paid every week." Everyone else was "family."

In the daytime, according to comedian and singer Dorothy Loudon, most of the clubs were undistinguished. At night, however, they assumed the glitter of a Cinderella Ball where every talented boy or girl turned into a prince or princess, and Mabel was ever the queen-regent.

The Onyx Room was dimly lit, long, narrow, and noisy. It had been a favorite stand of the best big-band musicians, who now operated out of their own club next door, modestly called The Famous Door.

Thelma Carpenter, a precocious mini-tornado from Brooklyn, who in her late teens was already a worldly graduate of the Apollo Theatre, first heard Mabel sing at the Onyx. Awestruck, she began dragging her show-business friends across the street from Kelly's Stable, where she performed. One friend she took to hear "this classy lady" was the tormented and hauntingly gifted jazz/blues singer, Billie Holiday. At twenty-five, Billie had already set her course through hell to early immortality. "No singer in jazz, before or since," commented Nat Hentoff, "has phrased with such supple inventiveness, as well as with such graceful, illuminating wit." When Thelma urged her to come and hear another master of phrasing, Billie did not want to go, protesting, "I can't be no classy lady." She had already been fired from both the Onyx and the Famous Door. Then, said Thelma, she almost got fired again, so entranced with Mabel that she balked at going back to do her own set at Kelly's.

Thelma, whose friends sometimes called her "Carp," was Irish-American, Native-American and African-American. She had grown up in a middle-class family and had no patience at all with hyphenated pretentiousness. "I am an American, honey, and don't you get superior with me. I stay brown the year around." At that phase in her life, she was constantly studying and insinuating herself as an apprentice into the company of the big stars: Ethel Waters, Lady Day, Tallulah Bankhead, and now Miss Mercer. Before the bad times, she and Billie had often practiced the songs from *Porgy & Bess* together at Billie's house, not far from Mabel's apartment, with the tiny Thelma protesting at always being pressed into singing the role of brawny, deep-voiced Porgy.

When Billie Holiday called Thelma to ask for money to

buy food for her dog, the latter knew it meant drugs "because usually she had just bought ninety-nine cans of 'dog food' the week before." Thelma could not forget grieving with Billie through her years of addiction, her twelve months in Lexington Federal Prison, and the final breakdown after her release. Even in the hospital, with a few remaining dollars (for dog food) concealed on her wasted body, the once beautiful singer and composer was harrassed by narcotics agents. At the end, the almost friendless Billie angrily warned Thelma against dope, ordered her away and told her never to come back. "When I went back," said Thelma, "she was beyond any help."

Among the artists Thelma proudly hand-delivered to Mabel was the brilliant and prickly Alec Wilder whose Octets had so fascinated her in Nassau. If any newcomer failed to appreciate Mabel right away, Thelma would make them stay and "listen to her, just listen, she's an acquired taste." Wilder did not have to be persuaded. Others who did not get it at first usually returned out of curiosity, often to join the thralldom.

None of them had heard anyone sing like that before, breaking all the rules, lingering on clipped consonants instead of rounded vowels, giving a special idiosyncratic emphasis to words that were usually ignored, imbuing lyrics with tragedy or humor that might end in a deep bosomy chuckle. Mabel sure as hell knew what she was doing, they said. But if another vocalist or composer or instrumentalist should claim to love her right away, like Margaret Whiting and dozens of others, Thelma Carpenter darkly suspected them of bragging. Carpenter also hung out with and studied the irascible genius Ethel Waters, and finally dared to urge her to "go and listen to this new high-yaller English lady named Mabel Mercer, really listen to her." Reluctantly Miss Waters went to Tony's Club on West 52nd Street, where Mabel had just begun her historic seven-year engagement. Ethel sat there and listened, recalled Thelma, "and Mabel didn't make any big fuss about her, she was just nice to her like she was to everyone."

Tony Soma didn't much like having either Thelma or Ethel as patrons in his club because they were undeniably off-white, but they sat there anyway, listening to Mabel sing in her strangely original way. When the Hearst columnist Dorothy Kilgallen walked in and sat down at the bar one evening, the haughty Miss Waters exclaimed in her famous voice, "Now what-in-hell is that damn bitch doin' in here?" The comment, recalled Thelma, reflected not so much on the columnist as on Waters' mood, which was usually testy.

In Mabel, Ethel sensed at once that she had met a talent as brilliantly original as her own, a woman who also had lived through childhood torment yet somehow gotten control of her life. While Mabel sang of understanding and love, Ethel's performances reflected the violent and destructive self-hatred of many American blacks. Mabel's poetry conveyed the vulnerability and tenderness of hard-won strength. Ethel struggled in song to find God even after she had found Him, never ceasing her war.

The young Jesuit priest Peter O'Brien, who idolized both artists, remembers Waters as "probably manic-depressive. She felt a lot of rage and anger. She never completed sentences. Some of her manner was camouflage, some of it professional, to raise hell with interviewers. I liked everything about her. She was brilliant. She made a big myth of her life...."

Although Ethel was often violent in those days, she never

threw a fit around the regal Mercer. Mabel, in her turn, undoubtedly felt complimented by the quiet attention of the temperamental artist. She must have known that they would never enjoy real friendship. They would remain equals in authority, but they met only at the point where opposites came full circle. Thelma Carpenter would sometimes drop into Tony's when Mabel was singing and see the haughty storm-cloud Ethel Waters lowering over a table, talking to no one, but listening.

Later, when this coruscating star of Broadway and Hollywood had been all but forgotten by her millions of fans, Thelma recalled making the mistake of taking her flowers and a hand-painted card on her birthday. Ethel glared at the tribute and the bearer. "What's this supposed to mean?" she demanded, and sent the eternal disciple away.

Mabel's kindness and her spiral to fame were therefore greatly valued by Thelma, the acolyte. Although Carpenter soon became celebrated in her own right, she needed another big sister just then. They would be friends over the years through thick and thin.

While Mabel's future glowed, Bricktop's abrasive personality and brittle patter were becoming eminently resistible in New York. The entertainment style of World War II and the early fifties was generally set by the discerning preference of horny youth for what the tabloid writers called "birds." Mabel triumphed at first because of her uniqueness. She was amused by the stream of blond girls who brought their boy friends to the club for the so-called "Mabel Mercer Sincerity Test for Young Lovers." Men who failed to be spellbound tended to fall by the garden path. Those who passed the test, on the contrary, became the maiden's dream. When Marilyn

Monroe brought Joe DiMaggio in the fifties, Joe melted instantly and won the girl.

Although she drew standing-room crowds every night, Mabel still tactfully gave her old friend Bricktop credit for making her a star. A nightclub hanger-on who fed gossip items to columnists noted that Mabel always seemed abstracted and unassuming, making no effort at all to advertise herself, whereas Brick was just the opposite.

Among the items at the Mercer archives in the New York Public Library's Schomburg Center is a contract scribbled on a cocktail napkin from "Tony's, 59 West 52nd Street," and dated Sept. 9, 1942: "It's hereby agreed that Miss Mercer is going to sing and furnish a pianist for $160 per week. This contract is cancellable on two weeks notice." It was signed by Tony Soma, the owner, and by Mabel Mercer in her childlike backward script. The contract would last for seven years. At the end are the words, "Witnessed by Cy Walter." He had recommended Mabel to follow him as the resident performer when he left to join the U.S. Army.

This inauspicious document marked the beginning of one of the most memorable and long-running appearances in cabaret history. Tony's West Side was an in-group bar and restaurant favored by journalists, theatrical folk, students, princes, and chic homosexuals. It became, as Carpenter said, like a schoolhouse for other singers and musicians. Everyone agreed that Mabel was underpaid; but so were Billie Holiday and most of the great vocalists, both then and since. Mabel later said, "It was a hand to mouth existence, but I didn't have the kind of voice and I wasn't the kind of entertainer to go to enormous places. I remained there for years. I prefer to stay in one place. It's the only way for people to know where to find you." Among those "people," perhaps she included her own never-forgotten father.

Tony's became home, her "chair of music" as master teacher six nights a week. Mabel had to share her $160 with her pianist, who probably got somewhat less than half. From her $90 she had to supply attractive gowns, so the frugal performer quickly acquired an expandable female tailor's form and began sewing her own simple designs for a figure of 5'1" and a weight now threatening to reach 165 pounds. She always wore her formal dresses with a long, brightly colored stole or sari, and satin pumps. As for her pianist, his tuxedo was likely to be his only suit.

Her budget also included a taxi back to Harlem every night and $65 a month for the nice apartment. But like most entertainers, she spent little if anything on her nightly visits to hear friends in other clubs, and was often given tickets to concerts and the theatre. Now that she was famous, she was always an honored (and half-price) guest at the Algonquin Hotel. At Tony's, however, her weekly pittance was stretched thin just to cover food, incidentals, clothing, and visits to the throat doctor.

Getting to Harlem by taxi at dawn could be a maddening trial for black entertainers, but so was getting anywhere. Bricktop loyally allowed that Mabel's accent and grand manner often served them well: really ticked off, Miss Mercer could be positively colonial to rude drivers.

The fuggy, smoke filled rooms and noisy crowds were again straining Mabel's voice. She frequently visited Dr. Leo Schwartz for throat treatments; and only one of his bills totaled $120. Mabel said that although she never smoked, "I must have breathed in more smoke than any heavy smoker ever did." Bart Howard added that, while it changed her voice, Mabel was careless and rather lazy about taking care of her throat. She would go into her act without ever warming up. "People who went to hear her should have waited for the second act."

In the Golden Age of Mabel, any impoverished music lover strolling along Swing Street in thin-soled shoes and a shiny suit could be magically whisked on waves of melody through the door of a funky no-cover-charge club crowded with romantic "duos" and "items." As his eyes adjusted to the gloom, he might notice that those of the girls were hopefully riveted on the expressions of their boy friends. When Mabel in her sweet vulnerability sang, "I *know* how it feels to have *wings* on your heels,"* they all knew that she understood their secret fantasies and was singing just to them. Nightly, lives were changed by her music. The pure bliss of the experience transformed the privileged listeners. Her music proclaimed that tenderness, humor, and beauty were not just luxuries, but everyday essentials for life's great struggle.

Bobby Short, for decades the crown prince of elite cabaret, recalled that a friend once took him to Tony's. He had just been rejected at a critical point in his New York career, "And a teacher appeared." He was introduced to Mabel in the rather faded room where she drew a packed house every night. Celebrities of theatre, film, and fashion were all "eager for her entrance through the narrow path between crowded tables to the throne-like chair in front of the piano. What a lesson to watch that entrance, her blue eyes glowing, her smile the smile of royalty."

But this was no aloof monarch; she was compassionate

---

* Lyrics from "Hello, Young Lovers," Rodgers & Hammerstein, 1951.

and understanding of her subjects. Short listened to her sing in "a high, floating soprano with faultless diction," and even though he had known many of the songs for years, the experience was a revelation. Never, he said, was a lyric sung "with more understanding perfection." From ballads to light, satirical Cole Porter numbers, she sang in a voice scarcely stronger than someone chatting with a nearby friend. "I was sure this was true love," said Short, "as the room filled with admiring sighs of 'Oh, Mabel!' instead of applause."

Obviously, Tony's belonged to Mabel. But Short noticed that the moment she finished her set, the owner of the club would rush to her side and stand on his head! A desperate cry for attention?

Regular guests began to observe a young hollow-cheeked guy with big blue eyes, hovering in a corner, always immaculate in a jacket and tie. Sometimes he would scribble notes on a napkin. "We all knew *he* was going to make it," said the watchful Thelma Carpenter. It was Frank Sinatra, Old Blue Eyes, the future Chairman of the Board who said, "Everything I knew ... I learned from Mabel." And wasn't that Dean Martin, sitting next to Tony Bennett? And Johnny Mercer? And Mel Torme!

Many of Mabel's favorite songs were as off-beat as Alec Wilder's "Have You Ever Crossed Over To Sneden's?" She was always looking for the sheet music of old favorites, like Kern and Fields' "Remind Me." Around midnight she might startle the audience with a melodramatic poem. "Ballad of the Harp Weaver," by Edna St. Vincent Millay, was one of her favorites, and a guaranteed weeper.

Loonis McGlohon and William Engvick, separately and in collaborations with Wilder, began to write satirical and romantic lyrics for Mabel. Engvick's "While We're Young," with music by Wilder and Morty Palitz, is a timeless favorite which James Thurber once described as the "finest piece of English writing" he knew:

"We must fulfill this golden time
when hearts awake so shyly, softly.
Songs were made to sing while we're young.
Every day is spring while we're young.
None can refuse, time flies so fast,
too dear to lose and too sweet to last.
Though it may be just for today
Share our love we must while we may.
So blue the skies, all sweet surprise
Shines before our eyes while we're young."

Mabel described to a *TV Guide* reporter the difficulties of intimate entertainment. "Once I cried while I was singing a song," she said. "It was 'The Last Time I Saw Paris,' and I got to remembering and feeling sorry and cried. I was lost. And the audience was lost. And the performance wound up a shambles. I'm not supposed to cry or laugh when I sing. I tell a story and it makes you remember something that once made you laugh or feel sad."

The writer added: "Happy or sad, Miss Mercer brings to the world of popular singing the same genius which Charlie Chaplin brought to the screen. The perfection of detail, the ability to find and project the hidden emotion in a story, situation, or song.... There has grown up around (her) a mysterious aura concerning her ability to handle a lyric, to make every word take on fresh, crystal-clear meaning."

Portia Nelson, the versatile creator of revues and lyrics who later starred at the Blue Angel, was afraid she had no talent when she first dropped in to hear Mabel in 1948. Mabel convinced her that she could sing. Nelson recalled the fifties as an exciting and creative time when "one could be walking down the street, run into someone, and start a revue. Mabel, a very kind and generous lady, made show music come alive as no one else did. She taught us all how to tell stories and that is what cabaret is—communicating."

Admirers never tired of trying to pin definitive labels on their idol. Philadelphia music critic Steven Levy, when Mabel was 75 and wryly describing herself as a basso profundo, prodded around in the mystery and wrote, "In any art form, there is a degree of attainable excellence that catapults the artist beyond the limits of mere artistry. Some call this genius. Whatever it is, this quality is very rare and involves a perfection in craft and a translation of feeling into form. . . .it emerges that the only indisputable Master in the field of popular music might be Mabel Mercer."

Some worshippers began to claim that when she sang, an aura shimmered around her frizzy head. Not a few began to think it a halo, which amused Thelma Carpenter. "If Mabel was a saint, would she have hung out with me?" she demanded. "Mabel was no saint, she was in show business!"

But each night when Mabel left her little stage, the magic story-telling ended. Going home to the bizarrely overcrowded apartment, applause still ringing in her ears, perhaps she sometimes wondered if success could ever fill the emptiness.

Chapter 12
Saints and Swingers

Mabel probably winced, in her middle years, when newspaper columnists began labeling her "Mother New York." While it was true that some of her followers in and out of show business seemed to aspire to be her children, the burden was a heavy one, especially when her own emotional turmoil felt more like adolescence. As always, she kept her deepest feelings mostly to herself.

When she unexpectedly received a wire from Europe about Harvey White's death, the news shocked her with a spasm of grief for what might have been. Perhaps only Ena Boucher understood how much she had loved her old beau, the high-spirited young black entertainer from her Paris days. If she had ever wanted a real marriage it would have been to Harvey. When news came of his death, Ena wrote: "I can't imagine him ill at all.... It's no use trying to disguise the fact that while Harvey was here, there could never be anybody else for you. I hope it's not too late for you to get some happiness out of life. You certainly deserve it...."

Only Ena may have understood why Mabel sang with such special poignancy, despite an underlying current of disbelief, the song that promised, "Time Heals Everything."

Financial security continued elusive as well; her bank account through the years showed little improvement. She watched some of her admirers selling millions of records with songs they had learned from her; and not a few of them, including Thelma Carpenter, were starring in roles on Broadway. When Jerome Kern revived *Show Boat*, she still yearned for the part of Julie. Friends, including Rosetta LeNoire who starred as Queenie many times, said that Mabel would have been wonderful in the role.

But life went on at Tony's Club. The program usually began at around 11 o'clock, after the singer had dined and perhaps seen a show or gone to another club. The dining tables would be whisked away and the star's highbacked chair brought forth. Mabel's appearance charged the room with a tension that needed no fanfare. Sitting down, she adjusted the long silk stole about her shoulders and turned to whisper to her accompanist. With a smile to the audience, she folded her hands in her brocaded lap and began to sing. Her repertoire, although it seemed impromptu, had obviously been worked out in her mind. If special friends appeared, she sang their favorite songs, no matter how off-beat. Her second set usually lasted until 4 o'clock in the morning.

"When you feel that to breathe would be an intrusion," said one fan, "you know you are in the presence of greatness." New York columnist Liz Smith claimed that her bathroom wall held photos only of her two heroes, Mabel Mercer and Tom Mix. She once reported in awe that the singer enabled one to remember even the most sleazy love affair with warmth and affection. As if she held a key to everyone's personal joys and sorrows, Mabel filled listeners with a sense that each moment was precious.

Kaye Ballard, the queen of cabaret satirists, created a Mercer take-off with deadly accuracy. "I adored her," Ballard said. "If the audience were noisy, she would stop and hold for five minutes until they grew quiet, and then say, 'I thought I heard some talking.' She commanded the audience's attention, yet in person was the shyest and most insecure. I have that insecurity and I recognize it."

Barbara Cook, who had starred in the original *Music Man*, was galvanized by her first exposure to Mabel at Tony's. She said, "I'd never heard anyone sing lyrics the way she did, so affective, so moving.....Judy Garland and Mabel were opposites and I learned a lot from both. Judy taught me to shape a song emotionally. Mabel seemed at a distance and regal.... Her take on a lyric was so personal, her sense of irony and humor greater than that of anybody I ever heard."

There were, of course, a few unrestrained critics. Jazz singer Anita O'Day, on hearing Mabel for the first time, is said to have burst out, "Man, this chick has got the weirdest...act in show business!"

Orrin Keepnews, a legendary figure in jazz recording, chuckled at remembering the first time he and his wife went to hear Mercer and found her singing Cole Porter's "Experiment," not one of the composer's more hummable tunes. In fact, Alec Wilder found it downright irritating, the title itself "uneuphonious," while the musical phrase that carries it exaggerated its "unwieldy unsingingness." Why Mabel often chose this song remains a mystery. Mr. and Mrs. Keepnews walked in at the moment of her highpitched injunction to "expeddd-iment, expeddd-iment" and found it "chilling." But after settling down and listening for a time, they too joined the ranks of the enraptured.

The Duke and Duchess of Windsor came often to New York especially to hear her, as did such luminous actors and directors as John Gielgud, John Huston, Zachary Scott, Frank Sinatra, and Ava Gardner. A diversity of show business royalty dropped in for her "workshops:" Nat King Cole, Dorothy Loudon, Ethel Merman, Blossom Dearie, Peggy Lee, Lena Horne, Howard Dietz, Leontyne Price, Sylvia Syms, Rod McKuen, Andy Williams, Stan Freeman, Faith Winthrop, Jimmy Lyon, Ronny Whyte, Travis Hudson, and many more.

Show-business bickering and jealousy were rife among Mother New York's group. "It was like sibling rivalry," recalled the unrepentant Thelma Carpenter. "I was always flipping off. Once we had a misunderstanding; a guy told Mabel I had said something about her that was not true. The next time I saw her, she called me right over and said, 'Darling, I sleep with whom I wish to sleep.'

"I said, 'Wait a minute! Who cares? Shit.'"

It was occasionally suspected that Thelma and Mabel were lovers, since they were so often seen together, a charge Thelma always vehemently denied and Mabel ignored.

The wandering Kelsey Pharr wrote from time to time. He addressed one long hand-printed letter to "La Duchesse," and enclosed a news clipping singling him out for "high taste and quality" in the Delta Rhythm Boys. Writing from California, he alluded to a recent reunion in New York with his "darling wife:" "I had a lovely visit home this week and a half, and I'm very proud of my wonderful wife and home-maker....thanks loads. You couldn't be lovelier." He enclosed household money he had earned playing musical bits in war-time movies. Despite Mabel's undeniable cooking skills, it may have been her only compliment as a home-maker.

After a significant silence of almost a year, Kelsey wrote again, this time from Portland, Oregon: "How have you been?

Thelma the Carpenter reports not so well.... Is that all over?"

He had not written, apparently, after hearing of Mabel's involvement with another musician, a temperamental black drummer. She spoke of the affair to only one or two intimates. Other friends knew little about him, and disliked what they knew: it was enough that he made Mabel unhappy, expressing love-hate feelings for light-colored women in forceful and unpleasant ways. Her friends were relieved when the interval ended. Kelsey also had lovers and suffered from similar emotional ups and downs. He commented acidly on the hardships of the road: "Dingy towns, dumpy hotel rooms, drippy people." Like Billie Holiday, he was doomed to enjoy his tumultuous life for only a short time.

In his next note, thanking Mabel for sending his IRS refund, he wrote, "I hope the Tony's trouble is a thing of the past now. Where is the Carpenter?" Tony's trouble may have alluded to Soma's abrasive racial attitude toward Mabel's friends. She once threatened to quit because of it, but Thelma dissuaded her. The Carp's strategy was to round up several flashy white Hollywood friends and drag them into Tony's, which she said temporarily quieted him down.

Thelma herself toured with Count Basie's orchestra. Not only could she belt, swing, and shout with the best of them; her exquisite vocal control was enhanced by her poise and beauty. Having started so young that the stage felt like her playpen, she had the opposite of stage fright. Her naturally combative spirit thrived on the conviction that "when you are on that stage, man, you are immortal."

Thelma told a story about being with a group of black band members who were trying to flag a taxi late at night in San Francisco. The men hung back in the shadows until she—

144

the lone helpless woman—charmed one down. When the driver swerved to a stop, she said, "I've got a band with me," and a dozen musicians with enormous instruments swarmed from the shadows.

In her youth, says Loonis McGlohon, Thelma was sometimes considered the most beautiful woman in New York. When she talked, the expressions that chased each other across her mobile, dusky Irish/Indian/Negro face were as hypnotizing as those of a totally self-absorbed child. Once she and Duke Ellington were sitting around after a television show and Thelma, as usual, was jabbering nonstop. She finally became aware that the composer of "Black and Tan Fantasy" was staring at her, and she stopped talking. "What?" she demanded. The Duke shook his head and grinned. "Nah," he said at last, "too much Indian."

And Thelma recalled that when Mabel first saw the handsome, beige-toned Ellington, she exclaimed with delight, "There's one like me!"

Thelma and Mabel had similar religious backgrounds. Thelma once spoke about their religion and what it meant to both of them, she believed, as women of color. "The nuns gave you a basic sense of self-worth and it stays with you. It was so ingrained that you did not dare to stray. ...If you were Catholic and black, you felt elitist. There was maybe one other black musician who dared to come to St. Malachy's, the actors' church at 49th Street and Broadway that Mabel and I went to early every morning; because being Catholic, to blacks, was like you had four heads. To me as I grew older, my religion seemed almost like a fairy tale...."

She recalled dramatic services at dawn when almost all of New York was still sleeping. "We would change our

clothes at the clubs when they closed around 4 A.M. A bar at
the corner stayed open just so people could eat before they
went to church. The church would be packed with a lot of
big stars, and the old Irish priest would say a whole Mass.
The strippers from Leon and Eddie's would be there, dressed
all prim and proper. But some of the believers would not be
able to get off their knees after they prayed and half of them
would be asleep.

"The priest knew what was happening. He was a former
boxer. He would get out there and rumble at us. If we were
feeling bad about being black, he'd tell us, 'Who told you you
can't be that way? You are the way you are, don't let nobody
turn you 'round.'"

Religion was particularly important to black female entertainers on the road. "Most of the time, traveling, we had
to live in whorehouses in the black part of town," said Thelma.
"Of course the musicians loved it. But when I was traveling
with Basie's band, I always made sure we got a hotel near a
church." She claimed also to have been strengthened by her
mother's homely wisdom about "keeping my dress down and
my pants up."

Visiting her friend's apartment, Thelma admitted, was
an unusual safari. Mabel always had cats, her favorite being
the large yellow American longhair named Winkle (after the
Paris Winkie) who presided at the top of a bookshelf in a
yellow mixing bowl. Mabel pretended Winkle was a heavy
reader, "He'll ruin his eyes up there." She and the cats constantly talked back and forth to the amusement of her guests.
Mabel chatted with Winkle in particular, and played elaborate mind games that made Thelma collapse in laughter.

"We would come into the apartment and Mabel would

look up at the big bowl and there would be no cat. Then she would say, 'Oh deah, I wonder where Winkle is? Thelma, can you see Winkle?' And I would have to crawl around peering under all that old furniture while Mabel called out, 'Winkle, darling, where are you? Oh, I'm so worried.' After about ten minutes, Winkle would get tired of this and we would see this huge yellow head with enormous yellow eyes slowly rising from the mixing bowl. And he would have that look on his face."

Thelma said that sometimes Mabel would come home to find the cat's big golden head just hanging over the edge of the bowl with a certain look. Then they would start talking back and forth about music or books or food. Sometimes they would just sit and blink at each other.

"Whenever Mabel left the apartment, she would always say, with her deep chuckle, 'Now, Winkle, you take care of the house, darling.' One day when a burglar somehow managed to work his way into the apartment, Winkle actually leaped out of his bowl onto the thief's back, and that S.O.B. went running out of there!"

No one, said Thelma, contributed more to her own musical education than Mabel. "She was so fantastic with words. The magic of her when she sang, 'Fly Me To The Moon!' She could swing too."

One night Thelma had just finished her last set at the Club Zanzibar, which was noted for the beauty of its African-American stars, when an elderly gentleman approached her. They began to talk. The man was a tumbler. When Thelma mentioned Mabel, he said, "Mabel Mercer! Why, I knew her before she was born."

The man claimed to have been a friend and partner of

147

Ben Mercer's and said he had a photograph to prove it. "So he brought this snapshot of her father," said Thelma, "and I took it to where Mabel was singing. It was very late at night when we were finally able to sit down at a quiet table alone, and I showed her the yellowed crinkly old picture. All I can remember of her father is that he was a very black man and I knew that she was partial to dark men. I wondered if she was going to want to meet the guy who knew him and find out more about her father. She just looked at the picture for a long time and then finally handed it back to me. She did not say anything. I could not tell what she was thinking. Maybe it was just too late."

Chapter 13
Midnight at Mabel's

For the regulars of New York nightlife in the late forties and fifties, it became customary at around midnight to say, "Let's go to Mabel's!" Any club she sang in was automatically "Mabel's." That passion was captured in an Atlantic album titled "Midnight at Mabel Mercer's," with such memorable numbers as "Wouldn't It Be Loverly," "Lucky To Be Me," and "Blame It On My Youth." Mabel was accompanied on the album by George Cory and Sam Hamilton at the pianos. She sang much loved ballads by Leonard Bernstein, Betty Comden, Oscar Hammerstein, Richard Rodgers, Lorenz Hart, Oscar Levant, and Alan Jay Lerner, as well as those of her friends Wilder, Howard, and Engvick.

After World War Two, the music industry proved itself more than eager for peacetime renewal. Wartime technology brought such advances as the tape recorder and the longplaying LP record, putting new life into the popular music industry. Gone overnight were the more soporific and jingoistic patriotic songs. Americans could not wait to hear the last of England's weepy "The White Cliffs of Dover," nor of Marlene Dietrich's equally bathetic "Lili Marlene."

Good sharp satirical humor returned to music, as in, "It's A Lie, It's A Fake!" a rakish number by Fogarty and Engvick, jauntily sung by Mabel. Her recording with Bart

Howard of Cole Porter's 1935 song, "Just One Of Those Things," which had withstood a thousand amusingly nostalgic renditions, went on and on, remaining popular well into the baby-boom generation.

During her long tenure at Tony's, Mabel felt secure enough to hang up a favorite portrait of herself, a delicately romanticized pastel by *The New Yorker* cover artist Lisa Rhana, who was also well-known for her paintings of ballet dancers. Another graphic artist who became a special friend was Beata Gray. She could drop in alone at any of the "Mabel's" without feeling uncomfortable. The singer always made sure she had a good seat and felt welcome.

By now Mabel was sought after and written for by all the leading composers. On December 31, 1952, the prolific Harold Arlen sent her a packet of sheet music and a note: "As soon as I get back I'll drop in to hear one of my favorite interpreters of songs. Happy New Year!" Enclosed were "When I Close My Door," which he wrote with Dorothy Fields, "One For My Baby," co-written with Johnny Mercer, and "Last Night When We Were Young," from the movie *My Blue Angel* with Betty Grable and Dan Dailey.

Mabel's personal sheet music tended to become tattered and lacy from too much loving demand. Favorites included "Blues In The Night," "Let's Take The Long Way Home," "That Old Black Magic," "This Time The Dream's On Me," "Get Happy," "Hooray For Love," and "Let's Fall in Love," among many. A note from music publisher H. Epstein said Harold Arlen had asked him to send her copies of songs from his new show, *House Of Flowers*.

Bart Howard reminisced fondly of Mabel in that era. "I'll never forget how she always insisted on putting on her nail polish in a bouncing taxi, and her dresses always needed a couple of stitches. She never came out of Macy's without two of their biggest shopping bags crammed with something like toilet paper for a year."

His appraisal of her private life, however, suggested that he might have been taken in like so many of her friends. "Sex was not important to Mabel, but surviving was. She kept that apartment for years, probably because she did not know how to get rid of all the stuff, or couldn't bear to get rid of it."

Mabel's upstate friend Muriel Finch, who assisted the singer tirelessly in her later years, commented regarding the Central Park North apartment that, "You inched in as best you could—and prayed to God you could find your way out."

Howard noted that in her middle years, "Her voice became less English as time went by. She was always like my sister. She called me Barty Balls and my friend was Buddy Balls, and she used to call us her two sons. When we drove the old LaSalle south, she had to eat with blacks and stay in the black part of towns. Then our transmission went. Harry Beard came and rescued us. And guess who got to go back later and get the car?"

Bart began to see a lot of the rather mysterious but handsome and cultured Mr. Beard of Philadelphia, who was always around, being helpful to Mabel and making a lot of her other admirers jealous. He (like everyone else in her sphere, as it seemed) was several years her junior. "I knew Harry from when we worked at Tony's," said Bart. "Mabel always had an entourage and he was part of it, and then he was missing for a time and someone said he caused her to lose money. But he came back and was her manager. He and his sister, Pearl Lemert, who owned a television station in Pennsylvania, took us to Florida another time and we spent a month on Joe Carstairs' island. It was Harry who got us to buy that old LaSalle."

Bart assumed, from the way Harry and Mabel acted when others were around, that they were not in love. Besides, Harry had a reputation as a hard-core womanizer. "At least with Harry she had someone to go out with besides the gay boys, who were fun," said Bart. All this suggests that Howard had lost touch with Mabel, or perhaps did not realize that the three words she lived by were discretion, discretion, and discretion. Mabel of course was Catholic, Harry was Jewish, both were married, and Harry had children. His ultimate divorce would prove trying for all concerned.

Mutual friends began to notice that whenever Harry Beard went to hear Madame, as he called her, he chose a seat away from others, the better to sink into his private reverie. He always seemed to be around, helping her.

Mabel, whose forte was never organization, grew to rely on him to handle the business details of her career. Their love affair was reported by some to be tempestuous, partly because Harry was so spoiled. He required, unfortunately, a well-kept home. More seriously, he did not care for cats. Mabel once laughingly admitted that sometimes they held hands just to keep from hitting each other.

Another love affair, completely platonic, soon developed between Mabel and Alec Wilder, the eccentric composer/ songwriter. Wilder's indifference to acclaim, except as it paid the rent, was one of the links he and Mabel shared. He adored her: she was "...the guardian of the tenuous dreams created by the writers of songs." That title, "Guardian Of Dreams," was borrowed by the Canadian Broadcasting Corporation

and used years later for an award-winning documentary film
about Mabel and her work.

One evening the prickly but sensitive Wilder came upon
singer Peggy Lee, another of his favorites, apparently feeling
depressed during her appearance with Benny Goodman's orchestra at the New Yorker Hotel. Wilder went home and,
hoping to cheer her up, wrote for her the lyrics and music of
the love song, "Is It Always Like This?" He later said, "I'm
quite sure she liked it, but so strange are the mazes of the
mind and the heart, she never sang it or as much as mentioned it." When Mabel and Wilder met, he played and sang
this song for her and told her the story. At first she declined
to sing it even though it was her kind of ballad, feeling it
would not be right. After she was finally persuaded to introduce it, it became one of Alec and Mabel's beloved "durables."

Loonis McGlohon and Wilder composed regularly on
long-distance telephone hookup between New York and
North Carolina. Alec, despite his acknowledged charms, could
be boorish, loud, and sexist, especially in the throes of a
practical joke. He loathed all females whom he suspected of
being "society women." One day while he was lunching at
the Algonquin Hotel, said McGlohon, he was spotted by some
of this noxious breed chatting at another table. One woman
was claiming that he had written "It's So Peaceful In The
Country" while he was a guest at her home. Foolhardily she
asked the waiter to invite him to their table.

Rising with his hat on his head, Wilder stopped to talk
with them. While the women gushed, he reached for a pitcher
of ice water, poured a fair amount into the crown of his
fedora, and tilted his head over the unfortunate creature who
was still describing the thrill of being his hostess. "Isn't the

weather beastly," he commiserated, wishing them good day. At the time of the Algonquin Round Table, rude pranks of that type were much admired.

But with Mabel, who could do no wrong, Alec Wilder was always a gentleman. The two were sometimes guests at the McGlohon home in Charlotte, where Nan Lovelace McGlohon presided as a model southern hostess, and was perhaps miscast as a society dame. She recalled wryly that Alec always completely ignored her, the McGlohon children, and anyone else present, except his beloved Mabel and his partner Loonis. He would spring up to get Mabel a glass of water at the frailest excuse, said Nan McGlohon, "even if I happened to be gasping and choking at his other side."

Far from a hostess's dream, Wilder was a guest who loved to go to bed with a book and a box of chocolates. While munching and reading, he carefully and logically wiped his fingers on the sheets to spare the book.

Mabel's ultimate departure from Tony's Club in 1949, after she had asked for a $10 a week raise and Tony Soma turned her down, prompted a legendary Mafia prank, perpetrated by Wilder and Frank Sinatra. Both men were outraged that anyone should dare say no to Mabel. One evening a group of burly gentlemen wearing broad-shouldered camel's hair topcoats, white silk scarves, and other tasteful accoutrements entered the club, ordered the most expensive champagne, and sat for several hours listening to Mabel, the diamonds on their pinky fingers dazzling her eyes. Very late in the evening, two of the gentlemen asked to speak privately with Mr. Soma.

They explained to Soma very politely that if business really was bad, they could understand that he might have to

154

fire Mabel. But clearly business was not bad. The way it worked out, see, if he really fired the lady, his club would be leveled within twenty-four hours. It is reported that Tony went pale and whispered this news to Mabel; Mabel trembled as she phoned Wilder, who had instigated the plot. "Alec, dear, don't you realize what you have done? This is no joke!"

Two weeks later, ostensibly because his club had to move to the other side of town to make room for the new CBS studios, Tony's was in fact closed down. The wrecking bars that finally arrived were legitimate.

Bob Lansdon, a former New York advertising executive, recalled the criminal underworld in which New York night clubs flourished. Lansdon had first met and heard Mabel when he was a young Navy man. One night in the mid-fifties he took philanthropist Raymond Jones to hear Mabel in a club controlled by mobsters. Lansdon became irritated by two men who talked through her songs. When their rudeness persisted, the normally quiet music lover whirled on them and was shocked to hear himself say, "Shut up or get out!" The men left soon afterward, but the bartender whispered that they were waiting outside to beat him up.

At 4 A.M. the mobsters were still lurking around. "Mabel had her Cadillac then, parked about a block away," said Lansdon. "We waited half an hour, then the three of us ran like mad to her car and she dropped us off.

"I would always take my Procter and Gamble clients to hear her," Lansdon continued. "Without exception she charmed the pants off them. When you were sitting at her feet, she was mesmerizing." Lansdon had a curious remembrance of Mabel "joining the church" at this time. In fact, she was experiencing a period of spiritual pain that for several years kept her from going to Confession and Holy Communion. As it turned out, she was waiting for the young Jesuit seminarian, Peter O'Brien, to be ordained a priest, hoping that because of his personal experience in show business, he would become a confidant to whom she could bear to speak of her shame and unhappiness.

Chapter 14
Searching

Bart Howard wrote a song for Mabel on her fiftieth birthday. "It Was Worth It (That's What I'll Say)," is funny, charming, and timeless, and she sang it truly. But she told the composer, "I never had any trouble about being fifty."

Bob Lansdon remembered the song as "Put On Me Pumps" because of the lines: "When down in the dumps, I can put on me pumps and dance again/ And who can tell—with a slight overhaul I could still be the belle of the ball! That's what I'll say!"

Howard's most famous song, "Fly Me To The Moon," was sung first by Peggy Lee, who wisely proposed that he change its title from the original "In Other Words." The song's immortality was further assured when Mabel lent it her unique interpretation.

Despite the worshipful crowds around her, it still troubled Bart and other friends that she seemed a lonely woman. "She was always busy," recalled the composer. "Cooking, caring for her cats and dogs, doing the things lonely people do. Well, aren't people who like cats and dogs supposed to be lonely?"

One journalist who went too far in speculating about the singer's private life incurred her rare and unforgettable wrath. Roland Wild, who had been a casual friend, wrote a long article about her in 1951 in a slick but short-lived publication, *Park East, The Magazine of New York.* Wild's piece might have been considered a rave except for his blithe reference to a female companion of many years "who manages Mabel with a practised hand, massages her regularly, and enjoys just about the same interests in reading, good cooking, and classical music."

The companion was Ena Boucher, who was often a guest of Mabel's in New York, as was Dicky Graden. Ena was both a professional nurse and a superior poker player, and both women were steady church-goers like Mabel.

On reading the Wild piece, Mabel phoned the reporter and raged that she would never speak to him again. He was, in effect, excommunicated. Her fury may have had little to do with sexual judgments, since she was unbigoted in that regard. This "friend," however, had violated her trust and possibly embarrassed her "sister."

More weighed upon Mabel than the real pressures of her profession and her growing celebrity. After many years of six-day weeks and over-exposure to cabaret "intimacy," she hungered for a private bit of God's earth. She often caught herself day-dreaming about the solace and stability of her grandmother's old cottage in Wales. For years she had carried around with her a watercolor sketch of a cottage, painted by her mother, as if it were a twin in search of its mate.

She did not require much: just a place to commune with weeds and flowers and trees, with cows in pastures and birds and running water. She longed to feel her hands in real dirt with real earthworms, to see mud beneath her painted nails, and to know the drowsy bliss of exhaustion after working outdoors all day. She wanted to walk by a reedy stream in spring, perhaps to surprise a mud hen like those in Wales rafting along with her yellow chicks on her back. Living without nature around her for so many years had left her with an intense hunger. Like all singers she also yearned for space in which to practice her songs without disturbing the neighbors or being made self-conscious by uninvited listeners.

She and Bart occasionally drove up into the magnificent north woods on Sunday, looking at first just for a weekend hideaway that she might be able to afford. The tall good-looking white man was her front. But he soon lost interest in the search and some of Mabel's female friends rallied around. Eventually they found for her a simple little cabin in the upstate resort of Kasoag.

Her friend Mildred Jones, also white, of Rome, N.Y., arranged the cabin's purchase and Mabel sent a down payment of $100 by Western Union. This modest place evolved into a rustic getaway for Mabels' women friends. The group included the artist Beata Gray, Barbara Probst, and Ena Boucher, plus the oil-heiress Joe Carstairs and her current retinue. A Mabelish haphazardness seemed to distinguish the activities pursued at the retreat. There were lengthy correspondences about a defective pickup truck, about whether it was possible to transport a mattress in a sedan, and the mortification of one of the group who accidentally spilled beer on Mabel's best coat. It was like being a girl again, and camping out. Mildred Jones congratulated Mabel on how quickly she managed to raise the full $500 for the purchase.

Then came the bad news. The "natives" discovered that a colored woman had invaded their turf. There was no way for Mabel to enjoy her weekend retreat while feeling such hostility. Once more she resigned herself to urban society.

The Byline Room where she worked at the time was a

narrow enclosure with space for about fifty persons. It was usually packed and she enjoyed being there. Not a fancy place, it offered only drinks and the world's foremost song stylist; and when she sang, it was necessary to turn off the music in the raucous Show Spot Bar below. Fancy critics were now describing her as the "doyenne of popular music." The royals, the millionaires, and their sycophants came as usual. Mabel sang for them all, known and unknown, managing to remember who loved "Dancing on the Ceiling," and who would rejoice in "Gimme A Pig Foot."

Herbert Jacoby of the Blue Angel asked her to sing for a charity benefit, with Bart Howard as her accompanist. Bart, now master of ceremonies at the famous club, wrote dozens of songs for the occasion. Mabel also appeared on the Dave Garroway television show and did a benefit for multiple sclerosis. Then quite suddenly one day she found herself singing opera, recording an aria written especially for her by a world-famous Italian composer.

Gian-Carlo Menotti, inspired after hearing her sing, wrote for Mabel the opening and deliberately unfinished aria for his opera *The Consul*. The production won the Drama Critics Circle Award for 1950 in New York and went on to garner a Pulitzer Prize. Everywhere it was a triumph, the Paris production being hailed as particularly brilliant. To make sure that Mabel's voice would always be part of the LaScala Opera Company's live productions, Menotti had her recorded singing the French street song, "Tu Reviendras." Mabel, always an actress at heart, relished her role, described vividly by *New York Times* critic William Hawkins:

"Here is a sharp imitation of one of those insidious, cheap, self-pitying, guttersnipe melodies, at which no one can top the French. As sung by Mabel Mercer, it captures the sirenish resignation that makes the song so loathsome…."

Said Menotti: "I've had many offers to finish it, so that it could be made into a pop song. Even Mabel Mercer herself, for whom I wrote it, begged me to finish it, so she could use it in her nightclub appearances. But I hate nightclubs. And so I never agreed."

Friends of Mabel's claim that for her contribution to the LaScala production that sold many recordings, she was paid a flat sum of $100.

Soon afterward, she registered at Doctor's Hospital in New York for an undisclosed illness. Upon her recovery, she celebrated by buying a big black yacht of a 1946 Cadillac to replace the finally banished LaSalle. When friends, including Bob Lansdon, politely observed that she still did not know how to drive and had no driver's license, Mabel said that she planned to learn; and she did.

Fred Henshaw's Body & Fender Works billed her $30 for removing dents and scratches from the automobile. The record failed to indicate, however, whether the damage occurred before or after she took the wheel. The new driver bought insurance for $16.21 and paid for other repairs of $55.50. Mabel's companions noted that her personal philosophy of never looking back applied also to driving.

Sam Hamilton, one of her accompanists, sometimes caught a ride home with her at dawn through Central Park. He mentioned that she was well into the Cadillac period before she mastered or showed any interest in the reverse gear. As for the forward mode, Mabel was just able to see over the dashboard by sitting on a cushion to reach the steering wheel. Despite the misgivings of timid passengers, she was thrilled to own the car and hoped to start driving into the country-side again in search of her dream.

Meanwhile, with the delightful team of Cy Walter and Stan Freeman on double pianos, she recorded *The Cole Porter Album*, and a 10-inch LP, *Songs of Mabel Mercer, Vol. II*. Walter and Freeman were a popular pair on the radio show, *Piano Playhouse*. Freeman recalled that Mabel was in splendid voice when they did the Porter album, which wasn't always the case.

"We began around midnight and worked until 3 or 4 a.m., taking breaks now and then for some champagne that Mabel had amply furnished," he said. "In the song, 'Looking at You,' there is a couplet that goes, 'Looking at you, I hear poets tellin' of lovely Helen of Troy,' with the words tellin' and Helen supplying the rhyme. Mabel was a stickler for diction but insisted on singing, 'I hear poets telling of lovely Helen of Troy.' When I pointed out to her that she was ignoring a carefully wrought Cole Porter rhyme, she said, 'Yes, I know, darling,' and proceeded to record it her way. It still bothers me when I hear it."

Freeman, who like many other composers had first met her at Tony's when he was a GI, says, "The voice was at its ripest then, and I remember being blown away—not only by her sound but by the new life she gave to anything she sang. I heard wonderful songs like 'While We're Young,' 'My Funny Valentine,' and 'All In Fun.' She also championed the latest songs by her friends Wilder and Howard. Her fans knew her repertoire by heart and there were certain rituals they'd perform—either chiming in on a line with her or clinking their swizzle sticks against their glasses in rhythm. This latter ceremony always happened when she sang the Hoagy Carmichael song, 'How Little We Know.' She was a rare lady, kind, generous, elegant, earthy—and a consummate artist."

Alec Wilder asked Mabel why she always sang the Hoagy Carmichael song as a fast waltz since it was indicated in 4/4 time. She had simply concluded that it would be more effective that way. "Well, she's right," Wilder said. "It's a happy, romping, delightful song in a fast three, and almost out of focus in four." Another Carmichael song that Mabel (and Billie Holiday) broke hearts with was, "I Get Along Without You Very Well." The finicky Wilder commented that he respected it more than he liked it.

Wilder also added that the first time he heard Rodgers and Hart's "Wait Till You See Her," it was sung by Mabel Mercer. "She told me," he said, "when I asked about the song, that she had received the full score of *By Jupiter* before it opened, and continued to sing the ballad though it had been dropped early on in the run. I believe that her faith in this song largely contributed to its position today as a standard. It is one of the loveliest of all Rodgers and Hart waltzes."

Once Mabel got her Cadillac and learned to drive forward, she resumed in earnest her search for a real place in the country, remote enough to escape the attentions of unfriendly white neighbors. Every Sunday after early Mass, she scanned the Farms and Acreage section of the *New York Times*. Then she and a friend or co-driver, armed with maps showing highways and the blue lines of back roads, would head north through the glorious Hudson River Valley and into the foothills of the Adirondacks. They would stop in villages to pick up local papers with more real estate advertisements.

Mabel read them and sighed, for the prices always seemed beyond her means. The real estate agents she consulted, even on sweltering summer days, always seemed cold and discouraging. After a vain search, the singer and her companion would usually attend some rural music festival and dine in a country inn before heading back to Manhattan.

Then Mabel would begin another six nights of singing for her supper.

Chapter 15
Landed Gentry

"A real estate agent phoned me one Sunday morning in the spring of 1951," recalled Adelaide Wallin-Beach, a long-time resident of "up-country" New York State. "He'd heard that the old Briggs place had been sold to a Black woman. And that she was moving in that very morning, at that very hour. I said, 'Why are you calling me? Does she have long green horns?' I was brought up to think that everyone should be accepted as an individual."

Mabel was lucky that Mrs. Wallin-Beach was the first person called when she put her money down in beautiful all-white Columbia County in the foothills of the Berkshire mountains. Adde, being curious, saddled up her horse any-way and rode over to the nearby 18th-century Briggs farm in the woods near Red Rock, a mere dent in the road not far from East Chatham. She knew the area intimately.

In the nearby forest was Edna St. Vincent Millay's iso-lated hideaway that would become Steepletop, a famous colony for writers and artists. As a girl, Adde often rode her pony through the woods past the cottage where the shy poet then lived in retreat with her husband. Millay, a political and social idealist, had already won a Pulitzer Prize for "The Harp-Weaver," a melodramatic poem of poverty and transcendent faith. Mabel Mercer, to the wonder of the uninitiated, sometimes recited the poem during her late-night cabaret performances. Young Adde had often noticed a woman watching from behind a tree as she rode by. One day the watcher stepped out and asked if she would like to get down and talk. It was Edna St. Vincent Millay. After that, Adde and the poet often sat at the kitchen table or under the trees and conversed while the girl drank milk and ate cookies. Millay had seemed to her a strange unearthly creature.

In her later years, Adde Wallin-Beach was a tall, strong-framed, patrician-looking woman with an easy and competent manner, who appeared to be on intimate terms with the surrounding hills and spruce forests. Her once movie-star blond hair had turned white. Since suffering a riding injury, she devoted any spare time from her family and grandchildren to playing golf and arranging benefit tournaments. It was not unusual to see her cutting the five-acre sweep of lawn around her house with a tractor mower.

After taking a course in engineering, she had designed and built, with timber-milling help from her son Peter Wallin, a sturdy replica of an 18th century Dutch farmhouse where she lived with her husband, real estate broker George Beach. The grand view from their hill overlooked a good-sized pond with beaver, Canada geese, and mallard ducks in residence. Perhaps the reason the real estate broker had called her regarding Mabel's incursion was that Adde gave the impression that she could, if so inclined, hand over keys to the whole Hudson River Valley and the Berkshire mountains.

The old Briggs farmhouse stood on more than thirty acres of forest and meadow off a winding red-dirt road in the network of hilly byways connecting the states of New York and Massachusetts. Strangers could easily get lost there, yet Mabel had found her place. On one of her Sunday searches for her lost childhood, she met the owner, Charlie Briggs, a retired grocer, postmaster, farmer, maple-syrup maker, and sly judge of character. Briggs had been born in the old house in 1912 and still tapped the maple trees for sugar.

When Mabel saw the farm, her hands flew to her mouth. It was an icy morning with snow on the ground but she trotted all over the field in her satin pumps. She found a brimming stream that burst from a ravine into a waterfall of scattering rainbows, and stood for a long time just looking at it and beyond into the forest. On the muddy verge of the creek, raccoons had left their sharp-toed tracks. Squirrels challenged her from ancient trees. No other dwellings could be seen in any direction. It seemed so much like Wales, the setting of her grandmother's cottage. Thirty acres of total seclusion!

She turned toward the old Cape Cod house standing in a sunlit meadow at the end of a short driveway. The basic house was two stories high with a jumble of small rooms. In front were two matching windows on either side of the unused central entrance. To the left was a 19th century add-on, a glassed-in porch leading to the kitchen door that now served as the front door. The place had only recently been electrified. An iron hand pump still brayed like a donkey when forced to draw water from the well; a venerable outhouse was further authenticated by an antique Sears & Roebuck catalogue.

Entering the house, Mabel was enchanted by the scenes framed in every window. She looked out on an old apple tree, an even more ancient sugar maple, and a windbreak of smaller evergreens, all surrounded by field and forest. She heard the faint sound of scampering feet, and peered hopefully into the pantry. Recent droppings. Charlie Briggs said smoothly that squirrels must have gnawed a hole in the floor and he would have to nail some tin over it. Mabel was doubtless thinking that nothing could be lovelier than having one's own squirrels in one's very own house. She asked if there were field mice too. Oh, yes, Briggs assured her, smiling. Briggs' own mother was still living in the old house. Mabel met the ancient woman and thought she was very beautiful. She may have been disappointed to learn that the older woman did not come with the rest of the property.

It would have taken Briggs a hundred pages to write down all the legalistic disclosures required by property lawyers today, were he to list the total charms of the old place. Mabel remembered that he made disparaging comments about it and even said that maybe it ought to be destroyed. She responded with a "Harrumph!"

Her trance remained undimmed even when he warned her that she would probably be snowbound in winter and have to sled her food in on foot for a mile up from the main road; furthermore, in spring when the snow turned to slush, not even a horse could get through. All this only added to the enchantment. The best thing, however, was that when they got to talking business, Briggs' price was compatible with the small bank balance she had been saving for so long. In her mind, Mabel had already named the farm "Blakely" in memory of her home with the nuns in Manchester.

The only question remaining was the neighbors, and she had to ask. Did they burn crosses in front yards? Charlie Briggs honestly said he didn't know how they would feel, but reminded her that she had her legal rights. Charlie promised to keep the field mowed for her, to cut her firewood, and to provide her with maple syrup collected from the trees. He also said that when she was away, he would keep an eye on the place for her. Visions of scones with maple syrup dancing in her head, Mabel closed the deal quickly, signing papers that very day before the word got out and Briggs could change his mind. Then they shook hands on it.

Briggs later recalled that some people nearby "were upset when I sold Mabel the house. But many of those people are now her best friends, which shows you something about her and about human nature."

Adde Wallin-Beach rode up to the farm a month later, in time for moving day. Turning off the road, she saw the driveway clogged with cars and trucks. A scattering of sleepy city people wandered around, bewildered. To paraphrase Margaret Halsey, they looked as if they had often heard trees described but had never actually seen one. Some were carrying chairs, suitcases, and boxes of sheet music into the house, while others delicately scraped mud from their heels ("Bart, that is not dirt, dear, that is God's earth!") Some repaired their makeup, while others wept over torn fingernails. One fragile fellow stared in shock at the outhouse, circling warily up to it and then backing away, certain that Mabel had been taken in by a country slicker.

As Adde approached, she saw a pale young man in a stiffly starched evening shirt standing on a flatbed truck, studying a refrigerator and a large square piano. Finally he climbed over to the piano, raised the lid, and began to play Alec Wilder's "It's So Peaceful In The Country." From the house came an answering chorus. Two dogs ran out and barked at Adde, who tried to look as if she saw this sort of thing every day in Columbia County. Swinging off her horse, she politely asked a man carrying a chair if she could speak to the new owner.

Someone went indoors to yell for Mabel, who was directing the placement of the all-important food and kitchenware. She took off her apron, sucked in a deep breath, and later remembered saying, "Oh, oh! Here it comes again."

As she left the house and walked toward Adde, however, she was smiling and the sun struck her blue eyes. Adde noticed that the new neighbor was short, wearing jeans and red sneakers with a scarf tied Jemima style around her head. Blond, slim Adde stood in her chic riding outfit, holding the reins of her horse. She spoke very quickly. "I just wanted to welcome you to the neighborhood and ask if there's anything I can do to help."

With a cry, Mabel threw her arms around Adde and then the sleek neck of her horse. When she introduced herself, Adde noticed at once that her accent was crisp and refined. It was the beginning of a special country friendship. Adde rode off soon afterward, promising to return the following Sunday to take Mabel to the Catholic church.

No one ever mentioned to her that Mabel Mercer was a famous entertainer, and it would be years before Adde learned it, quite by accident. Gradually she came to know that Mabel was some kind of a singer who could play the piano a little, but had no clue about her background, except for references to a childhood in rural Wales. Mabel tended to quote the sayings of Grandma Wadham whenever Adde mentioned her own mother.

When Adde left, Mabel was so relieved and happy that she couldn't go back indoors, but insisted on taking her skittish guests out to explore the farm. She led them to the ravine at the edge of the forest and the stream with its sparkling cataract. Floating logs and other debris swirled in the pool below, which was deep enough for bathing if anyone could stand the temperature. Joe Carstairs was sure to love it, and possibly Alec Wilder. Thelma Carpenter, who was there, recalled that Mabel suddenly went leaping across the stream from log to log, calling, "Come on, nothing to it."

Thelma, much younger, tried to follow. She remembered slipping off a log into the icy water and being rudely fished out by the more cautious. Mabel turned just long enough to make sure that she was still breathing, and splashed on down-stream along the shallows.

A pair of mallard ducks exploded from the ripples ahead of her. The bank was shaded by overhanging vine maples already leafing into tiny green umbrellas, and by thick clumps of willows. She recrossed the stream at a sandbar and turned back to find her friends running around and flinging them-selves to the ground. They were pouncing with strange little city cries upon the ruggedly beautiful wildflowers growing in the meadow: Johnny jump-ups, long-stemmed violets, and marshy patches of buttercups. Mabel first smelled and then saw the unfolding yellow scrolls of skunk cabbage, which would turn out, unsurprisingly, to be Alec Wilder's favorite flower. She understood that attraction: skunk cabbages were wild and strong and shy, but revolting in captivity.

She knew that Alec would adore this place, but was not at all sure whether Harry Beard would do so, or indeed whether she even wanted him there. Catching up with her friends, Mabel was unusually quiet. Harry had wanted to come along and advise her about farms, of which he knew noth-ing, but she had discouraged him; he would not like it unless everything were clean and in its place.

Harry was a perfectionist, not only about houses, but

171

also about clothes (hers as well as his own), and about diets (hers). She realized uncomfortably how much she had begun to rely on this gentle admirer in the management of her professional affairs. The tall, soft-spoken Philadelphian had recently begun to make it clear that he hoped to share her life, and it seemed the craziest thing she had ever heard.

It would have been a great relief to her to go to Confession and discuss the relationship, but she could not face it. What would the villagers say if they heard that the Black woman on the old Briggs farm had a white lover? This was not the liberated sixties, although in her quiet nonviolent fashion Mabel was already desegregating Columbia County. No other Blacks lived there.

Her plans for the property, indoors and out, began with building a bathroom, transplanting the garden weeds to more distant locations to make room for flowers, and getting acquainted with all the wild creatures. Peace, in the words of the old poem, might at last come dropping slow. As things turned out, predictably, Mabel was seldom to enjoy a solitary life there. It felt unnatural and wrong not to share all this beauty with as much of the world as possible, so she started at once planning the addition of rooms for special friends who might need them. It probably never occurred to her that not all her city companions would share her love of nature and tolerance of relative discomfort. But they all came, according to Thelma Carpenter, if only out of curiosity.

Harry Beard, with his immaculate tailoring, starched French cuffs, and diamond ring, began going to the farm at first for occasional weekends, along with other guests. Mabel may not have been his only conquest at the time, but he cared deeply for her. As her manager in the city, he understood the

172

stage fright that overcame her before every performance, and was able to give her the strength to confront it and go on.

As for the brilliant and tormented Alec Wilder, the farm became his refuge. He remembered going up to visit Mabel unable to compose, and feeling renewed within two days. "It isn't that she does anything—that there is any laying on of hands or such," he said. "She just putters around her house, and cooks, and feeds her animals. But there is some quality, some corrective force, in her very presence."

The irascible composer could never say enough about the miracle of Mabel Mercer. "As a person, as a friend, and as a singer, she is one of the very few great people I have ever known," he once wrote. This was no lightly considered judgment, for he had always studied famous people and made a special point of writing letters to them. He also urged his friends to write to great people; they were never told often enough, he insisted, of the public's feelings. Loonis McGlohon, who loved both Mabel and Alec, remembered a salient lesson from the composer on the importance of praising the famous.

"Alec told me 'I would have liked to meet Montaigne, the French philosopher, but he died. I think Pablo Casals is probably the greatest living human being. Who do you admire the most, Loonis?' I thought a moment and said Harry Truman. Alec said in his big outdoor voice, 'You should write a letter to him!' I said, 'Oh, the President would not have time to read a letter from me.' Alec said, 'Wrong! Wrong! We should tell the people we admire. They need to know that.'

"About an hour later, he asked, 'Have you written to Mr. Truman?' For three days while we were writing songs together, he kept asking me that question. Finally I wrote two

173

paragraphs to the President, telling him about our game of heroes, and that Alec thought Pablo Casals might be the greatest living person but that I thought he was. I got a reply in four days. President Truman wrote to me, 'Mr. Wilder is correct, and you should always let them know; and Alec Wilder may be right about Pablo Casals being the greatest person in the world.'"

Bill Engvick, incidentally, once noticed a letter in Wilder's wastebasket. Handwritten in French, it was from Dr. Albert Schweitzer. Fishing the letter out, he called it to Alec's attention. His fellow composer replied, "Oh, yes, I've read it." Throughout their musical collaboration, Engvick managed over the years to salvage many letters to Wilder from famous authors and other figures, which he ultimately sent to the New York Public Library.

On one of Wilder's visits to Mabel's farm (referred to alternately as Blakely or Ramshackle Manor), he took brought along a walnut tree and planted it. When it turned out to be hickory, she said to McGlohon in amusement, "Isn't that just like Alec not to know the kind of tree?"

Visitors reported differing impressions of Mabel's farm that all somehow added up to the same thing. Betty Aberlin, who played young "Lady Aberlin" on the *Mister Rogers* show, was rescued by Harry and Mabel one weekend when she found herself stranded in nearby East Chatham. They took her home. "The house was beautifully crooked and toasty and warm," she said. "To me it was like getting a make-believe family. I felt like a tired child. I did not know anything about Mabel and Harry as a couple, but I loved to see them together. My admiration was for a world I knew nothing about."

The *New Yorker* music critic Whitney Balliett remembered Blakely farm as "a masterpiece of disarray. She covered every surface—shelves, mantels, sofas, chairs, pianos, floors, stairs—with possessions, and prayed that the few navigable channels left would remain open. She also made a haven of the house, and those of her countless guests who arrived distraught left whole and at peace."

For almost a decade Mabel would commute to her farm every Sunday morning after early Mass and return refreshed to New York to perform again on Monday night. Although the drive was arduous in bad weather, her life seemed unbelievably and miraculously rich. She loved spending all week planning her many improvements to the farm and the weekend parties for her friends.

Chapter 16
Portents

On January 15, 1952, Mabel took what was a long-considered and drastic step for a loyal subject of the British Crown. She applied for United States citizenship. According to her certificate of naturalization she had grown both in height and weight since her last official documentation. She now claimed to be five feet three inches tall and to weigh 160 pounds. For some odd reason her bluest-blue, blue-green, or soft-blue eyes were described as gray, but perhaps this was the work of yet another clerk who knew better than she what color she was. Her complexion was noted as brown (she may have been tempted to write "inky dink"), her hair black, and she was still married and living at 45 West 110th street, New York. Mabel's photograph for the document was straightforward and very serious.

About this time an eager young singer named Bobby Short entered the New York nightlife scene. Once he had heard Mabel he said he knew his life had changed. When the two first met, he was an anxious twenty-one-year-old singing at the Blue Angel, and she was still at Tony's. It took several years for him to earn her friendship.

"When I returned to New York in 1952," he said, "she was very kind to me as she was to all young entertainers. I think she was shy. She was deeply religious and a lady; she never let down this manner unless she was in private and with very very close friends."

Short learned a great deal from Mabel, and so did a lot of other performers. "I often saw Sinatra and Billie and Lena and even Piaf in her audience," Short said. "Barbara Cook would be there, and Felicia Sanders. Mabel had firm ideas on taste and would not sing something she found offensive. She only sang songs she loved, but she would usually give requests." Short recalled that other more popular singers listened to her and sang her songs and reached the top of the charts. "Billie Holiday sang 'You Better Go Now,' and Lena Horne sang 'From This Moment On.' But they learned the songs from Mabel."

Margaret Whiting, who herself has recorded more than five hundred songs, recalled an experience similar to Short's: "One night Peggy Lee, Duke Ellington, Frank Sinatra and I were there at the same time, and we all agreed that we sat at her feet. She was a woman of the earth. Very unshowbusinesslike." Whiting added, "I think Mabel had the most respect of anyone in entertainment. She was very special and beloved."

What made her so unique and admirable to all those performers was the passion she instilled in the lyrics she sang. "Just mean them," Mabel said, and her advice turned singers into superstars.

Said Whiting, "I always thought she was royalty, yet so much of the earth, so warm and honest. She was majestic." Ronny Whyte is another creative contemporary of Mabel's who plays piano at the Carlyle Hotel, does concert work, and composes jazz for Audiophile recordings. He was in the U.S. Air Force in 1956 when he stopped at the Byline Club to hear her for the first time. "I just wept, it was such an incredible experience," he said. "I had never seen anyone so completely hypnotize an audience."

Comedic singer Dorothy Loudon said that she became one of Mabel's circle when they worked across the street from one another, she at the Blue Angel and Mercer at the RSVP Club on 55th Steet. Loudon and her husband, the superb pianist and arranger Norman Paris, once offered the singer a home in the lower two floors of their small brownstone house on East 83d Street. Mabel went to see it, no doubt measuring it for the guilty hoardings of her apartment on Central Park North. She said that it was "sweet—but too small." "Can you imagine our joy," said the former Broadway star, "if she had found it suitable?"

Pat Carroll, a natural comedian and another of Julius Monk's innocent small-town jewels at the Blue Angel, first started entertaining in New York supper clubs in 1950. Friends took her to the Byline, where Mabel's audience was "literally packed in like sardines." Carroll experienced the unusual impression in those generally rough-and-tumble days of a singer who was definitely in charge. "You didn't dast breathe too deeply, inhale too loudly, cough or sneeze, for you felt as if musical royalty were present.

"All of us working in New York at that time...lived the same hours, would go to see other performers in other rooms or visit jazz joints. But Mabel was different. You felt somehow that you were making a pilgrimage for some extraordinary reason. She made us feel the better for going to hear her. She illumined some old lyric with new meaning, she made the room spin with new ideas about a chestnut of a song, she cleared the air of celebrity watching. For when Mabel

178

sang you didn't care WHO was in the room, you watched and listened to HER."

For Pat Carroll and many of her generation, the fifties were a time of excitement and discovery. Carroll remembered hearing "Every kind of music, every kind of comedy, for the most part with taste and sophistication. Somehow Mabel reigned supreme, seemed a benchmark of what the best of cabaret was and could be. The tops of the industry came to study her, to distill or take apart her magic to see if it could become theirs." Ironically, in spite of all her many successes and the exorbitant homage she was paid, Mabel was still earning so little that she had to pinch pennies and condiments to make ends meet.

In her long tenure at the Byline Club Mabel took only one break. In early summer of 1954 she went with her accompanist Sam Hamilton to the Blue Angel in Chicago for a single Sunday night. She was lured there by producer Victor Lownes, III, who reported in *Playboy* magazine, "She packed that nightclub, with over eight hundred turned away at the door. This, mind you, in a city where she had never appeared before, on a Sunday, normally the deadest night in the week, and with an admission charge of $5.50. No funny hat comics, no chorus girls...just Mabel."

Mabel left a score of Chicago club owners wringing their hands because she would consider nothing so commercial as an extended return engagement (not even when the Mayor declared that they had passed an ordinance making her a property of the Windy City). She had now made three albums for Atlantic: *Songs by Mabel Mercer, Vols. I, II,* and *III,* which included the Cole Porter collection. While sales did not soar to the top of the charts, they ultimately proved that Atlantic had been farsighted. The records have been reissued in various combinations ever since, but somehow Mabel never managed to grow rich.

In 1955, she had been six years at the Byline, her second-favorite "chair of music," when both it and the East Side Show Spot below it were destroyed by fire. Lisa Rhana's treasured portrait of Mabel was burned. The painter and her husband, photographer Fred Bornet, made other portrait sketches and photos of her, but never again one she liked so well. As to security, Mabel had relied on her work at the club to support her new life in the countryside and the remodeling of the house. If she had taken fifty in her stride, she did feel portents at fifty-five. The new crop of entertainers in town were half her age or younger.

The singer who liked to keep her roots in one place sadly pulled them up again. For several months she and pianist Sam Hamilton brightened the tiny, cheerless Pin-Up Room at 34th and Lexington Avenue, attracting national attention from the press. *Newsweek* magazine wrote that Mabel Mercer was probably the only entertainer "who would dare face a bleary-eyed night club audience in the early hours of the morning and sing them a musical setting of A.E. Housman's poems." In the interim, until a new Byline Room opened at 28 West 56th Street, Mabel sang at various other clubs, including the Bon Soir in the Village, which was hosted by her friend Jimmy Daniels.

The reopening of the new Byline on a rainy November night in 1955 was a magnificent success. All of her loyals turned out. One writer compared it to "a subway express at rush hour." Frank Sinatra was quoted in the press as saying that when he was in New York he could always be found in her audience. "There is a singer there named Mabel Mercer.... When you see her you'll know why I feel as I do." Sinatra's new style, said Walter Ritchie, a fan of both singers "was a male version of Mabel's for phrasing; and he always had the wonderfully clear enunciation that was her trademark."

Celebrities tried to get to Mabel's, wherever she was, for the magic hour after 3 A.M. That was the time when she was likely to move from table to table singing their favorite interpretations of young love, old love, loss, and laughter. In her audience occasionally was concert pianist Van Cliburn, who also came to study her style. When he won the Tchaikovsky Competition in Moscow, he told Soviet television that although Miss Mercer recorded very little, he considered her "one of the three greatest popular singers in America, along with Frank Sinatra and Bobbie Short."

In 1957 Atlantic issued *The Art Of Mabel Mercer*, which included Wilder's "While We're Young," Cy Walter's "The End Of A Love Affair" and "Some Fine Day," as well as several songs she had recorded previously. But like the others, these LPs were not a great commercial success. It was the essence of Mabel in person that her fans longed for and missed on records.

The stresses of life undeniably were taking their toll on her voice. As the tones and range diminished, her perfection of delivery grew; admirers declared that her artistry had reached its full flower. Newer critics, however, found her puzzling. Telltale words like *cult* and *diseuse* and *legendary* crept into their reviews. Jazz critic Nat Hentoff wrote, "There are some who find Mabel Mercer over-stylized, and otherwise regard those of us drawn to her singing as mesmerized without musical cause. I was one of the unconverted for a while."

At about this time, Mabel's old Paris pal, Cole Porter, long said to be one of her staunchest admirers, allegedly left the fold. James Haskins wrote that Lew Kesler, Porter's rehearsal pianist and longtime friend, told him that when Mabel was at the RSVP (a locale that followed the new Byline), she asked him to tell Porter that she was singing his song, "Ours." Kesler claimed that Porter rolled his eyes and said, "God, that woman couldn't sing when she was young and she can't sing now that she's old."

Since the riding accident that had injured both his legs in 1937, Porter had been through some thirty operations. Although he continued to write hundreds of clever cosmopolitan lyrics and rousing musical scores until the mid-fifties, he was said to be in constant pain. Had anyone been so cruel as to convey this gossip to Mabel, she doubtless would have been crushed. What would she have said? Perhaps, as she had on learning of the backsliding of another old friend, "I don't think he's been himself lately."

The Duke of Windsor continued to stay in touch, perhaps because of Mabel's legendary discretion. "One day at her farm," said Stanley Crantson, "I saw a letter crushed into the sofa with a large W at the top, signed David. She came in and said, 'You are not to read that.'"

Chapter 17
Goodbye to all That

S am Hamilton, Mabel's gentle long-time accompanist from Indiana, had left her in disappointment during their tenure at the dingy Pin-Up Room, causing another spate of gossip. Hamilton felt so strongly that he was not sharing in the singer's success that he moved to Connecticut and went into business. But composer Bart Howard claimed that he was slow at learning new songs. Some said that Mabel, in a flash of irritation, would sometimes turn around and pound on the piano with her fist. Later on, however, she invited Hamilton to return, and he did. He left her permanently only after being stricken with terminal cancer.

Peter O'Brien, still a young seminarian working only part-time at the fringes of show business, recalled that the singer sometimes lost her cool when confronted with boorish behavior, but doubted that she would ever have pounded the piano. He was told that twice in anger Mabel had slapped men who crossed over the invisible line of decency. "Sometimes at parties," he said, "she would remonstrate with Will Craik, who was a real party man, one of those people who can be out of their minds at 4 a.m. and sober at 7. He was very intelligent, with a kind of Plimpton way of speaking, saying things like, 'Sapphire (his name for Thelma Carpenter), let us Simonize our watches.' He had an endless supply of money and could be relied on to buy drinks for poor Jesuit seminarians who made only three dollars a week teaching Shakespeare and Latin in the Bronx."

Mabel's temper flared again when her employer at the new Byline accused her of inappropriate behavior. One midnight she appeared in high spirits and fancily attired, apparently coming from a party, and the club owner commented that she looked lit up like a Christmas tree. Mabel thought he really meant "lit," and perhaps he did; perhaps in fact she was. Her retort in any event was a classic: "There are some things one would rather not hear." It was said that the singer then flounced to her dressing room and performed very badly that night, with a rare chill pervading the club.

Thelma Carpenter, who was singing across the street at the Valentine Club, never recalled any temperamental outbursts. Carpenter sometimes startled her own audience by singing about Porgy and Catfish Row to a tune that was unfamiliar to Gershwin lovers. It was the early piece from Lew Leslie's *Blackbirds Revue*, written by Dorothy Fields and Jimmy McHugh. Thelma may have learned the version from Mabel or Billie Holiday.

At the new Byline Mabel became acquainted with Buddy Barnes, a gifted young pianist with a classical background who would eventually become one of her finest accompanists. It was Ronnie Selby, however, who had played for her at the Pin-Up Room, who first accompanied her at the new club. Buddy Barnes was determined not to play pop music until a friend took him to hear Mabel. The encounter caused a major change in his career. "I was struck by her intelligence, her incredible honesty, and her unashamedness at revealing the human heart," he said. "And of course Mabel's great classical training…appealed to me. She did the same kinds of things that lieder singers do. I said to myself, 'My god, here's a lady doing in popular song the very things I love in classical music.' That was when I made my transition to pop, that is, to intelligent pop."

The new Byline Room, for whatever reason, proved to be a terminal case. By 1957 the star was forced to move on again, this time to the RSVP Room at 145 East 55th street. During Mabel's first months there, she took off every Monday night in October. She was helping to inaugurate a dramatic experiment or "diversion" at the little Cherry Lane Theatre in Greenwich Village. Among her mixture of little cameos, songs of city life, sophistication, and young love, she included deeper songs written for *Lost In The Stars*, by Kurt Weill and Maxwell Anderson. Her simple, evocative performances, both as singer and actress, won wide critical praise. John S. Wilson of *The New York Times* extolled them as a "rare treat," praising her timing, her subtle use of a glancing inflection, and her warmth and wit.

One such diversion consisted of a Eudora Welty play. Mabel's role was to sit in a booth and read the voice-over, which she did with her usual flawless diction and dignity. A friend recalled that the piece included nude dancing and that on opening night explosive snickers burst from the orchestra section where Mabel's two English "sisters," Ena and Dicky, were sitting. They realized she was completely unaware of the dancers' uninhibited gyrations outside her line of vision. Had she seen them, she might not have performed. Obviously, Mabel's intimates felt no compunction about teasing Her Ladyship, either in private or in public.

The brainy and amusing Will Craik was now a "regular"

in Mabel's life. He stopped in to hear her almost every evening after leaving the Wall Street brokerage where he headed the credit division. As his diabetes worsened, he retired to rural Columbia County to be near her farm. Mabel loved Craik's irreverent cracks and he appreciated her quick retorts, but she tolerated his drinking and gossip less easily. He recalled that Mabel was once approached by a rural gossip, who said she had heard that Harry Beard was getting a divorce in order to marry another local woman, and wasn't it wonderful news! Craik claimed that Mabel drew herself up and replied, "Oh, no, dear, I couldn't allow that. You see, she's my friend."

Stanley Crantson, a soft-voiced fan who was often her companion at parties and at the farm, told a revealing story about his favorite songstress: "I met her at Tony's when I was very very young, through a beautiful young woman named Cora Gibbs. She had been on Broadway and was very active in the theatre, until she got throat cancer and was sent to the Lew Hodges Memorial Center. Mabel phoned her often and we had planned to spend Christmas with her; but a bad snowstorm arose and the light plane was grounded.

"I phoned Cora on Christmas Eve and found her crying. But she said she was feeling better because she had just had the most beautiful present anyone could ask for. 'Mabel was on the phone for an hour,' she said, 'and she sang all my favorite songs for me.'" Cora Gibbs died the next day. (Incidentally, the English folk song "The Twelve Days of Chistmas" was rediscovered and popularized by Mabel.)

Crantson phoned Mabel to thank her and asked if he could repay her in some way. She said the only way was to spend a weekend with her at the farm. He did so on many occasions, and often went with her to show business parties.

186

"People would tell her their most intimate secrets—society people and celebrities like Ava Gardner—and she never betrayed their trust," Cranston said. "She never let newspaper reporters know if Frank Sinatra was visiting. She always collected things for her apartment—anything you didn't need she would accept. Her apartment was more than eclectic, so we began referring to all uncertain styles as being of the Mabel Period." Ava Gardner, incidentally, after her divorce from Sinatra, once commented that the best part of their marriage was when he played his Mabel Mercer records.

"Mabel had a lot of sadness," Cranston continued. "She was so sensitive to racial slights. Once at a party, when we were both dying our hair black, a woman came over and asked us if she could ask a personal question. She said, 'What kind of hair dye do you use? Because it looks like shoe polish.' We both laughed it off, of course, considering the source, but after that Mabel let her hair go gray."

One day the then-unknown young composer, Carol Hall, looked Mabel up in the telephone directory and was surprised to find her name. She called to ask if the singer would listen to one of her songs. Mabel agreed, and "Jenny Rebecca," the kind of song that sends program writers into flights of adverbs, like *unabashedly touching*, joined Mabel's repertoire of unusual popular classics. It was said that opera singer Frederica von Stade was so moved by her rendition, she named her first child Jenny Rebecca. In spite of such compliments Mabel would just say, "I don't have a voice, I have a noise."

In 1960 she received a saddening wire from the Delta Rhythm Boys: Kelsey Pharr had died in his forties. She went to Florida by train for the funeral. Staring for hours through the window, she remembered his troubled, mercurial life, how he had come forward to rescue her when she was stranded in Bermuda, and the early, frivolous aspects of their marriage. He had written on their fifth anniversary that he hoped to send her a piece of jewelry with five stones in it. In the same letter he teased that Diana Barrymore was running him ragged in 'Vegas. Thelma Carpenter noted that after Mabel became famous, Kelsey never pressed their relationship. Thus she had seen very little of him in recent years.

At the funeral, his musical brothers and sisters presented a poignant *mea culpa* to one who had set the standards as a decent, gentle, generous man. They praised "...above all that great musical style that raises the spirits, elevates the soul, takes you right up into the clouds of love and happiness." The brothers and sisters knew they had failed their gay brother and added, "Oh, God, that men could see a little clearer and judge less harshly when they cannot see...." Mabel said a heartfelt amen to that. A great deal had changed since those anxious months in Bermuda when she became Mrs. Kelsey Pharr, II. She had a country now and a real home; and so, she may have reflected, had Kelsey.

In 1960 Mabel and Harry drove to San Francisco for a triumphant twelve weeks at the Hungry i. The owner, Enrico Banducci, prepared a special area known as the Other Room for her performances. Bay Area music lovers were captivated, and feted Mabel at private parties. She told music critic Marian Zailian, "I wouldn't have come back to New York if I hadn't had a contract. I would have stayed there as long as Banducci could have kept the place going." But never mind: she would return in seventeen years.

Driving back across the country she and Harry made a vacation of it, dropping in on friends all across the country.

She returned to a few more short engagements in New York, before rock music exploded on the scene. All over America, adolescent hordes were turning up the volume on their electric guitars, while would-be composers discovered with awe that monosyllabic lyrics and simple chord progressions could win them fame and wealth.

The Beatles seemed such decent little chaps with their choir-boy haircuts and Peter Pan collars, as exciting to teenyboppers as Frank Sinatra had been to bobbysoxers. Who would have believed that the greatest pianists, horn blowers, vocalists, and composers could be routed into early retirement by such outrageous sounds? Mabel, like others of her era, thought that this would surely pass.

She struggled to rationalize the tribal tastes of the young. But later she spoke her mind to Richard Dyer of the *Boston Globe Magazine*: "Your ears would be bombarded with singers and instruments going full-pelt, the loudest they could. I have nothing against rock singing; obviously it pleases some people. But it annoys me because I don't really understand it. I can understand the movement because it's rhythmic and it's good for dancing, and dancing is a very healthy thing. But half the time I don't understand the words, even though the performers constantly repeat them. Yet there is an audience for that. They get up and they scream, so it must do something for them. To my mind it is not the right kind of release. It is too fiery. All is not lost, though. People get to be past 30, and then some of them come to hear other kinds of music."

She was too polite to say what she really thought of musicians who did not understand the preeminent role of lyrics and who felt it necessary to define such noble instruments as the piano as "acoustic." To be fair, there was no

reason anyone should have foreseen the siege of frenetic ki-
netics so dear to rock music. Nothing in history had pre-
saged it. Driven primarily by new recording technology and
portable transistor radios, it deceived even the "experts," who
failed to anticipate the social impact of rock on the brewing
civil rights revolution and the diabolic tar pit of Vietnam.

In the sixties, Mabel was often asked to join various
political causes, but she usually declined. She wholeheartedly
supported the NAACP, and along with Bobby Short gave a
benefit performance with Roy Wilkins for the NAACP Special Contribution Fund in 1969. Although public activism
was not her way, she knew the cruelty and injustice of racial
prejudice first hand. Once, going to meet Harry Beard's
mother in Philadelphia in the early fifties, a conductor had
ordered her to the back of a bus. She rose slowly and so did
Harry, and both went to the back, the American gentleman
and the English lady. The conductor was not pleased.

Another encroaching technology, TV, was also changing the cabaret music scene. Nightclub managers erred in
underestimating the impact of television on "live" entertainment and were surprised to the point of bankruptcy when
people stopped going regularly to hear ballad singers.

Entertainment moguls were delighted with the youth
rebellion of the period and its new mass market. Record
manufacturers, learning about all the new drug money on the
streets, quickly adapted, reaping fortunes from the music of
juvenilia. In their desperate search for the next new sound or
group, it seemed to Mabel all that was beautiful and true in
American music might be lost.

Hearing herself called a legend and the doyenne of cabaret, Mabel shuddered. Disk jockeys were referring to the popu-

lar classics as "golden oldies," or perhaps even worse, "standards." With her world of music spinning out of control, she found herself in her sixties, unemployed.

Mabel's retreat in the woods, it turned out, had been a wise investment. She finally moved to the country, but never pretended she was retiring: "There is a big difference," she said. Planning the remodeling of Blakely farm remained her salvation when all around her threatened to crumble. She began designing a lovely office for Harry on the second floor, with a balcony overlooking meadow and hills. And he was after her to diet again.

The nearby residents of Columbia County no longer complained about the black woman with a live-in white lover, at least not to her personally. Some apparently had made remarks to Charlie Briggs and Will Craik. Adde Wallin-Beach started taking Mabel around to flea markets and shops on weekends and introducing her, which had a soothing influence. What angered Adde was the way some local gossips changed to sycophants when they finally learned that Mabel Mercer was a celebrity.

Chapter 18
God and Miss Mercer

Not only were America's changing tastes economically and artistically threatening to her, Mabel was also burdened by spiritual self-doubt. Peter O'Brien, while studying to be ordained a priest, had been hovering in the background, listening to her sing whenever he could, as well as managing the career of the troubled composer and pianist Mary Lou Williams. Mabel had spoken to him a number of times about her need to confess and go to Communion again. Considering that they had met in 1964 and Father O'Brien was not ordained until the early seventies, her struggles of the soul were obviously lengthy.

O'Brien believed she was a born Catholic and that "going to Mass all her life was not negotiable." In any event, as she waited for the young Jesuit seminarian to become an official emissary of God, she needed forgiveness, perhaps for her relationship with Harry Beard. He had always meant so much more to her than her wandering bard and "paper" husband, Kelsey Pharr, but it had been drilled into her that their relationship would count against her when she had to add up her sins. Even knowing how many other Catholics had been involved in multiple and unofficial marriages apparently did not help assuage her guilt.

O'Brien first met Mabel at a gala opening for the portrait painter Richard Banks. His impression of her was of a "walking nun." It wasn't just the fact that she was wearing "sensible nun shoes," with a net over her frizzy black hair and a navy blue suit, but that she reminded him of television's beloved "Aunt Bea." He also noticed that she was the only person actually looking at the pictures, while others seemed mainly to be displaying themselves. On being introduced, he found her very polite and reserved, with perfect manners and quiet decorum.

"Of course, even in her suit and daytime clothes, she was sophisticated beyond measure—poised and profoundly knowing," he recalled. "There was often also a look of sly amusement that would cross her face, a bit of a smile, and now and then real mirth."

The seminarian, then also a dancer, felt comfortable only with other performers. "I felt right at home when I met her. My other world was the church, also an artistic arena. The Mass is a performance. My two worlds crisscrossed. Almost all performers are like locomotives, even Mabel. Until I was thirty my concerns were more artistic than social, but I also assumed a huge commitment to racial justice. I gravitated toward blacks. Once I said to Mabel, 'You should sing a spiritual,' and she just said, 'Harrumph!'"

O'Brien remembered especially her strength on the stage. "Some performers," he said, "hold it together with lipstick and grease paint. Mabel was very gifted and talented. She was powerful and had complete authority."

O'Brien was deeply interested in the brilliant Mary Lou Williams, whose career he managed until her death in 1981. For him, 1964 was a memorable year; he met and was influenced not only by Mabel and Mary Lou but by Ethel Waters (who, he said, "loomed large in my fantasy life after I read *His Eye Is On The Sparrow*"), and by Thelma Carpenter.

Of these great women artists he recalled, "They all listened carefully to others, all were full of life; all were intensely religious, and all were brilliant performers. The hold the church had on me (especially as an arena for performance and beauty) drew me very strongly to each of these older women."

When he met Mabel, she was attending the 4 a.m. Mass at either St. Malachy's or St. Francis of Assisi's near Penn Station every day. Early in their acquaintance, Mabel told O'Brien that something had troubled her for a long time. "She did finally confess to me, and went to Communion. I was happy to be able to do that. Mabel was a reverent person, and her performing was like that. Once at Downstairs at the Upstairs, I saw her sit and do a show as if she were at Carnegie Hall. There were four people in that audience.

"I was myself confused about certain church regulations, especially in the moral area, in those years. I did not know yet how to listen with full attention, but I did not encourage her anxiety and tried to allay or lessen fear with my own searching ways. She had confusion, worry about life, her future, the future of her work, Harry; and some of this confusion rested in her proper and steady religious beliefs, a great deal of which had to be contrary to the actual feelings, experiences, and lives of many of the people around her.

"In a sense the world, even the Catholic world in some areas, has caught up with experience more recently, but things were pretty staid then. I was searching in the same way she was searching.... My main effort was to offer solace and relief from whatever was worrying her. I was able to do this through the sacraments and also by inviting her to read on three state occasions in very large and beautiful churches, as well as more ordinary visits for Mass.

"Going to Mass was an absolute with her; but I think she was just as genuine in any other part of her life. There was nothing lightweight about her and I think some of the conflict that arose gave her great pain.... Without ever becoming overly specific, she approached me about things in a nervous, gingerly way. Mabel would twist her hands. I think that, like me, she had a profound reverence for God, and my guess is that her personal life was relatively uncomplicated. I may have relieved some of that with the confession. She was seventy-one or seventy-two then and her behavior was probably more decorous than it had been earlier."

The Sunday after Father O'Brien was ordained, Mabel attended the Interfaith Center on Riverside Drive in New York for a Mass for his personal friends, where she read from Scripture. Ethel Waters' pianist, Reggie Beane, was there, as was the Episcopal priest, Father Flye, a friend of the late James Agee. As always, Mabel was wearing her St. Genesius medal. Until her hands became twisted with arthritis she usually wore a ring with a green stone given to her by Zachary Scott. Her other jewelry, according to Father O'Brien, might include a beautiful jeweled bug on a pin, a strand of gray pearls, or sometimes just earrings with colored stones.

In 1975, Mary Lou Williams performed a jazz Mass at St. Patrick's Cathedral. During the service, Mabel Mercer read a selection from *Isaiah* and Thelma Carpenter presented the gifts of wine and water at the offertory. Mary Lou had earlier written and recorded "Music For Peace," which Alvin Ailey used in a ballet titled "Dances of Praise." He gave the musical score and his work a new title, "Mary Lou's Mass," which he presented with great success at New York City Center.

Both Mary Lou and Mabel had grown fat, the former only five feet two inches and weighing over two hundred pounds. Father O'Brien insisted that Ms. Williams wear a long gown, although she had tripped on her hem and fallen on the stage at the Apollo Theater. Mabel concurred, saying, "Oh, no, dear, we must be chic."

Father O'Brien recalled being at Mabel's farm once when she appeared to be especially disturbed, and saying Mass for her while standing at the strange square piano in her rehearsal room, with the cats looking on. "I said Mass with a cloth spread on the piano, a plate and stemmed glass from her own cupboard, and a host I had brought, with wine from her store. It was a very great moment. Mabel read from the Scriptures and gave all the responses and she was very peaceful. It was a great privilege for me to be able to do that. She was deeply content that Mass was being said in her own home where she got ready for the most important part of her life, her music and singing. Here we go again: the artistic and the divine coming together."

Even priests competed for her favor. Another of her admirers was Father Lee Smith, who met the singer through Will Craik in 1965 when both men were executives in Wall Street brokerage firms. Fr. Smith eventually became an upstate hospital chaplain at the Berkshire Medical Center and a resident of Columbia County, but at that time he lived on Park Avenue. He would walk down to hear Mabel at the St. Regis Hotel, especially to hear her sing his favorite song, "Mira." A frequent visitor at Blakely farm, he was persuaded to acquire a home near Mabel's.

"When you went to her house you knew you were home,"

he said. "A fire would be going and it would seem very welcoming. The refrigerator door always opened on the wrong side and there would be stacks of ancient *New Yorkers* and *Life* magazines around. People floated in and out. Mabel was a high-class dame. I tell you, she had a wonderful way. She could talk to anyone... She was a grace-filled woman. A good neighbor too, and it was an honor to know her." Mabel's friends often struggled with the apparent dichotomy between her stage and private selves, her plain and ordinary, sophisticated and elegant persona. It was not Mabel who changed, however, but only her context.

Loonis McGlohon said, "One of the last things she expressed a desire to do was to record the entire *New Testament* while I played a piano background. I mentioned this to Frank Sinatra one night at Carnegie Hall and he said, 'Well, let's get it done!'" Father Smith also encouraged the ambitious project, but it never happened.

When Father Smith's sister died, the priest invited Mabel to the memorial Mass and asked if she would do a reading. "She said, 'Oh, my dear, I don't have my glasses.' But she borrowed Willie Craik's and read from the Song of Solomon: '... My beloved spake, and said unto me, Rise up, my love, my fair one, and come away. For lo, the winter is past, the rain is over and gone; The flowers appear on the earth; the time of the singing of birds is come, and the voice of the turtle is heard in our land....' I had never heard the English language spoken like that!

"She had a great following among priests," Smith admitted. "They are celibate, but they are passionate men and Mabel touched them. She touched them because she understood what life was all about, she was celebrating life, and you can't do that unless you are a spiritual person."

Even Mabel's atheist friends saw the truth of that. Her artistic growth in the latter third of her life, the powerful dramatic control of a failing voice, imbued almost every little song with a truth that even seemed to surprise its composer. Medea, beating her breast, never gave a more galvanizing performance than Mabel Mercer seated, almost motionless, on a tiny night club stage. Finishing a set, Father O'Brien recalled, she would hobble off to stand in a greasy alcove behind the club's kitchen door; then come back and take her bow. Usually she sang three or four encores.

Father Jerry Dooley, another member of her spiritual court, quoted Mabel as saying, "The Church doesn't solve my problems, but it helps me face them." He often adapted nuggets of Mercer wisdom in his sermons.

And it mattered not that the majority of her night club followers were probably roaring skeptics and agnostics, for the song was universal.

Chapter 19
Wild about Harry

As with most aspects of Mabel Mercer's life, the remodeling of her farmhouse proceeded in response to a variety of idiosyncratic impulses. Mabel worked in increments of $600 worth of carpentering and materials. She informed her local helper, Mr. Macready, that he could work on any project—the bathroom, the garage, Harry's office, or Alec Wilder's meditation room, until the bill reached the magic number. Then he must stop until she paid him. This amused Harry because it was so irrationally Mabel, but he admitted that she was at least consistent.

Bill Engvick and his friend Read Arnow recalled visiting the farm before it had indoor plumbing. Eventually she added three bathrooms. "After Mabel had worked in New York all Saturday night and gone to Mass on Sunday morning," said Engvick, "we would all get in her big car. George Cross was working with her then and he usually drove us to the farm. Mabel would make a big breakfast, with the sun shining and the birds singing—or the snow falling. Then one by one we would all drift off and sleep. We would get up around 1 P.M. Mabel, whose energy never ceased to astound us, would sleep from noon until around 12:30. When we got up, we would all plan what to have for Sunday dinner. Little by little the old house became civilized and charming."

"When I first met her, I did not recognize her as black," Arnow said, "You did not think of color. She was Mabel, a charming lady. It was amazing how, as her voice deteriorated, her friends remained fiercely loyal. They had gone through her personality to her spirit. She was heartbroken when her voice went." He paused, then added, "She had that beautiful shade of grayish-blue eyes with a most endearing sweetness."

As for Harry Beard, said Engvick, he "ran interference for her. He reminded me of a Hollywood casting agent: brusque, a heavy beard, but very sensitive and protective. I can't help thinking that she liked Harry taking over. She was very private about her personal life. The only love of her life I ever heard of was Harry, and even their relationship was not often discussed.

"Alec [Wilder] always said she was vastly underpaid for her singing and her records. It was a curious thing but people were always saying they would take care of Mabel financially. At Red Rock I met a man who seemed to be quite well off, who said, 'No one has to worry about Mabel in the future because I intend to take care of her.' Sometimes she would ask, 'Why are they treating me as if I am some pauper?'"

Harry fretted that Mabel's professional image would suffer from the general disarray of her personal sanctuary. As she had feared, when Harry moved to the farm he was critical of her cleaning, or lack thereof. They quarreled about wads of cat hair on couches and dust bunnies under them. He became hysterical in midwinter when he found small, thinly-furred field mice cuddled around the hot water bottle in his bed. Mabel would be hysterical too, but with laughter. He always waited for her to get home, if she were performing somewhere, to clean up any pet messes, even to the ex-

200

tent of not opening the refrigerator door when he was hungry if there was a puddle in front of it. He would go out and meet the car when she arrived, to announce that he could not get into the fridge. One of Mabel's favorite later accompanists, Jimmy Lyon, pointed out that her music required intense concentration, with internal as well as external rehearsals, and that she just could not do it if she had to "think about going home and cleaning house or making dinner."

Mabel, who probably never thought of herself as a genius, demonstrated in her inimitable way how talent tends to command respect by simply letting the mundane aspects of life take care of themselves. Whatever was under the rug stayed there, adding to the mystique. Friends who appreciated how much she gave of herself were usually around to compete for the privilege of tidying up. Occasionally a regular like Will Craik would sort through the cupboards and pitch out rusted cans of beans or lethally leaking sauerkraut. Mabel, outraged, would say, "You Americans are so wasteful!" She molded thin old slivers of soap into multicolored balls and would not change her habits no matter how often people remarked that the War (whichever one) was over. She even exclaimed over the ethereal blue-green mold forming in the refrigerator.

She ignored Harry's grumbling, once telling him that if the cats had to go he would go first, which promptly subdued him. In return she eventually seemed to forgive his rumored romantic peccadillos. She refused, though, to let him use her car to visit a long-favored but suspect "medical specialist" in Rochester. He could take the train!

In addition to a fireplace in the living area that she called "the fire room," there was a small snug nook near the foot of the stairs, with brick flooring and a potbellied stove. When

Mabel was alone, she often sat there for hours with the cats and dogs, reading, reflecting, and dreaming. She had the habit of picking up and reading any printed matter that crossed her path, be it a seed catalog, an encyclopedia open to Astrology, or a telephone directory. All provided contentment if she had cats and dogs close by. Having made the mistake of letting her guests know that her favorite bird was the owl, she became the recipient of an endless menagerie of dust-gathering ceramics of the order *Strigiformes*.

She welcomed hungry raccoons into the house, put a splint on a squirrel's broken leg, adopted the neighbors' cats and dogs in addition to her own, fed a year-round murmuration of song birds, and continued to plan new rooms for human friends.

Many of her city visitors were inexperienced in the ways of the country. The gracious ones formed little teams to perform various tasks. Thelma Carpenter remembered a funny time when the amateur gardening team accidentally mowed down a bed of the hostess's favorite flowers and then tried to tape them all back up. "My mother approved of Mabel," said Thelma, "and always said she had 'mother-wit,' which Mama thought more important than education."

Gradually the colored newcomer had become acquainted with her white neighbors in the little towns of Chatham, North Chatham, Old Chatham, East Chatham, and Chatham Centre, not to mention the nearby hamlets of Austerlitz, Valatie, Kinderhook, and Spencertown. Slowly but surely she won them over—the children, adults, horses, and dogs. Columbia county was conquered without a drop of blood being spilled. A few other well-known African-American entertainers began moving into the area.

Edna St. Vincent Millay had died at Austerlitz before Mabel arrived, but the singer became a good friend of the poet's sister, Norma Millay. In addition to Adde Wallin-Beach, Mabel's most devoted local companion was Muriel Finch, a slim dark-eyed Valatie school teacher for students with special problems. Adde introduced Muriel, a music lover, to Mabel in a local restaurant one night around 1966, and she soon became the hardest worker in the corps of volunteers.

Almost from their first meeting, Muriel drove Mabel about, helped arrange her tours when she began to travel, and generally cared for her. When Harry was ill she also nursed him in Mabel's absence (which gave rise to local gossip), and later also took on his task as bookkeeper. "To see Mabel perform was indescribable," she recalled. "There are no words for it. Was I awed by her? No. I respected her for what she stood for, her art; but when you live every day with people, driving them and caring for them, it's just the way everyone has to live. She meant a lot to me and I cared a lot about her. She was a great lady. Mabel was Mabel."

The early friendly rivalry between Adde and Muriel may have been more a product of Mabel's temperament than their own. The two women often traveled with her and generally attended to her during the long, snowbound winters at Red Rock. Mabel was always glad to share every aspect of the excitement and glamour of her musical life with her friends. Loonis McGlohon felt, however, that she took Muriel's help for granted, did not treat her fairly, and was insufficiently appreciative of her personal sacrifices.

In the country, Mabel was more attuned to the relaxed style of Adde Wallin-Beach than to the highly organized efficiency of her other lady-in-waiting. Jazz concert impresario

203

Charles Bourgeois, who knew Mabel well, chuckled when he remembered how regally she used to pronounce Muriel's name and with what confidence she would say to him "Mur-iel will take care of it, Mur-iel always handles that." After a time it became unthinkable that Muriel might not always be at her beck and call.

Adde Wallin-Beach said, "Just being a friend of Mabel's was the greatest satisfaction. We used to go to silly old flea market sales and auctions together, and she would buy as much junk as I did. Mabel and I loved candy corn. Harry was always trying to get her to keep her weight down. He would say, 'What are you eating?' and we would mumble 'Nothing,' around our candy corn."

Mabel hated racial color classifications. "She was very sure of her views," said Adde, "never wishywashy, but also not opinionated. She had a strong will but in a beautiful way. Whenever I dropped something in the dirt she would say to me, 'Adde, that is God's earth. Dirt is what you get on your clothes.'" Only several years later, when Adde and her son Peter decided to go hear Mabel perform in New York and found her surrounded by awed stars of the entertainment world, did they realize how important she was.

Muriel, Adde recalled, was forever telling Mabel what to do. "We would go into a restaurant and she would say, 'Now Adde, you sit there, and Mabel you sit there so the sun won't shine in your eyes.' Mabel would mutter, 'Maybe I want the sun to shine in my eyes.' Or she might say, 'Your school teacher is showing, Mur-iel.' People would get upset with Muriel for shielding Mabel from her other friends."

When she was feeling crotchety from her arthritis or anxious about money problems, the singer was sometimes tart. She could not have gone on with her career for so many years without the care of such generous friends. She knew it, and Harry knew it as well.

"Harry came from a lovely family," said Adde. "I think Mabel's one and only true love was Harry. A lot of people spoke of Mabel's 'lesbianism' and a lot of her singing appeal was to the homosexual crowd. But I traveled with her everywhere for years, and never once did I see her behave in other than a straight way. Of course, she slanted her songs to gay people in the audience too. I loved her as a dear, dear friend, and a little bit as a mother. When Mabel hung up the phone after a conversation, she would always say 'God Bless' and I would say, 'Love you'. Often when I went over to see her in the later years, I would find her out weeding the garden. She would look up and say, 'Oh! Time for tea.'"

As the rock music barrage continued, Mabel retreated more and more into her beloved countryside. For nearly three years, her public wondered where she had gone; then they too turned to newer and younger icons. When Mabel started adding yet another room to her farmhouse, her country neighbors were surprised to discover that it was a first-floor addition for herself. Where once she had bounded up the stairs two at a time, she now must sometimes crawl on arthritic hands and swollen knees.

Her building projects had included dormers for the two front upstairs bedrooms to lighten the house and admit more air. One unfinished room was for Alec Wilder, whose health worried her. She added a sun porch and a brick floor in the kitchen, and then started building a new wing, which also remained unfinished. And she had a new well dug that was one hundred and eighty feet deep.

During the first long white winter that she spent entirely in the country, her stiffness got worse and she had constant pain in her joints. She stopped the dangerous habit of climbing onto a chair on the porch to refill bird feeders. Instead she started scattering seed on the snow, causing Will Craik to comment that no one could possibly slip and fall on her farm because the ice was studded with frozen grain. She loved the beauty and solitude of winter, the scrabbling noises of small creatures between boards, and her own long thoughts by the fire. Arthritis, however, was not part of her agenda; it stole her energy. She sent to a New York physician for medicine to make her feel better and was annoyed when the cooperative doctor was arrested for selling unauthorized painkillers.

When Ena came to stay with her, they played poker or canasta, and Mabel often read aloud from the prophecies of Edgar Cayce. When the snow was not too deep, they sometimes walked with the dogs through the brooding forest, being startled and then laughing when a branch exploded sharply overhead. As the roads became impassable they were connected to the world only by telephone.

She often phoned Harry and other friends who still had jobs in New York, but increasingly their stories sounded just like her own. Nightclubs were on a skid and no one knew if it was forever. Some of the big bands and jazz groups had found European tours more rewarding. Josephine Baker, Thelma Carpenter, and Bricktop returned to France and Italy. Some went to Hollywood or worked in television. To Mabel, the idea of returning to Paris was still haunting.

A time came when she was out of money for dog and cat food as well as for groceries. Her companions in the country argued that it would not be "welfare" to accept unemployment compensation, but her instincts rebelled against appealing to one of "those government agencies." They might ask her, like a voter registrar to whom she had never returned, "Gal, can you read? Can you write?" She was finally persuaded when Will Craik told her that Harpo Marx was driving up in his Rolls Royce to collect his check from the unemployment compensation office in Hollywood. She guessed if Harpo could do it, she could too.

Her checks when she got them were small, however, and Mabel had to scrape to maintain two households. She hoped to use the New York apartment again, and Harry sometimes needed it, and anyhow what would she do with all the stuff? She hated having to borrow money, even for her animal friends. The end of $600 installments had put all of her building projects on hold, which depressed her. And she missed Harry something awful during the long cold season.

Chapter 20
Winners and Losers

W ill Craik arrived at Blakely farm one day to find Mabel's next-to-worst fear realized; the absolute worst being the loss of her voice. She was down to a single box of cornflakes and had neither cat nor dog food. Harry would be pleased, she could not help joking, to find that she and the cats and field mice were slimming down.

Had neighbors like Adde and Muriel guessed her plight they would surely have sped to the rescue, but they were not to know. She was waiting in the yard for Will when he drove in and they went to the market, filling the shopping cart with food for the animals and birds. Then, as Craik told Jim Haskins, she asked if he "would mind, dear, if they got something for people." He said this scenario occurred over and over again. She would come out to meet him, saying, "Oh, thank God you're here. We must go shopping." She was then feeding four dogs in addition to any others that dropped in for dinner, as well as her cats, birds, and raccoons.

A letter from a lawyer in New York stated that she was in default on a loan of $2,297.64, the balance due being $357.88. In this period it was not unusual for a few of Mabel's better-off friends to send her rather generous cash gifts at Christmas. To her great embarrassment she learned that one friend was arranging a "For the Benefit of Mabel Mercer"

party in New York, with tickets at $25. Mabel had been asked
to sing at this function and had accepted, without realizing
its true nature. When she did, and even though the invitations were already in the mail, she phoned the party giver and
angrily insisted that it be cancelled.

In spite of the humiliating lack of funds, she always felt
rich in her life at Blakely farm, her soul in harmony with
nature and its ever-changing wonders. Occasionally she felt a
pang of regret at seeing her old and much-used dress form,
the ACME A-D-J-U-S-T-A-B-L-E, standing in the corner
layered in dust. She spent hours reading and daydreaming by
the potbellied stove where the bricks were warm to her swollen feet. She was addicted to science fiction books as well as
those on prophecy, and followed with keen interest the ad-
ventures of astronauts and moon-walkers. She kept a fire
blazing in the living room fireplace, a special force in her
dreams, even during the summer.

Still optimistic and determined to make the best of
things, Mabel played the lottery when she could manage it.
She read and chuckled over her horoscopes, and some said
she went occasionally to séances in New York. Her mind was
open to all possibilities. When spring came back to Blakely
farm and the voice of the turtle was heard in the land, the
field mice departed, the skunk cabbage bloomed, Harry returned, and they were happy to be together again.

Then, in 1963, a miracle happened. Muriel Finch remembered the occasion. It was late in the afternoon. She and
Mabel had just picked up Harry from the train station. Mabel
said, casually, "I had a call from Albany today, Harry." And
he said, "Oh. About taxes?" And she said, "No, it was from
the lottery." Harry, his interest picking up, said, "Oh. Did

you win?" When she said yes, he asked, "How much, a hundred dollars?" Mabel, looking sideways at him, and ready to burst, said no. And he said "Well?" And she said, "I won fifty thousand dollars, Harry."

At last she had hit the jackpot; her financial doldrums ended suddenly and spectacularly. She would no longer have to worry about the $600 increments for the carpenter. The interrupted additions to the house could proceed full speed, even new ones she had only dreamed of. She would build a lovely stone-enclosed pumphouse in symbolic memory of Emily and Tom Stonehouse, and she would never have to ask Will for food money again.

No sooner had Mabel found security than her career brightened as well. Her horoscope (Aquarius, the water-bearer) had predicted: "Other people, some of them very influential, stand ready to help you achieve your goals. You make headway in career pursuits. Leave the big financial decisions for next week. Relax at home this weekend." When Harry told her that Irving Haber was on the phone, wanting her to come work at his street-level club, Downstairs at the Upstairs, Mabel glanced up from her book of prophecy and said, "But of course, darling."

Haber's elegant cabaret was located in a brownstone duplex at 37 West 56th Street that had originally been the John Wanamaker mansion. Haber, a strangely unsophisticated owner, managed to draw the most brilliant of the sixties' revue entertainers. Among them were Lily Tomlin, Madeline Kahn (who, while studying classical singing, also found herself impersonating President Lyndon Johnson), Fannie Flagg, Joan Rivers, Bette Midler, and writer Michael McWhinney, all under the artistic direction of composer Rod Warren. Haber's interest in Mabel had been aroused by the composer/singer/pianist Ronny Graham, a longtime admirer, and it was Graham who phoned Harry Beard.

Mabel sent the cats flying as she sprang to her old Acme dress form and measured out a length of silk brocade. The news spread quickly and all her old fans prepared for the reemergence of their idol.

It was 1964, the 50th anniversary of her career in show business, and her opening at the Downstairs won a certain amount of national publicity. On opening night, Father O'Brien sat in a packed audience with Harry, waiting for Mabel. "I was a nervous wreck with my own problems. And Mabel said, 'I did not expect this. I thought I was finished.'"

For the next three years she captivated SRO audiences, showing up to perform as late as she liked. She sat on stage in her upright chair with a silk scarf draped casually around her shoulders, enchanting every listener with bittersweet wisdom and wit.

Haber himself could never understand what the guests saw in her, repeatedly carping that she could not carry a tune. A member of the staff, all of whom adored her, recalled that one night when the boss would not release her to go to the hospital although she was obviously ill, she sang all night because the house was packed.

Of course Mabel found many changes in the New York entertainment world. The grating tones of hard rock were ubiquitous and the streets near her old apartment dangerous. Father O'Brien said she was somewhat shocked by the broad new humor, particularly by Joan Rivers' crude and self-deprecating cracks about her own body. When Joan was on, Mabel would hover at the edge of the floor, twisting her hands and saying, "This won't do." But Harry was always there, protecting her from the crowds and the drunks.

Her compensation was the boundless delight of being with her fans again, hearing good new show tunes, visiting old friends at after-hours spots, and staying up 'til dawn. She sang the Joni Mitchell song about looking at clouds "from up and down,"* while admitting that she too really did not know clouds (or *lohv*) at all.

Photographer and novelist Carl Van Vechten, who had known Mabel when he was an itinerant jazz buff in Paris in the thirties and she the shy ingenue, made several stunning portraits of her at this time. Paul Padgette, a longtime friend of Van Vechten's, described how the photographer, then eighty-two, introduced him to Mabel at the Downstairs. They arrived before her first set and she joined them at their table in the front row to chat. Padgette remarked on her beautiful brocade gown. Mabel said she had bought the cloth in San Francisco's Chinatown while singing at the Hungry i, and had sewn it herself.

At one point during her performance that night, Mabel smiled at Van Vechten, seated only a few feet away, and asked what he wanted to hear. He said, "Mabel, you know what it is." And she sang "Sunday In Savannah," a tradition she followed whenever he was in the audience.

She rejoined the two men later and at Padgette's request autographed his cocktail napkin ("to prove to myself that I really had been there"). Van Vechten asked her to come to his Central Park West apartment the following week to pose for portrait photos. The result was four striking images of Mabel that looked like impressionistic paintings. In the best

---

* "Both Sides Now," Joni Mitchell, 1967.

known of these she sits erect against rich draperies, her intelligent face in a composed and contemplative mood, the arthritic hands resting on a glass-topped table.

For the celebration in New York of Carl Van Vechten's eighty-third birthday, she was there again to sing "Sunday In Savannah."

She was playing at the Downstairs on October 15, 1964 when word came that Cole Porter had died in Santa Monica. Everyone knew that the silencing of his pen marked another sad finale to the golden age of American popular music. Guests asked Mabel if she would sing a tribute to Porter, but she gracefully declined, fearing to lose control of her voice. They were surprised, therefore, when late in her second set she turned and spoke to the pianist. Facing the audience, she began to sing "Ev'ry Time We Say Goodbye," and at the end, bowed her head to unbroken silence.

By now many college students who were children of her regulars had begun to attend. She worried about their spending too much money and sometimes sent them home. One young girl who became infatuated with her hung around the club night after night, until Mabel reputedly telephoned her parents. Another young woman was said to have succumbed to the motherly *femme fatale* and attempted suicide. Mabel again intervened to help her sort out and redirect her "affairs of the heart."

Decca Records released *The Magic of Mabel Mercer* that autumn, including several of the songs for which she was most loved: "Year After Year," by Bart Howard; "Mira," by Bob Merrill; "I've Got Your Number," by Cy Coleman and Carolyn Leigh; "Run To Love" and "Trouble Comes" by Marvin Fisher and Jack Segal; "Ballad of the Sad Young Men,"

213

by Fran Landesmann and Tommy Wolf; and "This Is All I Ask," by Gordon Jenkins. Once again the critics did not predict a commercial success, and they were right. One wrote, "It seems we've never been able to give Miss Mercer anything approaching what she's giving us."

In October 1964, an article in *Life* magazine rather laboriously proclaimed her the "Durable Underground Doyenne." An obviously young and desperate reporter explained that Mabel was the grand dame of underground singers because this breed, "though talented, shy away from commercialism to perform in intimate clubs." Mabel and Harry surely had a good *lahf* over that. The article also described Mabel as a "cult" singer, the writer finding it astounding that she could still pack them in three times a night. There were several radiant photos of Harry and Mabel on the farm with Adde Wallin-Beach and the animals. They looked as domesticated as a Thanksgiving calendar picture, he with fashionable gray streaks in his thick dark hair, while Mabel had never looked happier.

For the next few years the singer commuted from her farm to ever shorter appearances at the Downstairs. In between she resumed and even completed several new building projects. Although there seemed to be more talented young entertainers than ever seeking discovery in New York, the nightclubs were closing one by one. Sixty-eight turned out to be both a good and bad year for Mabel.

Back in the early fifties, a pair of sophisticated jazz buffs, George Wein and Charlie Bourgeois, had started the Storyville Jazz Club in Boston. Wein was recommended by Mr. and Mrs. Louis Livingston Lorillard as a consultant for a festival at Newport, Rhode Island. The first festival was in 1954, and the Newport Jazz Festival was born.

Bourgeois, Wein's longtime friend and assistant, said that the two men sometimes launched a "most unenterprising project" from sheer love of music and entertainers. That was the case when they were inspired to sign Mabel to perform with Bobby Short in Concert at New York's Town Hall on May 19, 1968. By now both performers enjoyed considerable popularity. But the thought of singing in a thousand-seat auditorium terrified Mabel. The impresarios, who had persuaded Atlantic Records to record the concert in its entirety, could not have been more surprised by what happened.

Fans young and old flew in from London, Mexico City, Palm Beach, and Los Angeles, making the competition for tickets intense. An overflowing crowd was seated on the stage and perched in the aisles. Some even reported that devotees were swinging from the chandeliers. Critics proclaimed the concert an historic event. Kevin Kelly of *The Boston Globe* described the chemistry of Mercer and Short as "soul-touching." For his solos, Bobby sang the music of Cole Porter, Jerome Kern, Cy Coleman, Billy Strayhorn, and Duke Ellington, not to mention Bessie Smith's raucous "Gimme a Pigfoot and a Bottle of Beer."

For the second half of the program, when Mabel stepped on stage wearing a white gown and a turquoise stole, the audience rose as one. Rex Reed was present, and wrote the eloquent liner notes for Atlantic's album, *Mabel Mercer & Bobby Short at Town Hall*.

"…Everything had changed, yet nothing had changed at all. A new generation had discovered them all over again through the deliciousness of their songs. The rich and famous came, pausing briefly to observe the Andy Warhol superstars smil-

215

ing brokenly for flashbulbs. Youthful college kids came, only recently converted to the ageless cult of Mercer-Short worshippers. ....And suddenly, in the burnished hush of the concert hall, so jammed that pop society and old guard duennas crowded together onstage like Breughel paintings, Mabel and Bobby were there.... Like two butterflies on their way to the sun."

Chapter 21
Uptown Down-Time

The gay clubs that had functioned openly in Manhattan, and where Mabel's popularity began, fell one by one to a political reform that eliminated mob kickbacks and led, ironically, to a loss of civil liberties. With the club owners no longer paying protection money, their often distinguished patrons were no longer safe from police raids.

Time and trends created hurdles for many legendary entertainers. Duke Ellington, who had lost several of his finest older jazz musicians, including Billy Strayhorn in 1967, was struggling to keep his band together. Bobby Short became one of a dwindling number of cabaret stars who had a permanent Manhattan engagement, with a designer audience of well-heeled sophisticates.

Julius Monk confessed to John S. Wilson of the *New York Times* that during the late sixties he had begun to feel "hollow as an old gourd." He attributed his creative emptiness to the social preemption of "Race, Vietnam, the Young Lords, the Black Panthers...." People were so busy exploring sexual freedom that they had no time for other forms of recreation. Monk complained that the emphasis on youth distressed him. "It's as if a curtain...descended.... I really think we've all been drummed away for the time being."

In a desperately sad and temporizing effort, Monk's last

revue at Plaza-9 included a song titled "Take A Trippie With A Hippie."

Thousands of devoted Mabel Mercer fans were wondering what had become of their idol. One who felt a genuine need to find her was Donald F. Smith, who later became the creator and executive director of the Mabel Mercer Foundation and the sometimes controversial impresario of its famous Cabaret Conventions.

Smith was a youngster from Boston when he first met Mabel; he quickly developed a lifelong passion. He recalled, "My uncle...would take me to New York to further my musical education... I was about eleven when he took me to a night spot where a nice woman was standing, saying hello and good night to the guests. She wore a simple dress and a string of pearls. ... This same lady impressed me even more when she came over and sat down in a chair and began to sing.... I was convinced that everyone else knew her, because she sang as if for friends. When I went back to Boston, I went to Schirmer's on Boylston Street, asking for Mabel Mercer records. She had done a few records that were sold by a store called Liberty. What it was about that sound of her voice that got to me, I could not tell; but it was constantly there in my mind...."

As a volunteer for charity fundraisers in New York, Smith began bringing up her name at every opportunity. "Someone said they thought she had retired to the South of France. Someone else said she had been dead for years." At a party, he heard well-known singers and composers speaking of Mabel Mercer in the past tense! "I can remember blushing because it was like hearing something bad about someone I cared about. I did not say anything. But all the way home that night I was thinking that I could not be that different from others in the way I felt about her." Smith was right; on a small level people had begun to find Mabel again.

She was still doing short gigs in Manhattan. "I remember a night when she was singing and missed a key note," said Smith, "and I could see her look of terror. But I could also see that the audience was quite undisturbed." After the singer finished her set, he joined her and said, "You seem very upset." She said, "Well, it's my livelihood." He reassured her, saying, "But you are a great storyteller and it did not break the story."

Smith and the singer became friends and he began trying to help her as an agent. Mabel knew his heart was larger than his billfold. "If I took her to a restaurant," said Smith "and the entrées seemed too expensive, she would ask the waiter, 'Can you scramble me a couple of eggs?' If someone gave her a cup of tea, it was always the best tea she ever had. If you gave her a cracker, she said, 'I can't think where you get such good crackers.' She did this for me," he said, "these were her genuine reactions.

"I always felt that she had known great hurt. I think that when you suffer, everything else from then on seems so trivial, the things we worry about are superficial. When I got to know her, she had known everybody who was famous, and I am sure had been told every possible confidence, but one never heard them from her."

When Smith learned about Harry Beard, he wondered, "Was her great sadness the fact that he never asked her to marry him? He seemed to me like a man who had been quite spoiled when he was growing up…. I can tell you that when someone who has been catered to all his life gets a life-threat-

219

ening disease, it is only in Warner Brothers movies that he is ennobled. They just remain the same people with another set of problems."

In the late sixties Harry became seriously ill. "He could do very little, although he was devoted to her," Smith continued. "Mabel was then working in a large room with a hundred guests and on any given night you could see celebrities—Lauren Bacall, Sinatra, Mathis, Farrell.... Mabel was about sixty-seven. These artists were listening to her the way I go to school. I would watch Eileen Farrell's face and she would be mesmerized. Mabel would raise the emotional temperature of the room until sometimes it was exactly like a gospel meeting! They would get so moved." He paused. "Yet, she never had a hit record and probably did not know how good she was."

When Smith found only two minor clippings about Mabel in the New York Public Library, he talked to her seriously about her career. She did not seem interested in promoting herself. He tried in vain to convince her that, unless she gave interviews, people would go on saying things about her that were untrue.

He said that when Mabel was singing at the little clubs, she had an agreement about her hours that enabled her to go first to the theater to see other entertainers perform, or to explore the possibilities of some new musical that was in danger of closing. "She might come out of the theater saying, 'I think I got something there.' Composers of course loved it when every night she would sing one of their pieces that might otherwise have failed.

Among people in other branches of show business, going to hear Mabel sing became a routine when they were in town.

"You always took people to hear her when they were visiting New York. Sir John Gielgud, for example, Sir Laurence Olivier, and Dame Margot Fonteyn." To Donald Smith, it seemed destined that Mabel would rise again.

Almost simultaneously, in the autumn of Mabel's life, Smith, George Wein, Alec Wilder, Loonis McGlohon and others were individually inspired to mount a Mercer renaissance. Their efforts were so infectious that they brought on not only a resurgence of her career, but a rebirth of the endangered art of cabaret. New, young talent began slowly to appear, and other old-timers were rediscovered.

Jazz singer and composer Alberta Hunter, already famous when Bessie Smith first popularized her "Downhearted Blues" in 1923, was reborn at the age of 81, when Mabel insisted upon her presence at a party given by Bobby Short. There the reclusive Hunter was seen and coaxed back to her public for several years by impresario Charlie Bourgeois and composer Alec Wilder.

In another decade, having gone full circle, entertainers of the forties and fifties would again seem new and exciting: Tony, Ella, Mel, Frankie, Margaret, Eartha, Rosemary, Diana, Bobby, Lena, of course Mabel, and many more. At first some had fled from the ear-splitting racket of rock music. Or else, not wishing to be thought passé, they pretended to find it interesting as a short-lived phenomenon. They did not want to seem rude to the sensitive young, not realizing yet that civility and courtesy had been victims too. But now they were coming back with a civilized vengeance.

Chapter 22
Bless the Family

Mabel, Harry, and Will went to a cocktail party one evening and afterward strolled, as they often did, to Goldie's, a restaurant in the lower level of a brownstone at 232 East 53d street. There, Goldie (Lewis) Hawkins and his partner, Wayne Sanders, rattled out show tunes on twin upright pianos while the waiters served reasonably priced food with *vin ordinaire*. Goldie believed that conversation should not, as a regular thing, be interfered with by vocalists. Nevertheless, celebrities as hot as Ethel Merman, Art Carney, Jule Styne, Jason Robards, Lucille Ball, Fred Astaire, Gene Kelly, and Judy Holliday sometimes performed at Goldie's impromptu and unpaid if the spirit moved them.

That night, Harry tripped on a curb and was taken to the hospital with a broken ankle. Mabel took him to the new Harry Beard suite at the farm, and spent all her free time caring for him during the spring and summer of 1968. Scarcely had his leg healed, however, when phlebitis struck. While he was recovering from that painful and dangerous disease, Mabel was rushed to the Berkshire Medical Center with intestinal pain, and learned that she had diverticulitis. Harry was then sixty-one and she was seven years older.

In Mabel's case, the illness was not acute, but it did require her to pay much more attention to her diet. Thereafter guests at Blakely Farm were not so richly catered to as in the past. Mabel was forced to give up sesame seeds. Will Craik, who was diabetic, came often from his home in nearby Spencertown, sometimes with Father Lee Smith of Chatham Centre, who was unusual among them in having no significant ailments. He and Craik helped with chores according to their abilities. Alec Wilder came to visit and stayed to write music while basking in the singer's regenerative aura, which was becoming somewhat overtaxed. Mabel worried that Harry's phlebitis maight cause a blood clot. The pain did not improve his temper, either. Muriel Finch often drove over from her home in nearby Lavatie to help care for the entire household, and Adde Wallin-Beach telephoned every day to check on the patients.

That winter Mabel returned briefly to Downstairs at the Upstairs, which meant negotiating the often treacherous roads between Manhattan and the farm. Irving Haber's regular star was then Joan Rivers. When the Café Carlyle invited Mabel for the month of January, to replace Bobby Short, she was delighted to accept. Then Harry had a heart attack.

To describe it as an anxious winter is an understatement. Weather permitting, Mabel went home each weekend. Sometimes she had to park her car at the bottom of the hill and drag her suitcase through the snow with a belt around her waist, thus keeping her arms free for the inevitable large shopping bags. Only with much help from the local volunteers was the invalid Harry cared for. His doctor advised that he no longer handle Mabel's business affairs.

When it appeared that Harry might be recovering on schedule, other, mysterious symptoms developed that his doctor could not account for. The proud Philadelphian was losing too much weight. His head began to nod with a strange weakness. Tremors developed in his hands and he complained of stiffness. Mabel sat beside him one bitterly cold winter morning as he struggled to raise a cup of tea to his lips, sloshing and burning himself. Cursing, he looked up helplessly and moved his head from side to side. Mabel, in sudden terror, phoned Muriel, who arrived within minutes.

The two women drove Harry to his doctor in Albany. He sent him to another specialist, who believed his palsy to be the early symptoms of Parkinson's disease.

As they entered the farm driveway at dusk, greeted by the barking dogs, it began to snow. Mabel and Muriel assisted the tall, bent man out of the car, up the stairs, and into his newly remodeled suite. Snowflakes swirled against the window, framing the deep peace of meadow and treeline in a scene that always reminded Mabel of her childhood in Wales. Helping Harry into bed, she joked that the current crop of field mice had very short legs and would be unable to climb the stairs. His lips moved in a stiff and painful smile.

Muriel Finch shook up the embers in the kitchen stove, put on the tea kettle, fed the hungry pets, and scattered the icy yard with bird seed and dog chow for the nocturnal creatures that shared the space. She worried about Harry and wondered how her friends would manage, knowing that Mabel would never give up her singing. She started their dinner, checked Mabel's calendar for the following day, pocketed the grocery list and called upstairs a good night. Then she drove home along the treacherous but familiar country roads to her orderly, empty-seeming apartment. It was a difficult time for Muriel. She and her husband were going through the process of divorce.

Mabel, unable to sleep that night, hunted through book-shelves, on chairs and tables, beneath cupboards, and through an old refrigerator until she finally unearthed—between the wellworn works of Edgar Cayce and *Illnesses Of The Common Tabby*—an ancient medical reference book. Parkinsonism, she read, had no cure. It was not fatal as long as the patient's heart was not overstrained but "the cumulative burdens upon the sick person, his family, and his community are sufficient to try the patience of Job." While Harry might live for a long time, he would soon lose the expressiveness of his handsome face as the muscles stiffened; his voice would become a mumble; his hands would tremble.

The following day she dug out maps of Paris and London, which she had not visited since coming to America. She and Harry began planning a trip to Europe in the summer. They would go to the West coast again: San Francisco, maybe Los Angeles, Hollywood....

It drove Harry crazy when he began to stammer, particularly on the telephone. Mabel and her helpers began to screen his calls. One of the people who heard of his illness and telephoned with mixed emotions was Donald Smith. He was still faithfully going to hear Mabel wherever she sang, always unofficially promoting her name, and slowly building up his own talent agency. He now represented some of the finest Broadway entertainers and an occasional movie actor. He was still convinced that undiscovered millions of Mercer lovers would throng to hear his aging idol in person if only they were given an opportunity. Now, at last, it seemed that she might need him.

He knew that Mabel, in addition to being unwell herself, had never been a competent manager of her own affairs.

225

Certainly she was no self-promoter. Yet she wanted her life to flow smoothly, and tended to be irritable when things failed to arrange themselves according to her wishes. Harry had taken care of so many things for her. Now Smith was willing and eager to volunteer.

She hesitated at the offer, saying it was up to Harry. At this juncture, both Smith and Muriel Finch picked up the reins in their respective roles—she became nurse, driver, arranger of travel plans, and finally bookkeeper; he became Mabel's agent and publicist. Other friends, including McGlohon, Wilder, Wein, and Bourgeois, were instrumental in helping her get engagements, or in creating arrangements, writing new songs for her, even building concerts around her. Adde Wallin-Beach, her son Peter, and other Columbia County neighbors lent their comforting presence. Another friend and neighbor, horsewoman Judy Juhring, pleased the singer enormously by naming a new filly Mabel.

Thus, at a time when her responsibilities might have been crushing and when many entertainers of her generation were forced to retire, she not only survived but her career underwent an astonishing resurgence. It could never have happened without the loyal infrastructure of the "family." As usual, a certain amount of jealousy simmered beneath the surface. Mabel diplomatically discouraged gossip, although she herself was not entirely innocent when aroused. Family members were always invited to her openings; later on they went with her on her European junkets, and even to the West Coast and the White House.

Smith was never on Mabel's payroll. He noted that, "In more than twenty years I accepted only two checks, and both times it was when I had gone abroad with Mabel or on trips where I could not run my business at home. It was my privilege.... I would enter a room where she was singing and see her in ten minutes spellbind the audience, and I would think, 'That is why I do all this.'" He knew it was also because of the simple fun of working with her, the joy of her presence.

During his long, close association with Mabel, Smith said, he never heard her utter a cross word. Once he called to her attention the fact that a woman colleague had pulled an underhanded deal, and felt that Mabel should be aware of it. "But when I mentioned it, I found that of course she already knew. All she said about the matter was, 'I don't think she has been herself lately.'"

Mabel's own health deteriorated, and her everyday requirements grew. Muriel fretted about whether the singer was physically up to her aspirations; but what could one say? As Harry grew less mobile, Muriel also took over more of his care. If anyone asked whether she found her role too tiring, however, the slight, dark-eyed brunette would invariably smile stoically and say, "I am blessed." Adde Wallin-Beach began to resent Muriel's omnipresence, but tactfully said nothing.

Will Craik and the women all wanted to be Mabel's "best friend," said Donald Smith, who would have prostrated himself before his goddess in a second had she tolerated it. McGlohon and Bourgeois, for their parts, appeared to feel that Smith never quite qualified as "real family." Though some critics later disparaged his creation and stewardship of The Mabel Mercer Foundation, Smith, to his credit, ignored the sniping and carried on with his goal. He was defended by his own coterie of important artists, who were deeply impressed by his services to music and later to Mabel's memory. Father O'Brien, himself an artist's manager, felt that Smith did "ab-

227

solutely the right thing for Mabel, a truly great job...."

While Mabel was replacing Bobby Short at the spiffy Café Carlyle, Buddy Barnes became her accompanist. Their "chemistry" won high praise from audiences and critics. Bart Howard's professional opinion was that, "Buddy was crazy, but he might have been the best accompanist she ever had." The trouble with the gifted Buddy Barnes was the common one of excessive drinking, but also the fact that he liked to sing as well. Their partnership, unfortunately, did not last.

But under Smith's management, Mabel's career steadily gained momentum. She was honored by the Museum of the City of New York in an impressive affair sponsored by its Theater and Music Collection. Mabel presented the Museum with the Lisa Rhana portrait sketches that had survived the fire at the Byline and other disasters. Afterward in the auditorium, again accompanied by Barnes, she favored the sophisticated audience with an impromptu program of popular ballads and current show tunes.

Soon the team of Mercer and Short returned to Town Hall for a second performance, declared by their fans to be as marvelous as the first. One mainstream critic was puzzled and testy, however, describing Mabel's followers as "a fiercely devoted cult" who cherished "her guilelessness, emotional power, and phrasing gifts. But to the uninitiated, the fuss remains a puzzlement." Her voice was gone, he added, and her approach monotonous; yet, he conceded, "she can communicate feeling with sincerity, and there are no clinkers...." Atlantic recorded the second concert as *Mabel and Bobby Short, II: The Realm of Mercer and Short*.

Social observers have offered various theories about the surprising revival of cabaret's popularity in the early seventies, when the country was still trying to define the gestalt lunacy of Woodstock. Suddenly, it seemed, Mabel and several other old masters of pop were going strong. *Newsweek* reported that Frank Sinatra ("My Way"), Perry Como ("Seattle"), and Sammy Davis, Jr. ("I Gotta Be Me"), "were still in there slugging it out with the Beatles, the Stones, and the Archies." Henry Mancini was No. 6 on the charts, with the "Love Theme from Romeo & Juliet."

Curiously, another event in 1969, now celebrated annually by homosexuals as the Stonewall riot, inspired a rush to take back the streets and the nightclubs of large cities. On the hot June evening when a few police raided the Stonewall Inn, a hangout beloved of gays and lesbians on Sheridan Square in Greenwich Village, it proved the final straw in a long war of oppression. For some it was like Rosa Parks refusing to give up her seat. Suddenly the colorful habitués were furiously hurling rocks and bottles at the cops.

The result proved contagious. As the battleground spread across America, uniting the New York gay community with long active redoubts on San Francisco's Castro Street, on Hollywood Boulevard, and in Dallas and River City, gays began to claim their civil rights—in politics, in the courts, and at last even in the military. Asserting their right to sexual freedom, gay men and women again gravitated to funky rooms, torch singers, and good jazz. It went without saying that they craved the enduring humanity of Mabel Mercer.

The movie *Cabaret,* starring Liza Minelli as Sally Bowles, inspired what some hoped might be a resurgence of the sweet amorality of scandalous Berlin in the early 1930s. But although nihilism and fantasy pervaded the seventies, the period never achieved true decadence. The moderns were happily immured in simple vulgarity that had always had a home in the human psyche but until then had been somewhat restrained. It has been said that nearly half a hundred new night clubs both opened and closed in Manhattan during the decade between 1972 and 1982.

Even Bricktop returned to New York, forsaking her club in Rome. She soon made the only recording of her career, "So Long, Baby," with Cy Coleman. For several years she continued to appear sporadically in New York and Chicago and at the Playboy Club in London, always warring spiritedly with managers about the treatment of her "clients," and about her hours and conditions of employment. When she and Mabel were both working in New York, they kept in touch.

Whitney Balliett, doyen of music critics, wrote what seemed like a eulogy for Mabel in *The New Yorker* of Sept. 18, 1972, in which he lamented America's tardy attention to its greatest artists. But how could he or anyone have guessed that the Icarian Miss Mercer at seventy-two was poised on a launching pad for the most meteoric flight of her career?

Undoubtedly his profile contributed to the "Mabel Mercer Madness" being assiduously promoted by Donald Smith. After singing for three seasons at the Café Carlyle during Bobby Short's absence, Mabel was moving on to the splendid St. Regis Room. Now she was working for the queenly sum of $500 a week.

Chapter 23
The Honors Brigade

A provision of Mabel's contract with the St. Regis was a room in the hotel whenever she was appearing in its famous cafe. When Whitney Balliett managed to reach her through an intermediary, she was dubious about being interviewed for a feature article in the influential *New Yorker*, wondering what they could possibly talk about, since there really wasn't much to her life. She had been in show business since she was fourteen and that was it. Harry was consulted to help, and between them, with Donald Smith's tortured soul presumably hovering in the wings, they set a date.

When the music critic arrived for their appointment, there was no response to her room telephone. As he debated what to do, "a short stocky figure in a brown tweed coat and a long woollen scarf" descended to the lobby. In her low elegant accent she said "Oh, my!" and clasped her hand to her mouth. Mabel, on her way to pick up some gowns for an appearance on Dick Cavett's TV talk show the following day, had forgotten all about Balliett. To console him, she gave him a peek into the gold and mirrored St. Regis Room with its cerulean ceiling, and invited him to go to the Cavett taping with her and Harry.

Harry spoke to Mabel about her clothes bag of gowns in a concerned way "like a nanny clucking over a charge." He

231

told Balliett later that in the hours before going to the studio she had been afraid of forgetting her lines and had behaved "like a child who has to go to the hospital."

A young, good-looking priest rushed up and Mabel embraced him. It was Father O'Brien, just stopping by "to give Mabel a cheer." He had recently relocated, he explained, to a church on Eighty-third and Park Avenue. Harry, with a flash of his old humor, said, "Well, Peter, you've moved that much closer to Heaven."

After the taping, and outside the TV station, Mabel was besieged for the first time by a crowd of autograph seekers. Signing her name with difficulty, she expressed surprise. Harry said, "You're a living legend, Mabel," and she asked him please not to say that. To Balliett he said, "Mabel has walked alone. She has never deviated from what she knew had to be done. It has never been a question of money or vogue."

The *New Yorker* critic, while conceding that her voice had diminished over the years, wrote that her "insuperable diction and style remained inspired, with rests now supplanting the flow of melody between tones. Her singing in her prime was unique...somewhere between concert hall and jazz.... Her phrasing was jazzlike in that she often placed her notes in surprising places and often used jazz timbres." She was able in an uncanny way, he said, to make her voice encompass not only many moods but their attendant colors—the purples of love, the blues of sorrow, the yellows of humor and good cheer, the black of despondency.

After the Cavett interview, the singer and her friends went to Michael's Pub for lunch. Mabel's stomach had been in an uproar for the past seventy-two hours, so she celebrated with a Bloody Mary, soup, and a spinach salad. Later, at the hotel, a television set was placed in the King Cole Bar so they could watch the complete show. Harry Beard was mesmerized, as always. Balliett wrote, however, that she leaped up midway through her first song, saying, "I can't stand this." Her companions found her later, sitting alone in the St. Regis Room. She sighed. "I just don't know," she said. "I've never had any wish to be famous…."

Biographers had often sought her permission to write her story but she wanted no part of them or it. After she was gone, she said, they could say whatever they liked, but while she lived she would have peace and privacy.

Donald Smith despaired of his diffident "client" yet never ceased to believe in his own vision for her. The phrase, "Mabel Mercer Madness"* kept spinning through his mind. He could almost see it happening. It was surely close. Whether she wanted peace and privacy or not, universal adulation was what she deserved.

Mabel reigned appropriately in the St. Regis Room, a stage highly coveted by entertainers; and the gifted if impulsive Buddy Barnes performed with her. Thelma Carpenter recalled putting on her finery to join many other celebrities and the country "family" for Mabel's opening night. For the first time Thelma sensed, however, that the vibrations she was getting from her old friend had somehow changed. According to others who knew both women well, Mabel had grown impatient with her disciple, having tried without much success to get Thelma to hone the edges of her picturesque speech. Miss Carpenter, although she could not be expected to forgo her First Amendment right to "flip off," had no recollection that Mabel ever spoke to her on the subject. The

---

* Phrase attributed to Walter Winchell.

St. Regis Room being such an upper-crust *boite*, and Mabel wanting very much to see it stay that way, she was in fact nervous that evening for a more upsetting reason, having nothing to do with Thelma. She forgot her lines a few times, and had to be cued *sotto voce* by Barnes. Her confusion was noticed by a critic.

The message Thelma got, unfortunately, was that while their friendship had been good enough for the old days, Mabel in these tony surroundings did not need her any more. Father Peter O'Brien recalled that once when he, Mabel, and Thelma had been in an after-hours club, he suddenly noticed Thelma was missing. "Where is Thelma?" he asked. Mabel replied, "I told her, 'Go home, Thelma.'"

Carp, in addition to being a vocalist with Count Basie's famous orchestra, had achieved success in Hollywood movies, and on Broadway in such roles as "Dolly." She herself had sung at the Maisonette in the St. Regis during the sixties. Although she was richly talented and beautiful, with Mabel she would always be the disciple.

When Mabel and Buddy Barnes completed their triumphant month at the St. Regis Room, they were invited to return in the autumn. Between the two engagements, she and the Café Carlyle's premier performer, Bobby Short, joined forces to help recapture "the golden age of cabaret" for a television documentary. The 1972 special, produced by South Carolina Educational Television Network, was titled, "An Evening With Mabel Mercer, Bobby Short, and Friends."

If Mabel was Mother New York, Short at the crest of his career was surely Mr. Manhattan. The "Friends" included Bart Howard, pianist William Roy, Alec Wilder, and Cam Walter, widow of the revered Cy Walter. Wilder coaxed Mabel to talk about the glamorous times at Bricktop's in Paris, and she and Short joined forces to sing a Cole Porter medley. Mabel did her jaunty interpretation of "Just One Of Those Things," to which Bart exclaimed, "Amen!" Then, with the familiar break in her voice that always dissolved her fans, she sang, "These Foolish Things," and Bobby was transported.

Buddy Barnes accompanied Mabel sublimely, whispering words when she seemed to forget them. Howard said that Barnes never stopped watching her, "like she was a baby." One critic noted that the show left viewers with the sense of an art form gliding away before their eyes, too elegant and fine for the modern world. Despite her few memory lapses, Mabel seemed in effortless command of the mood.

To everyone's astonishment, Buddy Barnes left Mabel's side just before they were to return to the St. Regis Room. Some said he had married a woman older than himself and gone on a European honeymoon, from where he wired that his return was delayed by a strike. Father O'Brien said, "When Buddy finally joined Alcoholics Anonymous, he was delightful. As far as I am concerned, there was nobody who played like Buddy—so unobtrusively beautiful."

Playing background to Mabel's unique phrasing was no easy matter for the best of pianists. She was demanding not only of herself. Fortunately, Jimmy Lyon happened to be available and agreed to join her, although they both feared he could not master her repertoire in the short time available. They met daily for intensive rehearsals. Lyon told his wife Christine that he was amazed by the number of songs she remembered—at least a thousand. By opening night they were as prepared as possible. He played the role of ventriloquist as she forgot words that any singer but Mabel might have chosen to fudge. The audience found them sweet together and giggled about it, but to Mabel the performance was torture. The critics, as usual, could not find enough superlatives to describe the joy of seeing the queen on her throne again.

As much as Mabel loved the excitement of being at the white-hot center of Manhattan entertainment, she could not stop worrying about Harry, back at the farm, and longing to be with him. It was still possible for him to get around, but he preferred living in retirement to being seen with his affliction, or so he led her to believe. Nevertheless, gossips clacked that he sometimes enjoyed periods of remission, when old flames would beckon and he responded. In times past, she had been furious about his casual philandering, but Will Craik believed that Mabel was never prepared to be without Harry nor he to part with her.

Father O'Brien shed light on Harry's "medical expert" in Rochester. He recalled accompanying Mary Lou Williams to an engagement in a night club there in 1973. On a stormy evening in January, Harry walked in slowly, accompanied by three women who, to the experienced eye of the priest, all looked like "church ladies." Harry's hands shook so badly that Mary Lou said she could not play the piano with him nearby. O'Brien found them a booth behind her.

Now in her seventies, Mabel grew steadily more famous. She sang regularly at the St. Regis until the spring of 1974. Then a Canadian film crew came to feature her in the award-winning documentary, "Guardian of Dreams," one of a series produced by CBC under the title *People of Our Time*. The programs were designed to profile "men and women of remarkable character and experience."

She was invited to Harvard University for a concert at

the Sanders Theater, whose manager was afraid that few students would come, but he needn't have worried. Two thousand clamored for admission. She was given a standing ovation and defined as "a trip." Mabel also became something of a regular visitor to the Copley Plaza Hotel's Merry-Go-Round Room in Boston. The *Boston Globe* critic declared that she recreated "an age of charm and innocence...from whose lyrics only she could extract the last touch of humor or pathos." Told of a young man who thought her material "too limited and too New York," the unruffled Mabel remarked, "Excuse me. That doesn't sound like a very receptive mind to me. Perhaps age will broaden his views."

The Berklee College of Music in Boston awarded her an honorary degree the following year. Most of the "family" went along to share the glory, among them Harry, his sister Pearl Lemert, and Will Craik. Pianist Marian McPartland attended, as did composers Cy Coleman and Alec Wilder—the latter towering and beaming paternally over the little singer in her cap and gown. She had been the first woman artist of any color to be so honored. A few blocks away on that Saturday morning, students rioting over some racial conflict clashed on Boston Common, ignorant of the fact that civil rights history was being made, bloodlessly, nearby.

The television special featuring Mabel, Bobby and Friends was followed by a fifty-six show series on National Public Radio titled *American Popular Song*. Also produced in South Carolina, it aired from 1976 to 1978. It was based on Wilder's witty and erudite literary masterwork, co-written with James T. Maher, *American Popular Song: The Great Innovators*, which was nominated for the National Book Award. Wilder himself hosted the radio series, with Loonis McGlohon as collaborator. Mabel was a charming and authoritative participant, along with most of the great stars, writers, and composers of popular music of their era. Among those honored was Teddi King, a much-loved Boston jazz singer with a richly evocative contralto voice. She was a friend of Mabel's who had sung with big bands and was noted for her haunting ballad recitations.

The radio series brought long overdue fame to the shy, eccentric Wilder, and a serious new interest in popular song. A rare small book, *Songs by Alec Wilder Were Made to Sing,* recounted "song stories" and included the music and lyrics for many of his popular compositions. It was published with a biography written by his friend Engvick and an endorsement from Mabel.

She herself was beginning to receive the awards and honorary degrees that some had feared might arrive too late. She now blithely described the St. Regis Room as her home base, saying she did not know whether the management felt the same way about her, but she liked the fact that her friends always knew where to find her. That was where William Livingstone, editor of *Stereo Review,* found her when she was chosen at age seventy-five to receive the magazine's new Award of Merit. Later called the Mabel Mercer Award, it was presented, among other distinguished recipients, to Frank Sinatra.

Livingstone confessed that he had "pestered" her for two or three years for an interview before she said yes. All the raving about her, he wrote—though true—was somewhat unfair: "...some writers make her sound like a forbidding educational experience, something that's probably good for you but you'd just as soon put off for a while." To bolster his courage, he invited Don Smith to join them on a Saturday afternoon in the King Cole Bar of the St. Regis; it was lunch for the two men and breakfast for Mabel. "We just ate, laughed, and talked all afternoon," he recalled.

Livingstone found Smith still convinced that "Mabel Mercer Madness" would yet sweep this country." Mabel, "a short round little woman who looked taller than she was," wore a red dress for the occasion. Her skin was "the color of cream with a little coffee in it, and her head is topped by a crown of shortish hair. She doesn't begin to look her age."

She said that age made her feel no different, except that she was beginning to creak a little, but there were pills for that. The only thing she regretted was that she could no longer hold a note for a long time. She had had to learn to achieve the desired effects in other ways.

She alluded vividly to her ordeals as the "golliwog" of the convent school, who could never get married. Inadvertently or not, she allowed Livingstone to continue believing an account of her father that he had gathered from *Current Biography*, i.e., that "he was a black American who died before she was born." She made it very clear that she would not have traded the years in Paris for anything.

Their talk drifted to her views of other performers. Mabel said she was planning to go hear Tony Bennett, Johnny Mathis, and Lena Horne, and that she hoped to catch Cleo Laine's new show. She liked dozens of singers and was partial to "good robust voices, although I don't like the style in which many of them sing." She thought that "Sarah Vaughan had a divine voice, as did Michelle Lee in *Seesaw*, and Susan Johnson, who sang 'Big D in Dallas.' She noted that Karen Morrow, who had recorded *The Grass Harp*, was "a good show person's singer. You know it's all there." She loved Ethel Merman as "a downright robust performer. She doesn't care if it's a right note or a wrong note. She's gutty. I like Lena's voice, and Ella Fitzgerald has a truly gorgeous quality."

But she could also deal sharply with her colleagues when it seemed to her that they failed to understand what they were singing about. "The first time I heard 'The Way We Were,' I thought, 'That's a beautiful song, and nobody knows what they're singing about.' The melody's nice but when they get to the second part, they screech it out, especially Barbra (Streisand) with that beautiful voice of hers. She has absolutely no perception of what this song is about. Most of them think you have to sing loud or soft. Loud and soft are the only nuances they seem to understand, and they don't get the meaning of certain phrases."

Although she had grown to like the exciting rhythms of rock music, it irritated her that rock singers usually threw away the words. If Mabel noticed that the lyrics often deserved their fate, she did not say so that day.

Don Smith observed, "When you sing these songs…you make it seem as though you know the things that will always be true. You have a gift for insinuation. You somehow manage to be wise without pontificating."

"Well," she said, "I've had my experiences, and I happen to know what I'm talking about…. I thought I'd never survive certain things in my life, that if it didn't go the way I wanted it to, life was not worth living. Later you learn to shrug your shoulders and say, 'well, it was great fun.' 'Just One Of Those Things' is not a sad song; it's very cynical, and I like to get a laugh on the line about a trip to the moon where nothing happens. We've all been in that situation, and some people…respond to it with a laugh; others can't. It's often from the audience that I get ideas about how to handle certain lines, but I've never tried to analyze that. I feel that I'd start imitating myself and ruin it."

Of her lasting appeal to youth, she said, "The young are very sensitive. They haven't experienced very much.... Nothing hurts like young love that's been slapped in the face.... I've known a great deal of suffering and young people sense that in my songs and are comforted by it. This all becomes easier as you grow older."

Livingstone commented wryly that he had not noticed life becoming one bit easier. Mabel smiled, patted his hand, and poured him another cup of tea. "Don't fret," she said. "Whatever it is, I assure you by the time you reach my age it won't hurt any more."

For her birthday in February 1975, *Stereo Review* carried the interview, with a cover reproduction of her Lisa Rhana pastel portrait. Critic Rex Reed warned that record collectors were guarding their Mabel Mercer albums "the way Elizabeth Taylor guards her diamonds." Five had been reissued, including Rod McKuen's Stanyan label of her only album for Decca, now titled, *Mabel Mercer For Always*. The other four Diamond Jubilee reissues consisted of fifty-five songs in a single package from Atlantic Records, called *A Tribute to Mabel Mercer on the Occasion of Her Seventy-fifth Birthday*.

"These albums are classics...and absolute requirements for any serious music library," wrote Reed. Of his own favorite, the *Blue Moon* album, he added, "The arrangements by George Cory...are classics in themselves; every time I hear them I am filled with admiration. Everything about this beautiful album seems to have been produced, performed, and embroidered with love. The two Noel Coward songs, 'Sail

Away' and 'If Love Were All'…and the Gershwin 'Isn't It A Pity' are beautiful enough to bring tears to the eyes. The septuagenarian wink in her deft handling of Lerner and Loewe's 'I'm Glad I'm Not Young Any More' proves that humor has no season, and the childish enthusiasm of 'Sunday In New York' makes me feel sorry for anyone who has never lived through one." But his favorite, he confessed, was "the story-song of the world-weary sophisticate planning a trip back home to recapture innocent times and feelings ('Guess I'll Go Back Home This Summer')."

Mabel had moved, with her audience, into modern times that were often baffling and bitter; she would outlive us all, Reed predicted.

Stereo Review threw a diamond jubilee party for her, attended by distinguished members of the entertainment industry, old and young. Mabel was photographed reminiscing with musical-comedy pioneer Eubie Blake, in his nineties. Livingstone gave much credit to Don Smith for the acceleration of her career "at a time when many of her old fans thought she was dead." As for Smith, having announced in the special Mercerized edition of *Stereo Review* that "Mabel Mercer Madness is sweeping the country," he proceeded like any good agent to make it happen. He rushed the article to the attention of entertainment managers, television producers, critics, and editors. Her story was parlayed into reverberations that left Mabel wondering what on earth all the fuss was about.

Another "surprise" 75th birthday party was held in her honor on the St. Regis Roof, attended by some five hundred people. The guest of honor found out about it in advance, says Smith, because the press started asking her questions.

242

This was not remarkable, considering that the St. Regis had started sending out invitations months before. It didn't help when the planners began whisking away bouquets of flowers sent to the singer's private suite and using them to decorate corridors and the ballroom. A muff of orchids was sent by Donn Harmon, an elderly admirer who had never met her. The card said simply, "Thanks for everything." One bouquet with balloons floating above it was signed Francis Albert.

Mabel said to Smith, moments before the affair, "You've done all this for me! And I don't do anything for you." She entered the room on the arm of the proud Harry Beard, accompanied by Jimmy Lyon. Rudolph Nureyev was there, Angela Lansbury, Warren Beatty, Jack Nicholson, Mabel's favorite accordionist Ed Moreno, Roy Wilkins of the NAACP, and Bricktop herself, all "lined up like kids to talk to her." She was overheard saying it was "the kissiest party" she had ever attended. That night Mabel was entertained by the greatest stars of Broadway and cabaret. Mary Lou Williams played "My Funny Valentine," then picked up a nosegay and carried it over to Mabel and hugged her. Sylvia Syms and Cy Coleman performed, "The Best Is Yet To Come," an allusion to Mabel's taking the stage at around midnight. Bobby Short sang "Looking At You," his eyes following her everywhere.

The manager of the St. Regis Hotel announced that the room in which she sang would bear a plaque naming it the Mabel Mercer Room. New York's Mayor Abe Beame presented her with the keys to the city. Every major newspaper and wire service photographer scrambled to cover the event.

Mabel nodded to Jimmy Lyon at the piano, then smiled at the audience and began to sing the timeless poetry of America: "Blame It On My Youth," "While We're Young,"

"'S Wonderful," and "My Shining Hour." When she sang "Being Green," from Sesame Street, she forgot the words, was cued by Lyon, smiled wryly at the audience, and said, "I told you, it's not that easy being green."

The singing and hugging went on until 1:30, when she concluded with an upbeat favorite and guests exclaimed, "It's history!" It seemed the standing ovation would never end.

Just as Mabel was allowed to leave the party, a guest confronted her and asked how old she felt. She looked into his eyes and said, "As young as you are, my dear." Then, presumably taking a second glance, she corrected herself with a smile: "No, as young as you look."

Chapter 24
Transitions

The tempo of Mabel's life continued to escalate. One evening in the mid-seventies Don Smith escorted her to a show where she thought she might find a new tune. Afterward they went to a club or two, returning at around 1:30 a.m. to the Algonquin Hotel where she was staying. She turned to him in the lobby as he started to say goodnight and said, brightly, "I wonder who's playing at Frankie and Johnny's?" Smith replied that he did not know but, as for himself, he was going home to bed. He left her at the elevator.

Next morning he was talking on the phone with a friend in show business who said, "Guess who I saw at Frankie and Johnny's last night?" Mabel had been invited out by an admirer in a chance encounter and got home at around 5:00 a.m. Smith said, "I was never able to keep up with her."

Father O'Brien took her into the sacristy of the Church of St. Ignatius one day, where the priestly vestments were kept. She tried to conceal her amusement at the spectacle of several holy fathers nervously primping and adjusting their robes in front of the mirrors. When O'Brien heard her familiar little "bosom chuckle," he asked, "What's the matter?" She whispered, "Look! It's just like our business."

In June, the septuagenarian was off to Philadelphia with accompanist Jimmy Lyon for a "major event" at the smart

Café Lafitte. She was the first singer to be booked there for an entire month and the first to perform twice nightly. Asked by a reporter about her style, she said, "My mind is always on the lyrics. Some young ladies today give you a lot of lovely sounds but there's nothing to remember."

One of Mabel's shows at the Café Lafitte was taped for a television appearance, *The Mark of Jazz*. She conquered the City of Brotherly Love with her usual flair, and hardly remembered that fifteen years before, she had been ordered to the back of a Philadelphia bus.

Week nights in New York she continued to enjoy her very own "room" at the St. Regis, where she knew the staff by name and everyone knew her, where the finest musicians in the world dropped in to hear her, and where the best composers still brought their songs for her to introduce. Occasionally she was accompanied at the piano by a newly arrived classical composer, Richard Rodney Bennett, who had come from England to teach at the Peabody Institute in Baltimore and particularly wanted to meet Miss Mercer. They became warm friends. Mutual acquaintances say that Bennett's appearances with her at the St. Regis helped advance his own long and successful career as a composer of symphonies, ballet, operas, film scores, and show tunes. He has been a featured entertainer at many Town Hall Cabaret Conventions.

From Berkeley, California came word that a professor of English was assigning Mabel Mercer recordings to his students seeking the proper enunciation of the mother tongue. The singer went to Washington, D.C. several times to sing at a Georgetown club called I'm Tony, and received as a staff departure gift a box of Screaming Yellow Zonkers, which she opened and then carefully rewrapped. At the office of

246

Donald F. Smith Promotions, Inc. in New York, clippings from all over had begun to fatten the Mabel Mercer file.

In March 1977, Mabel appeared for the first time since the late sixties at Carnegie Hall with her old friend Bobby Short, singing a long program of twenty-seven solos plus three exuberant duets. Critic John S. Wilson detected a renewed vocal power.

Such pleasures helped her forget, for a time, her chronically painful arthritis, although the anxiety of rehearsal did not soothe that other misery, diverticulitis. As if these problems were not enough, she now began to have attacks of vertigo that sent her world spinning without warning. The sudden terrifying loss of control made her feel more dependent than ever on Muriel Finch and the other family members. Adde Wallin-Beach noticed that when she took Mabel shopping and the latter happened to finish first, she now sat down on a ledge to wait. This was totally unlike her.

"One day at the farm," Stanley Crantson remembered with a smile, "she was not feeling well. I suggested she get up and I would straighten up her bed. So she did. And under the bed I saw twelve boxes of candy." Even in her twilight years, Mabel never lost her fear of want nor her love for sweets.

As for Harry, he seldom came to New York any more except to get a haircut from his favorite barber. He looked old and thin yet still dressed immaculately for special occasions. Mabel helped him in and out of cars; he soothed her nerves before the big performances.

She left the St. Regis that spring to sing at Cleo's, a popular new West Side spot, where fans new and old found that she could "make the most banal tune sound like Robert Frost's poetry." *Cue* magazine saluted her as "Cabaret Performer of the Year." One enthusiastic critic exclaimed, "It's her room from the time she sits down to sing that first number ('Autumn In New York') till she finishes.... Listening to her is like taking a Ph.D. in singing."

In midsummer of 1977, Victor Lownes III, director of London's Playboy Club, invited Mabel to open his new Playmate Grill on Park Lane on the Fourth of July, and to stay in London for four weeks. She was flabbergasted. Why would all those young rock fans want to listen to her? And a new generation of royalty? She and Harry gravely conferred. Could they? Dare they?

The two consulted with Don Smith, Muriel and Adde, Harry's sister Pearl, Jimmy Lyon and his wife Christine, and Loonis and Nan McGlohon, all of whom knew there would be no stopping her. Mabel Mercer was going home after forty-one years. Would there still be anyone she knew? What if she had a vertigo attack and fell off her fancy gilt chair in front of Lord Hmphmphmph and the Archbishop of Canterbury? They all decided that after London, she should go on to Paris. Mabel thought her Chinatown silk brocade was still quite good enough, but Harry said definitely that she must have new gowns. The old ACME dress form was dusted off again.

Mabel worried about forgetting her lines, but Jimmy Lyon said "Why do you think I'm going?" And so, after a *bon voyage* party thrown by Bobby Short, the Mercer entourage left for London on the Queen Elizabeth II. Mabel and Jimmy gave two concerts on shipboard.

When the Mercer Party arrived, the headlines proclaimed that there were two Queens of England in London. In front of the cheering toffs and Bunny Girls, Mabel curtsied beside the grand piano and was presented with a bouquet of flowers larger than herself. In truth, most of the young guests had no clue who she was. *The Daily Mail* asked, "What makes Mabel the most exciting woman at the Playboy Club?" and answered that each song she sang was "like three acts of your favorite play condensed to a few fleeting moments of bliss. Here is a truly great actress who tells her stories in song." Londoners loved her sophistication, her lack of "ingratiating chatter, and no clutching of the microphone." Members of the press outdid each other in proclaiming her "the most remarkable woman in London."

Don Smith recalled that BBC-TV filmed three evenings in the Playmate Grill with the original intention of editing it for an hour's show. Instead, they scheduled a whole week for a series of late-night half-hour broadcasts billed as *Miss Mercer in Mayfair*, "an honor never before accorded any entertainer." If this was not Mabel Mercer Madness, Smith thought deliriously, then he didn't know mad.

After the grand splash of her London conquest, the singer summoned her courage once again and crossed the Channel to Paris. She found the old city vastly changed—still beautiful, but in some ways deeply disturbing. She was driven at night through Montmartre, "...and it was like walking at night down 42nd Street," she said. "I don't know. I couldn't live there again, I couldn't believe it.... All the ugly pictures— oversized nude pictures of girls. It's all so wrong." Mabel remembered that even thieves and gamblers had behaved like gentlemen in the old days, and that people wore their best clothes to the theater.

When she returned to the U.S.A. and to Cleo's, overflowing crowds came nightly as before. Critic Patricia O'Haire exclaimed, "Hurray! Hurray! We can all rejoice today." That same fall, Mabel stopped the show at New York University's 50th Anniversary Gala, *A Salute to Richard Rodgers*, where her single number brought a standing ovation from the all-star cast and audience. In January of the following year she left for the West coast for a San Francisco Ballet benefit. That was followed by a four-week engagement (later extended to six) at the Club Mocambo, where she was hailed "as a legend in her own sweet time." Bill Engvick recalled that at some of the Mocambo performances, Mabel alienated people by not showing up until 11 P.M.

"They didn't realize," said Read Arnow, "that she was ill and it was a miracle she even showed up at all."

A highlight of her return to San Francisco was a celebration of her 78th birthday given by friends, after she had spent the day autographing records. BBC sent a camera crew from London to record yet more events in the life of America's premier song stylist. After an extended run at the Mocambo, Mabel and the family were off to Los Angeles for a performance on the imposing, not to say terrifying, big stage at the Dorothy Chandler Pavilion. Her old friends Jack Nicholson, Warren Beatty, and Lily Tomlin awaited her in the first row orchestra section. After "cavorting" through more than two dozen numbers in two sets, "without a falter" (*Variety*), she was honored at a reception and more parties.

During this trip Mabel suffered periodically from the frightening dizzy spells. As for Harry, Pearl, Donald, Muriel, Jimmy, and other members of the group, they were all exhausted by the end. The strain of traveling had been horrendously difficult for Harry. Returning from the West coast trip, he and Mabel retired to the country where she was content to care for him and rest from her triumphs. For the better part of the next two years, New Yorkers heard little of Mabel Mercer. Despite their illnesses, they spent a pleasant and relaxing time with old friends.

Bricktop, who had been appearing at a club in Chicago, suffered a heart attack and was hospitalized in New York. Julius Monk called Mabel and Jimmy Daniels at her request. Mabel phoned Father Lee Smith in the city, asking him to call on Brick. The priest, who at the time had never heard of Bricktop, remembered with a smile that he went to her hospital room as requested and was informed by a nurse ("like something from Cornelia Otis Skinner") that "Madame is indisposed." The tough Brick rallied, however, and for a time returned to work. Plagued with anemia and chronic arthritis, she appeared for the last time at "21" in New York with the famed saloon pianist, Hugh Shannon.

Father O'Brien often visited the farm when Mabel was not working. "I did not think her farmhouse looked cluttered or unkempt," he said. "It was just—packed. Lots of tea cozies and vases of dead flowers. Behind the house she was pouring some big concrete thing. Willie Craik said, 'Mercer is laying the Merritt Parkway.'"

O'Brien, while searching for an answer to his own depression, spent his thirties serving God by day and standing in the backs of clubs at night helping Mary Lou Williams. The important thing he learned from Harry Beard, even after he was ill, was always to be right there, protecting his star from the crowd and the drunks.

Mabel and the family went to Boston on May 18, 1980, where she received another honorary degree of Doctor of Music from the New England Conservatory.

When Alec Wilder came to the farm that year, Mabel

and Harry noticed how tired he looked, and how loosely the uniform of tweed jacket and flannels hung on his tall frame. He and Mabel walked in the meadow and along the creek, inhaling the rejuvenating odor of the yellow skunk cabbages.

When Mabel was not slippering around the kitchen, banging pots—she, Alec, and Harry gathered in front of the blazing fire. Sometimes they moved to the big square piano to practice an old song or study a new one. Harry might burst into a raucous story with his old élan, and Alec would roar. Then they would all fall quiet and thoughtful, wrapped in their separate but interwoven skeins of memory.

Among the many songs Alec had written for Mabel was one called simply, "Up The Hill In Red Rock." In 1976, the prolific team of Wilder and McGlohon had written two deeply affecting songs, "Blackberry Winter," and "Be A Child," both of which were recorded by Mabel Mercer and three other superb vocalists, Eileen Farrell, Teddi King, and Marlene VerPlanck. Alec's final compositions with McGlohon were prophetic: "A Long Night," and "South to a Warmer Place." Frank Sinatra recorded them both.

Wilder died of lung cancer in Gainesville, Florida, on the morning of Christmas Eve, 1980. Ironically, he abhorred that holiday, along with all others. He would not be buried until after the ground thawed in Rochester, New York. It was Mother's Day, and several mourners almost thought they could hear him roaring, "Oh God! Not Mother's Day!"

Most of Wilder's public recognition came posthumously, including his induction into the Songwriters' Hall of Fame, and the 1991 dedication of the Alec Wilder Reading Room in the Sibley Music Library at the Eastman School of Music in Rochester. Among his many admirers, Alec was also famous for his aphorisms. He had once said, "I am not well informed, but I know too much."

Mabel climbed slowly up to "Alec's" room under the roof at the farm and stared out at the snow through the newly framed picture window. Wilder had never seen this modernization. She could almost hear him shouting, "No! I don't believe it!" She later told McGlohon she felt he was actually in the room. "He's there, I'm sure of it."

The holiday season following Alec's death seemed strange at the farm. Sub-zero temperatures gripped the house and all its creatures in brittle silence. Mabel found it hard to grasp that they would never hear Alec's booming, irascible voice again. Harry looked so ill that she was reluctant to leave him, but invitations had been sent out. She was to be the honored guest at the first of a series of black-tie fundraisers for the Whitney Museum of American Art—a benefit inspired by Don Smith for its Composers Showcase. It was all she could do to muster enough energy to face the crowds in New York.

The museum and the City of New York presented Mabel with the Handel Medallion for her "unique contribution to the culture of New York City." The finest talents in show business were there to sing the songs she had made or helped make famous. Rex Reed noted of the $150-a-plate event that, "All the Missys and Chessys and Buffys and Muffys were there—enough swells to fill the society pages for months." Bricktop was there, as were Buddy Barnes, Ronny Whyte, and Cy Coleman. The program was not far along when the guest of honor almost cracked up. An apparition swam onto the stage "in a finny purple gown," her famous elbow-length gloves, and her gardenia. The Incomparable (and Unpredictable) Hildegarde, veteran of many a Stage Door Canteen during World War II, sat down at the piano, smiled at the audience, and began to play "The Warsaw Concerto" with her gloves on—"not hitting a single key," as Mary Lou Williams whispered to Father O'Brien.

Bart Howard sang "It Was Worth It," and Ronny Whyte dedicated a new song to Mabel, "Let Me Show You My New York." Sammy Cahn had written special lyrics for her to the tune of "It's Been A Long, Long Time." As Mabel was receiving awards from ASCAP and the American Theater Wing, Reed overheard someone say, "Look at the aristocracy in that face," and another replied, "She should be knighted."

In June of that spring, Whyte joined with other entertainers to present five Sunday concerts in Alec Wilder's memory at Spencertown, near Red Rock. "It was at the little Spencertown Academy; the weather was beautiful and Mabel came to all of them," he recalled. "David Allen was there, Suzanna McCorkle, Jackie and Roy, Marlene VerPlanck. We ran the gamut of every performer's best things and it was simply beautiful. Judy Juhring…gave a reception and about fifty people went to her house, including Mabel—who would sometimes sing to my accompaniment. Songs like 'Just One Of Those Things,' or 'By Myself.' She had not been performing at all in those days, because she was almost 81 when Alec died. People would stand and cry. We would all talk with her. And this was really the last time I sang with her…."

Mabel went to New York that spring for a tribute to honor the 90th anniversary of Cole Porter's birth. Friends noticed that she had again let her hair go back to its natural gray. The stiffness in her hands made it impossible for her to tint her hair and style it with her old-fashioned, stove-heated curling iron.

One morning at the farm, she made her usual cup of strong English tea and struggled up the stairs. Her manager, friend, and lover was lying on his bed. He seemed to have dozed off in the process of dressing. She touched him and called his name. Then she telephoned Adde Wallin-Beach, crying, "I can't wake Harry!"

Chapter 25
Kool Jazz

Harry Beard died at the age of seventy-four. He was buried in the tiny pioneer cemetery at Red Rock, which occupied a hillside in a clearing blazed long ago from the surrounding spruce forest.

Harry's grave, marked by a simple bronze plaque in the grass, could be discerned from the driveway at the foot of the hill only by its lonely proximity to a small evergreen tree. The old cemetery had a rugged, timeless quality, enclosed like a harbor against storms, yet open in fine weather to the ambient beauty. Local folk noted that from Harry Beard's grave, you could see the top of Mabel's hill.

That same year, Father O'Brien lost his dearest friend, whose life and career he had passionately guarded, the great jazz composer and pianist Mary Lou Williams. He himself went into treatment for drugs. In Williams' later years she was described as a kind of one-woman retrospective of the entire jazz movement. Like Ethel Waters, she had been something of a religious fanatic, but claimed she had returned from semi-retirement because of the sounds she was hearing in modern jazz. "They're disturbed and crazy," she said. "They're neurotic, as if the Negro was pulling away from his heritage in music. You have to love when you play. Lord, I've talked talked talked music to young musicians, but they don't listen. So I've decided to show them, make them hear the soul."

You could almost hear Mabel saying Amen to that. At this juncture of her life, she could easily have withdrawn into the isolation of her farm and the company of her animals, had the rest of the family not rallied around. Several times she visited the McGlohons in Charlotte, N.C. Every afternoon Mabel would say, "I must see Queen's Road," and they would give her the grand tour of broad streets, majestic oaks, and unfenced, palatial homes of the nouveau-riche textile manufacturers. It was spring, and the lawns were bursting with white and red azaleas. Mabel, her fingertips to her lips, would exclaim, "Oh, my, my, my!"

Even in her eighties, Nan McGlohon reported, the singer could always bend over and touch the floor with flattened hands. Her normal walk was almost a run, which in her later years became a rapid shuffle—except of course when she was on stage. Then she moved slowly.

As she and Loonis rehearsed songs after dinner, she once surprised him by saying, "Something I've never done in my life but have always loved is the 'Kerry Dance.'" He said he could not imagine her singing it. Mabel explained, "It's one of the saddest, most poignant songs ever written. It's about lost youth. No, I wouldn't want to do it as a jig. It's very slow." So Loonis played it slowly and she sang. Later she sang it—of all places—at the Kool Jazz Festival, in a strangely beautiful and original rendition.

"But she also loved contemporary music," said McGlohon. "One of the songs she fell in love with in the last years of her life was the Sergio Mendez song, 'So Many Stars.'" Bill Stowe, McGlohon's drummer, was in his mid-twenties and one of the youngest musicians ever to play with

Mabel and Eileen Farrell at Carnegie Hall, and later at other engagements. "Because I was always seated behind her," he recalled, "I was unable to see her face, but I could watch the enraptured effect of her on the audience and even on the face of Miss Farrell."

The McGlohon trio also accompanied Mabel in her segment of Eileen Farrell's *American Popular Singers* for National Public Radio. That led Charles Kuralt (host of the CBS television show, *Sunday Morning*) to feature the collaboration of the opera diva and the cabaret singer on one of his shows. When this performance in turn was seen by millions of viewers, Loonis had a call from John Langley, principal of the Rockingham, N.C. junior high school, who each year presented a two-week arts festival for his students. In that poor area, children might see an occasional rock concert but never in their lives be able to go to a symphony, a ballet, or a major museum. Langley phoned Loonis: "How can I get in touch with Mabel Mercer?"

McGlohon explained that she lived in New York. The Principal asked him to call her and ask if she could come down to do the arts festival. Loonis said, "I don't think so." He was thinking of her age and physical problems, but mainly, he did not think she would feel comfortable performing for junior high students.

Langley said, "I never saw her before *Sunday Morning*, but I have never seen anybody communicate like that lady. Don't undersell my kids. They would dig her and they would know what she's doing."

The only question in Mabel's mind when Loonis put the suggestion to her was, "Do you think the children would *lahf* at me?" He said, "Mabel, nobody would ever laugh at you."

She said, "Well, then, I'd love to do it." So the composer/ arranger and the singer began to put a program together. "Mabel wanted to sing a railroad song, of all things," he recalled. It was "Run For the Roadhouse, Nellie." She wanted the drummer, Stowe, to do a chookachooka kind of sound. McGlohon found a recording of the number, and asked her to listen to herself, which was very painful for her.

At the appointed time, Mabel went to Rockingham. She sat on stage in a brocaded chair borrowed from a local furniture store. With Loonis at the piano, she was prepared to sing to eight hundred kids, aged around thirteen, who had never heard of her. Loonis didn't want to sell her too hard because he had worked with the kids before.

"They are exceptional. When John Langley tells them he's bringing in somebody good, they know it's somebody good, even though it may not be anything they'd like. He tells them, 'You may not like this, but I want you to listen and hang onto every note and every word, because years from now you may look back and say, 'That was a wonderful experience, and thank God I got to hear that person.'" Understandably, both the kids and Mabel were nervous during her first number. For the second, Loonis had suggested a song they would have heard before, so she sang "Both Sides Now."

"During the second number," said Loonis, "it was very obvious that the kids knew something special was happening on that stage, and by the end of it, Mabel had won the audience over. They gave her two standing ovations during the performance, and I remember looking out from the front and seeing the superintendent of the North Carolina schools, who had come over from Raleigh, and some other adults, and the tears were streaming down their faces."

Bill Stowe, at the drums, was watching faces as usual. He recalled that when she sang the cat song, "Chase Me, Charley," the kids were entranced. "Partly because of the lighting, I could see this aura around her head with her back to me and feel the effect of her presence. She was like that even in rehearsals. She was always the center of attention, but not because she drew attention to herself.... The kids did not think she was playing down to them."

On their drive back from Rockingham, McGlohon recalled that Mabel was very thoughtful. Finally she said, "You know, I think I received my favorite compliment today." He asked what it was and she said, "Well, as I was leaving, a little black boy, a very tiny boy, came up and touched my hand and looked up at me and said, 'Miss Mercer, you done good.'"

Back in New York, the big boys were waiting for her. George Wein, the emperor of jazz productions, had decided to create the Kool Jazz Festival New York, a weeklong hydrahead that would swallow up the Newport Jazz Festival and all its clones around the country.

Coincidentally, photographer Barbara Bordnick, an artist with distinctive ideas on character portrayal, was preparing to embark on a portrait series to be called *Women in Jazz*. She discussed with Wein's assistant, Charlie Bourgeois, the possibility of publishing a Kool Jazz Calendar. He took her to Cleo's, to hear Mabel Mercer for the first time.

"I could not believe it," she said. "I was hypnotized." She knew little about jazz at the time. "Although Mabel was not a jazz singer, she was very much what jazz was all about. She had the most sophisticated star quality, the most incredible evocative skills of anyone I have known. I think part of her elegance was her unassuming quality. But her ability to touch you so gently and so deeply and delicately was what I found the most amazing.... At first you did not know what was happening, and suddenly you were being emotionally manipulated to exactly where she wanted you to be. I mean the word manipulated in a gentle sense, like a petal blown by the wind, that lands on you." Of course, she arranged to photograph Mabel for the collection.

The Kool Jazz Festival opened on June 25, 1982, with programs at the Forum Room of the New York Sheraton, Avery Fisher Hall, and Carnegie Hall. Many old familiar artists performed the brilliant melodies of Benny Goodman, Lionel Hampton, Teddy Wilson, and others. The following night impresario George Schutz and a German colleague presented a three-hour concert, "Jazz and World Music." On June 27 and 28, Mabel Mercer, a non-jazz singer who was eighty-two years old, would take the stand. Loonis McGlohon had produced the show in honor of Alec Wilder, with the finest musicians in New York singing and playing a dozen of his songs. Marian McPartland played "Jazz Waltz For A Friend" with her usual brilliance, and a combo performed Wilder's famous Octets.

Music critic Nancy Q. Keefe wrote, "...I was really dreading that Mabel Mercer would break my heart. She came out on the arm of the master of ceremonies, more secure about herself than he seemed to be for her. She sat in an armchair...put on her glasses to read from a script on a music stand. Her voice was shaky. I definitely should not have come.

"Loonis McGlohon... played the opening bars to the poignant song, 'Did You Ever Cross Over To Sneden's.' She began to say the words.... I felt a lump in my throat, remembering the rich mezzo.

"Then suddenly musical notes came floating out across Carnegie Hall, and Mabel Mercer was singing again. The audience seemed to be holding its breath. There was no other sound but the light piano and the singing voice of Mabel Mercer, enunciating every word with perfect diction. Backstage, the other performers listened with tears streaming down their faces; out front, hardly anyone was dry-eyed. Miss Mercer was her usual unassuming self."

Mabel later said, "I had a good mike," as James Joyce might have said he had a good dictionary.

The following morning Miss Mercer and Eileen Farrell, seated regally side by side at Alice Tully Hall, sang thirty songs and seemed "in their ease and artlessness to be at the very center of music—a pair of goddesses telling us what all songs should sound like…." Near the end of that concert, Mabel read A. A. Milne's "Vespers," and Edna St. Vincent Millay's "Ballad Of The Harp Weaver."

On June 29th and 30th the Kool Jazz Festival continued with the avant-garde, and then more of what Alec Wilder had dubbed the derriere-garde. It sailed on into July with a concert of songs composed by American women. The festival concluded on the fourth of July with Lionel Hampton's big band, and finally a monster jam session.

It was over! Mabel, following her second performance, led Eileen Farrell off the stage doing a buck-and-wing, demonstrating how easy it was to be eighty-two.

One afternoon in the spring of 1983, she was out in her garden transplanting God's weeds to make room for flowers, when she was summoned into the house by Muriel Finch. The White House was on the phone. President Reagan's assistant told Mabel that he wanted to give her the Presidential

Medal of Freedom in a ceremony at the White House, and could she also have lunch with the President? Basically apolitical, Mabel was puzzled by the proposed award and her response was somewhat wary. She did, however, accept.

Being the granddaughter of slaves, she asked Muriel about the medal: "Freedom from what?" Muriel explained that it was the highest honor the President could bestow on a civilian. Mabel said, "But why me?"

Muriel, who was excited and wanted to start phoning the rest of the "family" right away, explained, "It's because you're famous, Mabel; because you have done so much for our music." Before long it seemed everybody in Chatham, Chatham Centre, East Chatham, Old Chatham, Red Rock, Lavatie, Austerlitz, and Spencertown had heard the news and wanted to congratulate her. In New York, Don Smith was euphoric. Mabel never did get back to her gardening.

On a Wednesday in late February, she took the train down to Washington along with Muriel and Adde, and by that time she was getting excited. In the Blue Room of the White House, President Reagan presented the Medal of Freedom to her and nine other worthy Americans, including former Congresswoman and writer Clare Booth Luce, ballet master George Balanchine, Senator Jacob Javits, and architect Buckminster Fuller.

Mabel's citation said, "... Her talent, her elegance and her unique way with a lyric have gathered a devoted following all over the world. ...With her incomparable talent she has helped shape and enrich American music."

After her lunch of Chicken Véronique, seated on the left of the Commander In Chief, Mabel and her group returned to New York, where a party was being given in her

263

honor, arranged by Donald Smith, at the Algonquin Hotel. That night she made a rare admission: "I'm just so exhausted."

But there were still more honors. Her old friend, Frank Sinatra, sent a composition titled, "A Love Letter To Mabel Mercer," to the Rev.. Fr. James F. Hinchey of the Cathedral of St. James in Brooklyn, to express his delight that the Church was giving her its Compostela Award. He wrote, "... She has indeed illuminated the horizon of human experience in her profession. Her gift with a song is enough to make other vocalists seek a different occupation.... See how gracefully she sits, quietly and with elegance. Mabel has enriched my life and the lives of all who were fortunate to know her, or even to see her and hear her.

"Thank you, dear Mabel, through all these years you've made the world a brighter and warmer planet. God loves you and so do we."

On several occasions Mabel had performed at benefits for the SLE Foundation, to aid persons afflicted with lupus erythematosus, the disease that had taken the life of the much loved singer Teddi King. As usual, she and Loonis McGlohon met in New York in November 1983 to prepare for the program. Susan Kuralt, whom McGlohon had invited to meet the singer she had long admired, remembers the rehearsal in an apartment on Central Park West: "She was having trouble then, not only with her voice, but remembering lyrics. He took me over and sat me down on a sofa beside her. I was so overcome that I literally could not talk. We sat there. She was thinking music, and I was thinking, 'Oh, God, what can I say?'"

When Mabel walked on stage that evening, however, McGlohon felt immediately reassured. He saw her transformed before his eyes. "... There was this energy that came.

264

I think that's true with a lot of performers, but it was rather strange to watch because I would never have bet she could pull off a great performance. That night some kind of magic happened. She looked absolutely radiant and she sang as well as I'd heard her sing in years and years."

The program included her unique slow rendition of "Kerry Dance," and the ever-charming "While We're Young," which she had long ago rescued from oblivion. "A fantastic performance," McGlohon remembered.

Chapter 26
Coda

On a bleak day in January 1984, Mabel was rushed to the Berkshire Medical Center at Pittsfield, Massachusetts. She had felt the first excruciating stabs of angina pectoris, a disease of the heart that is accompanied by suffocating contractions in the chest. When the attack struck, she shot straight up in a frozen position, unable to move or breathe. Will Craik, who had experience with the affliction, said that he usually took a nitroglycerin tablet and the spasm went away; but this did not work effectively for her. In the hospital, the attacks kept recurring. The acute-care staff fastened tubes all over her and made her as comfortable as possible.

A few days later, Craik and Muriel Finch were sitting in her room and Muriel, whose intense dark eyes betrayed more strain than usual, suddenly said, "What do you want to take with you when we go to the West Coast?" Craik said he nearly went into cardiac arrest. Apparently Mabel and Eileen Farrell had a joint performance scheduled in California, and Muriel was planning to take her there.

Adde Wallin-Beach, who was planning a vacation in Mexico, also worried about Mabel's health if she tried to keep the singing engagement. Muriel, whose stoic nature concentrated on wellness, told Craik, "The doctor said it would be all right if she felt up to it." Craik recalled, "I had a vision of

Muriel getting her out in California somewhere, and that would be the end of Mabel." Although the singer felt terrified of more paralyzing angina attacks, she could not stop fretting about all the people who expected her. Craik finally said bluntly, "Well, make up your mind, dear. Would you rather disappoint somebody, or kill yourself? Which?"

She took her time answering. Muriel told Craik in an aside, "Well, she's never happy unless she's working." He knew this to be true, and he understood her drive to keep going. But to everyone's relief, she finally decided not to go. She was feeling better in the last week of January, and they took her back to Blakely farm. Her physician said there was little more they could do for the angina, since she was far too frail to undergo surgery.

On January 31, Mabel's almost-oldest friend, the fabled Bricktop, died in her sleep in New York. The family discussed whether to tell Mabel. When she was informed, she asked Father Lee Smith to represent her at the funeral services, which he did.

Craik went to stay at the farm, as he had done periodically. Some of Mabel's friends felt she would not want the public to know she was ill, and decided at first to keep it secret. This could not last because she began fretting about why she had gotten no get-well cards or phone calls. Craik settled the matter by announcing that it was all nonsense and he was going to tell everyone he knew. Since he knew a great many people and also wrote a column for a local newspaper, Mabel was soon cheered by mailbags full of messages. She remained weak, but her spirits picked up remarkably. She saw a select few visitors and was constantly surrounded by old friends and her beloved pets.

Will and Muriel grew accustomed to the pattern of her illness: a painful recurrence of angina one day, followed by rapid "recovery," when they might find her sitting up watching television or chatting and laughing with callers. This lasted through Mabel's 84th birthday on February 3, which they celebrated quietly, and on through March. Peering through the window, she could see the lilacs blooming and hear the rowdy chorusing of birds.

In her good periods she sorted through boxes of old letters and threw nearly everything of a personal nature into the blazing fire. She sorted photos and mementos and some of her beautiful scarves into boxes, marking one of them with the name of Adde Wallin-Beach. When Harry Beard had died, Mabel had not allowed his sister to take his things until she had a chance to sort through them. The things that were still with her she put into boxes marked for Pearl.

During one remission, Muriel took her to a dinner party nearby at Judy Juhring's home, which was also attended by her old friend and admirer Ronny Whyte. Whyte recalls, "After dinner I went to the lovely grand piano and said, 'Mabel, would you care to sing?' She said, 'Oh, no, no, no, no, no.' That was the last time I saw her."

A week later she was rushed back to the hospital at Pittsfield. Adde Wallin-Beach was in Mexico, but had asked Muriel to phone her at once if their friend's condition became more serious. Adde felt uneasy. She kept phoning Muriel who, she said, continued to reassure her that Mabel was holding her own and there was no need to return. Finally Adde's son Peter telephoned her and told her he thought the singer's condition was extremely grave.

Meanwhile Will Craik, Father Smith, and even Muriel

had begun to worry about the fact that Mabel had made no provision for the disposition of her property. Of course it was a delicate subject; the superstitious Mabel believed she would die as soon as she made a will. Craik warned her vividly that if she did not do so, Uncle Mario Cuomo would take her farm for a parking lot, and the animals were likely to get nothing. He said, "...please, for our peace of mind, tell us how you want it...." He later told James Haskins he did not think it was so much a matter of superstition with Mabel as her habitual procrastination.

Still she delayed. She had another heart attack. Dicky Graden was then too ill to come visit her, but Ena Boucher was driven up to see her by a member of her church. Joe Carstairs kept continuously in touch and remained helpful. Peter Wallin flew to Mexico to drive his mother's car home. Adde returned at once by airplane, angry and hurt at not having been called earlier.

Father Smith anointed Mabel, then phoned the White House and told President Reagan of her illness. The Reagans sent her a cheering card. Someone notified Frank Sinatra, whose telephone call came as a thrill. Although Mabel was not supposed to receive calls in intensive care, the hospital staff had been alerted to bring her the phone. The two singers talked and joked together for several minutes.

"On Wednesday of Holy Week," recalled Father Smith, "I chatted with Mabel and asked her if she had made a will. I suggested she think about it, because the tax office up in Albany would be glad to take her property if she didn't. She had nothing then except the farm. She said she would like to leave her place to 'the children of Chatham.' Like they were going to come out to the farm and run around? I suggested maybe the Morris Memorial that ran a local youth center."

Ultimately Mabel decided to leave the proceeds from her farm in three equal sums: to the youth center, the United Negro College Fund ("for scholarships to be given in my name in the field of music,") and to her "sisters" Ena Boucher and Madeline Graden. She also left property she had inherited from her mother to an animal welfare group.

The nurses, who had grown to love Mabel, stood around while she signed her will so that no one could claim she had been coerced. After she signed it, Father Smith left her. He recalls that every time he talked with her during her illness she was "totally clear in her mind. As to her thoughts, well, she remained a very private person."

Mabel was acutely aware that it was Holy Week and that for the first time in her life she would not be attending any Easter celebrations; Adde promised to pray twice as hard. The tubes that had hurt her throat were removed at her request; she breathed lightly and regularly. Her face that had seemed so small and drawn in recent weeks looked smooth beneath the silvery frizz. Her once rounded body seemed to have shrunk. Although the famous blue eyes looked tired and distant, they burned with a light of certainty.

She died at 6:40 the morning of Good Friday, April 20, 1984, and was buried two days after Easter Sunday. Within minutes of Will Craik's receiving a call from the hospital saying that she had passed away, all the "family" knew; long distance telephone and telegraph wires were humming.

A great sense of loss touched the thousands whose lives had been warmed by her presence and her art. People who had been close to her had always felt that her spirit was in synchronicity with the stars and other mighty cosmic forces.

Even those who only thought they had known her felt a strange sense of orphanhood. The music critics searched (some as far as *Revelations*) to find the elusive phrases that might help their readers understand her gift and their loss.

While the Mass of the Resurrection was being said at St. James Roman Catholic Church at Chatham, "rain as light and soft as her voice" began falling outdoors. The church was packed to overflowing. On the altar in a straight row sat a phalanx of priests, six in number. In addition to her many professional honors and the Presidential Medal, Mabel had been an honorary member of the New York State Council of the Arts, a member of the American Guild of Variety Artists, the American Federation of Television and Radio Artists, the Spencertown Academy, and the Columbia-Greene Humane Society; all those groups were represented. Father Dennis Corrado paid tribute "to a most remarkable woman, whose life and voice will never be forgotten."

The honorary pallbearers were famous for their contributions to music and show business: Bobby Short, Frank Sinatra, Tony Bennett, Sammy Davis, Jr., Johnny Mathis, Charlie Bourgeois, Cy Coleman, Jimmy Daniels, Bart Howard, Jimmy Lyon, Loonis McGlohon, Thomas McNamara, Rex Reed, Will Craik, Stanley Crantson, and Donald Smith.

Adde Wallin-Beach could not believe it; as she left the church she saw all the press and television photographers and a long cortege of cars with their lights on, stretching out of sight. Two thousand mourners, someone said. Bart Howard said it was "the biggest damn funeral" he had ever seen, and it surprised him.

The Red Rock cemetery was just a hillside clearing in the forest, laid out long ago to accommodate the brief lives and abrupt departures of early settlers. Few people could look at it without thinking it an enchanted place. One mourner, visiting the cemetery two weeks later, was reminded of the snowy grave scene blanketed in frozen flowers in the movie *Snow White*. In the pioneer section, crazy old tombstones careened in every direction; to the other side were the newer, concrete monuments.

Just as members of the funeral party began staggering up the hill, the rain poured down. It melted into the tears that streaked their makeup, gushing in icy rills from hatbrims, soaking the mink and ermine and rolling off the heavy-weather coats of local tradespeople. The long procession of umbrellas wound slowly as near as the owners could get to the grave where the red earth was blanketed with Mabel's favorite spring gladiolas. A huge bouquet of perfect roses lay on the coffin with a card inscribed, "I love you, Mabel," and signed "Frank."

"There's the tree," Adde Wallin-Beach told me. We had spent most of a fine summer day together talking about Mabel Mercer, almost a decade after the funeral. She hesitated only a moment to get her bearings from the flagpole. Hiking up the steep path, she veered right toward the sentinel evergreen and the two simple bronze plaques that lay side by side in the grass, bearing only the names and important dates of Mabel Mercer and Harry Beard.

She reminisced about how the cold sky had opened up that April morning just as the pallbearers, including her son Peter, staggered and slipped up the hillside. They had paused at the half-turn to wait for the long line of mourners to catch up. It was almost like some strange opening, rather than a closing, with the wobbly black caterpillar of umbrellas winding up from the dirt road. On that day the players were merely segments of a long, sad, black stage property. They were like children devastated by the warmth that had gone from them. One by one the mourners placed flowers on the casket. Someone, in denial, remembered the lines of Mabel's favorite poet, Edna St. Vincent Millay. *Dirge without Music* was an expression of the poet's own railing at death:

"...Into the darkness they go, the wise and the lovely.
...Gently they go, the beautiful, the tender, the kind;
Quietly they go, the intelligent, the witty, and brave.
I know. But I do not approve.
And I am not resigned...."

A decade later on that warm June day, Adde Wallin-Beach laid a rose from her garden between the two plaques and began to pull some weeds. Then she tilted back on her heels and laughed at herself. Mabel had loved weeds.

She spoke simply, "I want to say, Mabel's life is not over. She lives on and on in all our hearts. I loved her very much."

References

DISCOGRAPHY
(Courtesy Institute of Jazz Studies, Rutgers University;
Rhino Records, Tower Records)

Art Of Mabel Mercer, Atlantic, 2 LP12, AT 2-602.

American Popular Song, Smithsonian, CDO5

American Popular Song, Six Decades of Songs and Singers, 7 LP

Atlantic Jazz Vocals, *Voices of Cool,* Vol. 1, CDO5

Cole Porter, *American Songbook Series,* Smithsonian, CD05.

For Always, Stanyon, LP12.

From This Moment On, Songs of Cole Porter, Smithsonian, CDO5

George Gershwin, *American Songbook Series,* Smithsonian, CDO5.

Jerome Kern, *American Songbook Series,* Smithsonian, CDO5.

Mabel Mercer and Bobby Short at Town Hall, Atlantic, 2 LP12, SD 2-604.

Mabel Mercer, Second Town Hall Concert with Bobby Short, Atlantic, 2 LP12, SD 2-605.

Ertegun's New York: New York Cabaret Music. Atlantic 3-CD 7 81817-2.

Mabel Mercer Sings, Decca, LP12.

Mabel Mercer Sings Cole Porter, Atlantic, LP12.

Mabel Mercer Sings Cole Porter, Rhino/ Atlantic CD, 1994.

Mabel Mercer, Tribute On Her 75th Birthday, 4 LPs #1213, 1244, 1301 and 1322, Atlantic reissues.

Merely Marvelous, Atlantic, LP12, ATL 1322.

Midnight At Mabel Mercer's, Atlantic, LP12, ATL 1244.

New York Cabaret Music, Atlantic, 6 LP12 box.

Once In A Blue Moon, Atlantic, LP12, ATL 1301.

Songs By Mabel Mercer, Atlantic, DLP 10, Vols. 1, 2, and 3.

You're The Top, Cole Porter in the 1930s, Indiana Historical, CDO5.

Echoes of My Life, Audiophile LP, Audiophile and Rhino reissues, CDs, 1990s.

FILM

Everything Is Rhythm, Harry Roy & His Orchestra, London, 1938. ("Black Minnie's Got The Blues," recorded by Electrical and Musical Industries.)

VIDEOS

Mabel Mercer, A Singer's Singer, V.I.E.W., 1986.

Mabel Mercer, Cabaret Artist, V.I.E.W. Catalog, New York, 1989.

BIBLIOGRAPHY

Abbreviations

IJS: Institute for Jazz Studies, Rutgers University; **MCI**: Margaret Cheney interview; **MMP**: Mabel Mercer Papers; **NYPL**: New York Public Library; **NYT**: *The New York Times;* **SCRBC**: Schomburg Center for Research in Black Culture, NYPL; **SR**: Stereo Review; **TNY**: *The New Yorker*

What the Stars Said

Balliett, Whitney, *American Singers.* New York: Oxford University Press, 1979.

CBS, Inc., *Six Decades of Songwriters and Singers,* 1984.

Morris, James R., *American Popular Song.* Smithsonian Institution, 1984.

Smithsonian Collection, *American Popular Song.*

Wallin-Beach, Adde, "not opinionated but firm...."

Wilder, Alec and Maher, James T., *American Popular Song: The Great Innovators, 1900-1950.* New York: Oxford University Press, 1972.

Text References

Anon, Mabel Mercer telephone interview, n.d.

Ayerhoff, Stan, "Django Reinhardt (1910-1953)," Los Angeles: Introduction to *Jazz Masters.* New York: Consolidated Music Publishers, 1978).

Bach, Steven, *Marlene Dietrich: Life and Legend.* New York: William Morrow & Co., Inc., Outpost Productions, Inc., 1992, p. 126, 242-246, 470-477.

Baggi, Denis L., *Aspects of European Jazz In The Thirties,* http://www.cimsi.cim.ch/-dbaggi/

jazz-i.htm. Victor Record liner, *Quintet du Hot Club,* 1937.

Baker, Jean-Claude, *Josephine: The Hungry Heart.* New York: Marlowe & Co., 1995.

Balliett, Whitney, "Profiles: A Queenly Aura," TNY, Nov. 18, 1972, p. 60.

_____, "Our Footloose Correspondent: In the Country." TNY, Sept. 6, 1982, p. 44, 49.

_____, "Profiles: Julius Monk, Regisseur," TNY, Apr. 6, 1992, p. 37.

_____, TNY, "Notes and Comment," Jan. 12, 1981, and May 7, 1984.

_____, *American Singers.* New York: Oxford University Press, 1979.

_____, *American Musicians: 56 Portraits.* New York and Oxford: Oxford University Press, 1986) p. 209.

Bornet, Fred, MCI , April 27, 1993.

Bourgeois, Charles, MCI Oct. 16, 1992.

Bricktop and James Haskins, *Bricktop.* New York: Atheneum. 1983, p 173-175, 192.

Bell, Arthur, *The Village Voice,* April 11, 1977.

Carpenter, Thelma, MCI, April-Aug. 1993. (Mabel's apartment and mode of life, personal and professional.)

Cecil, Robert, *Life in Edwardian*

England. New York: G. P. Putnam & Sons, 1969.

Christian Science Monitor, "Commencement 1975," (honorary degree ceremony), May 20, 1975.

Cohen, Edgar, "The Truth About The Charleston," in *The Melody Maker & British Metronome*, July 5, 1926, p. 7. Archives IJS, Rutgers University. (See also letter from Max Rivers.)

_____, "Song Writers Walk," in *The Melody Maker*, 1920s.

Cook, Barbara, *American Popular Song*. South Carolina Public Radio Series, National Public Radio, 1976-1978.

Converse, C. Crozat, "Rag-Time Music," in *Etude*, June 17, 1899, p. 185.

Crantson, Stanley, MCI, June 28, 1992.

Delaunay, Charles, trans. by Michael James, *Django Reinhardt*. London: Cassell & Co., Ltd. 1961; *The Jazz Book Club*, by arrangement with Cassell, 1963, p.66, 67, 88.

Dooley, Father Jerry, *Catholic New York*, June 6, 1991. (Condensed from *The Progress*, newspaper of the Seattle Archdiocese.)

Draper, Tom, "Music Scene," in *The Courier-Post*, Camden, June 14, 1975, p. 45.

Dyer, Richard, "Mabel Mercer: A Remembrance," in *The Boston Globe Magazine*, June 3, 1984.

Embree, Edwin Rogers, "The American Negro Cultural Contributions," in *Encyclopedia Brittanica, Vol. 16*, p. 196.

Engvick, William, Introduction to "Songs By Alec Wilder Were Made To Sing," by Alec Wilder. TRO/Ludlow Music, The Richmond Organization, 1976.

Ewen, David, *All The Years Of American Popular Song*. Englewood Cliffs, N.J.: Prentice-Hall, Inc., 1977, 470-471.

Fauset, Jessie, in Carolyn Sylvander, Jessie Redmon Fauset, *Black American Writer*. Troy, NY: Whitson, 1981.

Finch, Muriel, MCI, June 29, 1992.

Flanner (Genet), Janet, ed. Irving Drutman, *Paris Was Yesterday, 1925-1939*. New York: TNY; Viking Press, 1972, p. 61, 62, 221.

Fleming, Shirley, *Mabel Mercer: A Legend In Pop Music*,
HiFi Music At Home, March, 1959.

Frazier, George, Liner notes for *Mabel Mercer Sings Cole Porter*. Atlantic Recording Corp.

Gavin, James, Intimate Nights. New York: Grove Weidenfeld, 1991, p.66-70, 131-33, 285-86, 336-339.

Goddard, Chris, *Jazz Away From Home*. New York: Paddington Press, 1979, p. 9-59, 88-89, 218, 298.

Gruen, John, *Menotti: A Biography*. New York: Macmillan; London: Collier Macmillan, 1978, p. 99.

Hansen, Arlen J., *Expatriate Paris, A Cultural & Literary Guide to Paris of the 1920s*. New York: Arcade Publishing Co., Little Brown Co., p. 27.

Haskins, James, *Mabel Mercer: A Life*. New York: Atheneum, Macmillan Publishing Co., 1987, p. 10-33, 39-42, 54, 58-59, 74, 78.

Hasse, John Edward, *Duke Ellington: Beyond Category*. New York: Simon & Schuster, 1993, p. 82, 232, 253, 372, 308-309.

Holden, Stephen, "From Billy Barnes to Mabel Mercer with Love," NYT, Sept. 16, 1983.

Horne, Lena and Richard Schickel, *Lena*. Garden City, NY: Doubleday & Co., 1965, p. 55-60.

Howard, Bart, MCI, Sept. 4, 1992. (In England and Paris...that first day.)

Jefferies, Wayne, "Django's Forgotten Era," http://ourworld. compuserve.com. Also "The History of Django," by Fred Sharpe, ibid.

Keefe, Nancy Q., *The Berkshire Eagle*, Feb. 11, 1975.

Kelly, Kevin, "Short-Mercer Concert Historic, Soul-Touching," in *The Boston Globe*, May 23, 1968.

Kimball, Robert, ed. *Cole*. New York: Holt, Rinehart & Winston, 1971.

Levy, Stephen, *Philadelphia Bulletin*, 1975, n.d.

Life, "Durable Underground Doyenne," Oct. 15, 1965.

Livingstone, William, letters to the author, Oct. 1992.

_____, "Mabel Mercer," SR, Vol. 34, No.2, Feb. 1975, p. 60-64.

London Daily Mail, "Return Of Mabel," July 4, 1977. Also *The Sunday Telegraph*, July 17, 1977;

The Sunday Times, July 17, 1977; *Evening Standard*, Aug. 19, 1977.

Lownes, III., Victor, liner notes for *Midnight At Mabel Mercer's*. Atlantic Recording Corporation. Reprint, *Playboy*, 1955.

Marcovicci, Andrea, NYT, Oct. 16, 1994, Section 2.

McGlohon, Loonis, MCI, April 25-26, 1993, (When she was in public....")

Mercer, Mabel, Foreword to *Songs by Alec Wilder Were Made To Sing*, by Alec Wilder. New York: The Richmond Organization/ Ludlow Music, 1976.

Mialy, Louis-Victor, "Frank Sinatra, Voice Of America," in *JAZZ HOT*, July-Aug. 1998, No. 552, p. 24-25.

Millay, Edna St. Vincent, "Dirge Without Music" from *Collected Poems*. New York: Harper Collins, 1956.

New England Conservatory of Music News. Boston, May 9, 1980.

Newsweek, "A Singer In The Night," Aug. 22, 1955, p. 86.

_____, Aug. 8, 1994, p. 44.

NYT, Sept. 7, 1962.

O'Brien, Father Peter, letter to author, n.d.; MCI Oct. 18, 1994.

O'Haire, Patricia, *New York Daily News*, Oct. 6, 1977.

Padgette, Paul, *A Moment In Time*, author's collection, Aug. 30, 1994.

Parker, Jerry, "The Singer's Singer," in *Newsday*, April 21, 1984.

People Weekly, Feb. 17, 1975.

Placksin, Sally, *American Women In*

Jazz, 1900 to Present. Wideview Books, a Division of PEI Books, 1982, p. 6, 7-10.

Raymond, Cynthia, "On The Record: Mabel Mercer, Cleo's." IJS.

Reed, Rex, liner notes for *Mabel Mercer & Bobby Short at Town Hall.* Atlantic Recording Corporation, May 19, 1968, by Valyr Music Corporation.

_____, "The Essential Mabel Mercer," in SR, Feb. 1975, p. 90.

_____, "The Sweet Survival Of Mabel Mercer," in *Sunday News,* New York, Feb. 16, 1975.

Riva, Maria, *Marlene Dietrich by Her Daughter.* New York: Alfred A. Knopf, Inc., 1992.

Santosuosso, Ernie, *The Boston Globe,* May 1, 1974, p. 41.

Santoro, Gene, *New York Daily News,* Sept. 15, 1994.

Sark, John, "A Legend In Her Own Sweet Time," *San Francisco Examiner,* Jan. 31, 1978, p. 18.

Shales, Tom, *Washington Post,* Feb. 5, 1975, B1.

Shirer, Wm. L., *Rise And Fall Of The Third Reich.* New York: Simon & Schuster, 1960, p. 738.

Short, Bobby, with Robert Mackintosh, *Bobby Short, Saloon Singer.* New York: Panache Press, Clarkson Potter Publishers, 1995, p. 87, 88, 207-208 et seq.

Smith, Donald F. MCI, Apr. 30, 1995.

Smithsonian Institution Traveling Exhibition Service, *The Jazz Age In Paris, 1914-1940,* 1997.

South, Eddie, *Biographical Sketch and Discography.* Newark: IJS.

Stone, Desmond, *Alec Wilder In Spite Of Himself.* New York: Oxford University Press, 1996, p. 81-84.

Stovall, Tyler, *Paris Noir: African-Americans In The City Of Light.* Boston, New York: Houghton Mifflin Co.,1996, p. 39.

Summerscale, Kate, *The Queen Of Whale Cay.* New York: Viking Penguin, 1998, p. 88-99.

Sylvester, Robert, *New York Daily News,* Nov. 1955 n.d.

Taylor, David, Manchester (England) City Council, Department of Libraries and Theatres: letter to author, Sept. 28, 1992.

Thurber, James, "Letter From The States: Back Home Again," in *The Bermudian,* n.d.

Time, Oct. 10, 1938: "In German schools… 'disloyal facial expressions.'"

_____, Feb. 17, 1975, Vol. 105, No. 7.

TV Guide, Aug. 25, 1964, p. 50-51.

Variety, "Mabel Mercer, Bobby Short," June 27, 1962; May 28, 1969 p. 26; March 23, 1978, p. 14.

VerPlanck, Marlene, MCI, Feb. 1996.

Wallin-Beach, Adde, MCI, June 29, 1992.

Wasserman, John, "In The Presence Of Greatness," *San Francisco Chronicle,* May 29, 1972, p. 40.

Waters, Ethel, with Charles Samuels, *His Eye Is On The Sparrow.* New York: Doubleday & Co., 1951.

Watson, Steven, *The Harlem Renaissance: Hub of African-American Culture, 1920-1930.* New York: Pantheon Books, 1995, p. 157.

Wild, Roland, "She Never Looked Back," in *Park East*, Mar. 1953, p. 16-19.

Wilder, Alec, interview with Mabel Mercer for liner notes, "Echoes Of My Life," in *Audiophile*, July 1976.

_____, *American Popular Song*, South Carolina Radio Series, National Public Radio, 1976-78.

_____, Address at Mabel Mercer honorary degree ceremony, Berklee College of Music, Boston, May 1975.

_____, and James T. Maher, *American Popular Song: The Great Innovators, 1900-1950*. New York: Oxford University Press, 1972.

_____, *Alec Wilder: An Introduction to the Man and His Music*. Margun Music, Inc., Broadcast Music, Inc., TRO, p. 78.

Wilson, John S., NYT, Oct. 7, 1958; July 27, 1970.

_____, "Mabel Mercer Hailed at 75," NYT, Feb. 4, 1975.

_____, NYT, March 7, 1977.

Winchell, Walter, *New York Mirror*, Sept. 16, 1955.

Yoors, Jan, *The Gypsies*. New York: Simon & Schuster, 1967. p. 251-256.

Zailian, Marian, "An Ageless Enchantress and Her Timeless Songs," *San Francisco Examiner & Chronicle*, Jan. 29, 1978, p. 17.

Index

282

285

289

Permissions and Credits

Permission to use the following copyrighted materials is hereby acknowledged with thanks:

Instrumental score, "Mabel," by Django Reinhardt, 1937 (renewed). Publications Francis Day; all rights in North America controlled by Jewel Music Publishing Co., Inc.; all rights reserved; international copyright secured.

The Richmond Organization (TRO), five lines from "It was Worth It (That's What I'll Say)," by Bart Howard, TRO/Hampshire House Publishing Corp., 1956, 1984.

In its entirety, lyric from "While We're Young," by Alec Wilder, William Engvick, and Morty Palitz; Ludlow Music, Inc., 1943, 1971.

Williamson Music Company, two lines from "Hello, Young Lovers," by Rodgers and Hammerstein.

Elizabeth Barnett, executrix of the estate of Edna St. Vincent Millay, copyright 1956, lines from "Dirge without Music," from *Collected Works of Edna St. Vincent Millay*, HarperCollins.

Warners Chappell, Warner Bros. Publications, Warner Bros., Inc., and Robert Montgomery, Jr., trustee of the Cole Porter Musical and Literary Property Trusts, lyrics from "Love for Sale" (Harms, 1930).

Every effort has been made to credit original sources. If an error or omission has occurred, the author will be pleased to rectify it in forthcoming editions.

291

Mabel

Main Theme

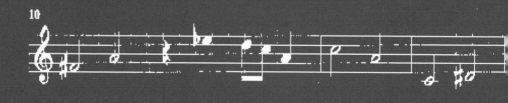

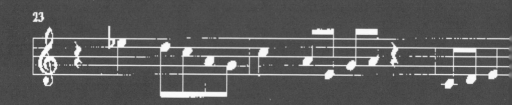